TESS IN THE THEATRE

University of Toronto   Department of English
STUDIES AND TEXTS, No. 4

MRS. FISKE
Courtesy of Harvard Theatre Collection

Tess
IN THE THEATRE

Two Dramatizations of *Tess of the D'Urbervilles* by THOMAS HARDY
One by LORIMER STODDARD

Edited, with an Introduction

by

MARGUERITE ROBERTS, Ph.D.

UNIVERSITY OF TORONTO PRESS
Toronto, 1950

Copyright, Canada, 1950, by University of Toronto Press and printed in Canada. London: Geoffrey Cumberlege, Oxford University Press.

Reprinted in 2018

ISBN 978-1-4875-7336-2 (paper)

All rights reserved

For My Mother and Father

"To be a great novelist and a great poet and to have the potentialities of a great dramatist—what a destiny for a man!"

St. John Ervine on Hardy

"Everything written by a genius is interesting, whatever his aesthetic ideas may be, and in spite of all his mistakes and imperfections."

Sibelius on Brahms

PREFACE

MARCH 2, 1947, marked the fiftieth anniversary of Mrs. Fiske's first presentation of *Tess of the D'Urbervilles* in the Fifth Avenue Theatre in New York. November 26, 1946, saw evidence of the theatre's revived interest in Hardy's novel when Miss Wendy Hiller first appeared in London at the New Theatre in Ronald Gow's dramatization of *Tess*. It seems to be particularly fitting at this time, therefore, to present the half-century's history of *Tess of the D'Urbervilles* on the stage together with the texts of significant dramatic versions.

Gathering material for this volume has led me into some fascinating corners and archives which it is a pleasure to remember, but which purpose and space keep these pages from reflecting. Two places are so important, however, that they merit notice here: Max Gate and Gordon Villa in Dorchester. At Max Gate, the late Mrs. Thomas Hardy shared with me her memories, her opinions, and the Hardiana which permeate these pages. Through her good offices, she made the dramatic scripts available and placed in my hands Hardy's correspondence with the world of the theatre, a correspondence which reveals for the first time many of his associations, personal and literary as well as theatrical. The many references to Max Gate manuscripts indicate my indebtedness to Hardy's private papers found there. Gratefully I acknowledge Mrs. Hardy's generosity and co-operation, which made this volume possible, as well as many unforgettable associations of my visits to her in Dorchester and at the old Adelphi Terrace in London. Miss Irene Cooper Willis and Lloyds Bank, as trustees of the Hardy copyright, have kindly given me permission to include the texts and the other hitherto unpublished Hardy material contained in this study and the Macmillan Company, owner of the copyright of the published works, has given its approval to the idea of this book.

At Gordon Villa, the late Mr. T. H. Tilley, honorary stage manager, coach, and producer of the "Hardy Players," entertained me for many hours with reminiscences of the amateur productions in general and of *Tess* in particular. He generously placed in my hands dramatic scripts, programmes, pictures, and other mementoes of the Dorchester productions.

I am deeply indebted to Harper and Brothers for their cooperation in enabling me to publish the Lorimer Stoddard text as well as the original Hardy version. Letters from their files have been important in tracing the history of negotiations with managers and actors. Professor Carl J. Weber has kindly sent me several Hardy letters from the Colby College collection. Mr. Carroll A. Wilson of New York and Professor Richard Purdy of Yale have allowed me to use their private collections.

To St. John Ervine, Professor George Herbert Clarke, Miss Gwen Ffrangçon-Davies, Miss Christine Silver, Mrs. Gertrude Bugler, Mr. F. E. Hansford (a nephew of Mrs. Tilley), Frank Carlos Griffith, and the late Hector Charlesworth I am indebted for letters and other information about various productions. For notes from the files of the late Adam Fergusson in Edinburgh pertaining to the whole field of Hardy research, I am indebted to Dr. Howard P. Whidden, whose interest in this study has been an inspiration. Among the many actors and actresses who have allowed me to use their letters to Hardy about *Tess* are the late Sir J. Forbes-Robertson, Miss Olga Nethersole, Miss Elizabeth Robins, Miss Lillah McCarthy (Lady Keeble), Dame Sybil Thorndike, and Miss Gwen Ffrangçon-Davies. First drafts of many of Hardy's letters to people of the theatre, fortunately preserved at Max Gate, were among the papers given me by Mrs. Hardy. Others have come from sources indicated. Baron Frederic d'Erlanger not only gave me permission to use his letters to Hardy (found at Max Gate), but also sent me Hardy's original letters to him about the opera, *Tess*. Doris Arthur Jones has permitted me to use her father's letters to Hardy, and Colonel C. Archer has given me permission to include letters to Hardy from his brother, William Archer.

Throughout the preparation of this study the vast resources of the Harvard Theatre Collection and other Harvard libraries have been continuously at my disposal. Dr. William Van Lennop, Mr. R. H. Haynes, and Mr. William A. Jackson have shown much consideration in making these resources available. The newspaper articles bear the identification and dates as given in the Theatre Collection. The Introduction to the plays, in an earlier form, presented as part of a larger work in partial fulfilment of an official requirement at Radcliffe, was read by Professor Theodore Spencer and Professor Howard Mumford Jones. In preparation of the entire study, I was especially indebted to Mr. Spencer for his kind interest and encouragement, and valuable criticism.

In presenting this volume as one of the University of Toronto, Department of English Studies and Texts, I wish to express my appreciation to Professor A. S. P. Woodhouse, Professor N. J. Endicott, and several of my other colleagues, and to the management of the University of Toronto Press, for their co-operation. The texts have been faithfully reported with the exception that spelling has been made consistent throughout, that obvious errors have been silently corrected, and that minor changes in punctuation, which are a matter of current editorial taste, have been made.

M. R.

March 15, 1947
University College
University of Toronto

CONTENTS

PREFACE vii

INTRODUCTION

    I. Hardy and the Theatre: 1867-1893   xv
    II. Dramatizing *Tess of the D'Urbervilles*   xxii
    III. Lorimer Stoddard: The Play for Mrs. Fiske   xxxiv
    IV. Hugh Arthur Kennedy's Unauthorized Version   l
    V. Baron Frederic d'Erlanger's Opera   lix
    VI. Hardy's Contact with the Theatre: 1908-1925   lxx
    VII. Hardy's *Tess* on the London Stage: 1925   lxxxvi

TEXTS

    I. Hardy's Original Version (1894-5)   1
    II. Lorimer Stoddard (1897)   73
    III. Hardy's London Version (1925)   131

APPENDIX 205

PLATES

Mrs. Fiske	*frontispiece*
Tess Returning from the Dance	*opposite page lxxxviii*
Mrs. Fiske	*opposite page 125*
Mrs. Gertrude Bugler as *Tess*	*opposite page 138*

INTRODUCTION

I. Hardy and the Theatre, 1867-1893

THE drama appealed to Thomas Hardy. Like Keats he wanted to write a few fine plays. Apart from lyric poetry Hardy's earliest literary aspiration lay in the field of poetic drama. His interest in contributing to the theatre extended over a period of nearly sixty years, from 1867, when he first considered writing for the stage, until 1926, when he still desired to see *Jude the Obscure* dramatized. Although, as Mrs. Hardy reminded me, most people do not think of Hardy as a dramatist, his private papers reveal the fact that there were times when he was interested in writing drama not only to be read but also for the stage. At certain times this attraction to the theatre was especially strong; but unfortunately at these crucial moments he was repulsed, frustrated, and turned in some other direction either by the advice of a friend, the conditions of the contemporary stage, or the break-down of negotiations with actors and managers. As a result Hardy never devoted his full energy to the practical art of writing plays. But, despite that, his interest in the folk-drama of Wessex, and in the Greek and Elizabethan tragedy, as well as in the current productions of the London stage, is marked in varying degrees throughout his long life. And his correspondence with actors, managers, and dramatic critics, as revealed in this study, shows that his attitude toward his own work in the theatre varies from indifference to enthusiasm.

In 1867, Hardy had formed the idea of writing drama in blank verse and planned to make a first-hand study of the theatre for six or twelve months from the vantage-point of a supernumerary. He even sought advice from Mark Lemon, a dramatist and amateur actor (and at that time editor of *Punch*), and Mr. Coe, the stage manager of the Haymarket under Buckstone's lesseeship. Their counsel and the first sight of stage realities, however, so discouraged

Hardy that he gave up his initial idea of writing plays in blank verse.[1]

Hardy turned to the stage again in the early eighties when he allowed J. Comyns Carr to adapt *Far from the Madding Crowd*. Dramatized novels were enjoying a golden age in Victoria's reign. Indeed Mr. Reynolds remarks: "Original drama stood little chance beside versions of books which had already won national fame."[2] Under ordinary circumstances, Hardy and Carr should have had some success with a stage version of a novel so popular as *Far from the Madding Crowd*. Unfortunately, however, an acrimonious newspaper dispute[3] arose between Hardy and Carr on the one hand and Arthur Wing Pinero on the other because of the resemblance of the dramatized novel to Pinero's play, *The Squire*. The *Critic* (New York, April, 1906) speaks of "tiresome litigation" over the two plays, but Mr. Carl J. Weber could find no evidence of litigation in the British courts.[4] The wordy dispute over the coincidences of the two plays, however, was bitter and involved John Hare, the Kendalls, and R. C. Carton, as well as Hardy, Carr, and Pinero. Carr charged Pinero with appropriating Hardy's work and robbing his play thereby of commercial value. Hare and Kendall were suspected of betraying the Hardy-Carr version to Pinero. Strong denials from both author and producers naturally followed in the press. Pinero was especially sarcastic, with the condescending attitude of a successful dramatist toward the failure who falls back upon the charge of plagiarism to belittle a successful work. He was, however, probably quite innocent of being (as Carr called him) a "literary somnambulist who trespasses on other men's dramas."[5] The unpleasantness of the controversy and the consequent failure of *Far from the Madding Crowd* resulted in a repugnance for the

[1] Cf. Florence Emily Hardy, *The Life of Thomas Hardy* (London: Macmillan & Co., 1933), I, 71.

[2] Ernest Reynolds, *Early Victorian Drama, 1830-1870* (Cambridge: W. Heffer & Sons, 1936), p. 145.

[3] Cf. the *Era*, December 31, 1881—January 21, 1882.

[4] Hardy, *Far from the Madding Crowd*, ed. Carl J. Weber (New York: Oxford, 1937), p. xvii, foot-note 16.

[5] *Boston Evening Transcript*, April 6, 1900.

stage on Hardy's part lasting a decade or so. In 1892, it is distinctly reflected in his little article, "Why I Don't Write Plays."[1]

To understand the change of mind evident in Hardy's dramatizing of "The Three Strangers" in 1893 and *Tess of the D'Urbervilles* in 1894-5, it is necessary to remind ourselves of the revival of interest in the drama in the latter part of the nineteenth century. There were attractions, some vague and some definite, both at home and abroad, which lured Hardy to the theatre at last. It is true that throughout the century there had been good acting. The classics had been produced, and French plays imported, but before Shaw finished *Widowers' Houses* in 1892, the numerous unrealistic native plays had shown little relation to contemporary culture. In 1879 Matthew Arnold had written:

> We have our Elizabethan drama. We have a drama of the last century and of the latter part of the century preceding, a drama which may be called our drama of *the town*. . . . But we have no modern drama. . . . We have apparitions of poetic and romantic drama . . . , because man has always in his nature the poetical fibre. Then we have numberless imitations and adaptations from the French. All of these are at the bottom fantastic. We may truly say of them that "truth and sense and liberty are flown." And the reason is evident. They are pages out of a life which the ideal of the *homme sensuel moyen* rules, transferred to a life where this ideal does not reign.[2]

In the following decade, however, new activity on the part of dramatic critics and producers became manifest, which culminated in the nineties. William Archer battled enthusiastically for the producing of Ibsen's plays in London, and with some success. J. T. Grein, who founded the Independent Theatre and inaugurated its career with Ibsen's *Ghosts* on March 13, 1891, also encouraged native dramatists, particularly George Moore and Bernard Shaw. A foreign development which affected the future of literary drama in England was the passing of the American Copyright Bill in 1891. This new copyright convention was especially encouraging to men of letters, since it meant that published plays were not only pro-

---

[1] *Pall Mall Budget*, September 1, 1900.
[2] Matthew Arnold, "The French Play in London," *Nineteenth Century*, August, 1879, pp. 238-9.

tected from exploitation on the American stage but also that those which failed in the theatre were not necessarily doomed to oblivion. Authors could look on plays as literature worthy of the literary finish which would recommend them to a discriminating intellectual reading public rather than as mere toys of the moment needing "garish artificial light."[1]

English producers like George Alexander, John Hare, and Beerbohm Tree began to produce the plays of contemporary novelists, if only to charm and delight the few. In 1891, Tree presented *Beau Austin* by Stevenson and Henley, and in the same year, Edward Compton produced *The American* by Henry James. For Henry Arthur Jones and William Archer, the hope of the theatre lay in luring other men of letters into writing for the stage. In a letter to Barrett H. Clark, Jones wrote (April 15, 1916) that he had always tried to show "that no nation can have a drama that is worth consideration unless it is or becomes part of the national literature—that all plays outside this are mere toys of the theatre—that therefore the highest aim of those who are working for the drama should be to bring it into relation with literature, and to draw men of letters to an understanding of, and a sympathy with the theater, so that they may exercise their authority as to what is produced."[2] To show the literary possibilities of the drama, William Archer, in an article, "The Stage and Literature," exalted Ibsen's ability to combine theatrical technique with literary beauty. He cited the fusion of character, action, and dialogue in *Hedda Gabler* into an indissoluble whole with an intensity and multiplicity of meaning: "The simplest sentence," he wrote, "proves, on examination, to be cut in many facets."[3] Archer challenged men of letters to write for the English stage: "So soon as we have an English playwright who possesses the literary vigour and technical skill of Dumas, or Meilhac, or Becque, we shall cease to dispute as to the possibility of a literary drama."[4]

[1] Henry Arthur Jones, Preface to *Saints and Sinners*, in *The Renascence of the English Drama* (New York: Macmillan Co., 1895), p. 310.

[2] Quoted in *European Theories of the Drama*, ed. Barrett H. Clark (Cincinnati: Stewart & Kidd Co., 1918), p. 458.

[3] *Fortnightly Review*, February, 1892, p. 232.

[4] *Ibid.*, p. 231.

INTRODUCTION

The *Pall Mall Budget* decided to follow up Archer's challenge to men of letters. On September 1, 1892, it said:

In the recent discussions on the Drama a good deal has been said about what is called "the divorce of literature from the stage." Mr. William Archer, in particular, has been greatly pained at this unhappy incompatibility, and in a recent number of the *Fortnightly Review* urged strongly upon the parties the desirability of reunion. Certainly he has found experience on the side of his appeal. In France and in Germany almost all the great novelists have been playwrights as well: as, for example, Victor Hugo, Balzac, George Sand, Sandeau, the Goncourts, Daudet, Zola, Maupassant, the two Dumas, Freytag, Heyse, Turgenieff, Tolstoi, Bjornsen, Kielland, and many others. Why is it that in modern England, on the other hand, scarcely any of the popular novelists are known as writers for the stage? Mr. Archer, in the article above referred to, suggested that the novelists were to blame. "To glance," he said, "down the roll of living poets and novelists is to pass in review writer after writer who owes it to himself and to literature to make some essay, at any rate, in dramatic form." The question seemed to us, however, one on which Mr. Archer's was hardly the last word; and as one on which the opinions of novelists themselves were likely to be of great interest. We ventured, therefore, to invite a few of the best-known writers of fiction to answer, in such form as they might think fit, the following questions:—

(1) Whether you regard the present divorce of fiction from the drama as beneficial or inimical to the best interests of literature and the stage;

(2) Whether you, yourself, have at any time had, or now have, any desire to exercise your gifts in the production of plays as well as of novels; and, if not,

(3) Why you consider the novel the better or more convenient means for bringing your ideas before the public whom you address.

Of the twelve answers furnished by novelists Hardy's was published first,[1] along with that of W. E. Norris. Hardy wrote:

1. Inimical to the best interests of the stage: no injury to literature.

2. Have occasionally had a desire to produce a play, and have, in fact, written the skeletons of several. Have no such desire in any special sense just now.

3. Because, in general, the novel affords scope for getting nearer to the heart and meaning of things than does a play; in particular, the play as nowadays conditioned, when parts have to be moulded to actors, not actors to

---

[1] In the same issue of September 1, 1892.

parts; when managers will not risk a truly original play; when scenes have to be arranged in a constrained and arbitrary fashion to suit the exigencies of scene-building, although spectators are absolutely indifferent to order and succession, provided they can have set before them a developing thread of interest. The reason for this arbitrary arrangement would seem to be that the presentation of human passions is subordinated to the presentation of mountains, cities, clothes, furniture, plate, jewels, and other real and sham-real appurtenances, to the neglect of the principle that the material stage should be a conventional or figurative arena in which accessories are kept down to the plane of mere suggestion of place and time, so as not to interfere with the high-relief of the action and the emotions.

This statement betrays a strong interest in the drama—an interest stronger, in fact, than that of any other novelist who answered the questions of the *Pall Mall Budget*. But despite his interest, Hardy makes it clear that he does not care to write for the stage on its own difficult and circumscribing terms. Some months before his "Why I Don't Write Plays" appeared, however, reviews were making him more and more disgusted with the craft of the novel. Mrs. Hardy quotes his diary for Good Friday, 1892, in which he records reading a "smart and amusing article" on *Tess of the D'Urbervilles* in the *Quarterly*. He concludes: "If this sort of thing continues no more novel-writing for me. A man must be a fool to deliberately stand up to be shot at."[1] It was time for Hardy to try a new medium, and the obvious one for 1892 was the drama.

Of all the greater Victorian novelists, Hardy could probably best have taken his place in the theatrical world. Unlike the gifts of Henry James, so little of whose mind, as Max Beerbohm has said, could be transferred to the stage, Hardy's gifts were essentially dramatic. His whole theory of writing consisted in making tales unusual enough to stop wedding guests, as he wrote in his diary on February 23, 1893: "We tale-tellers are all Ancient Mariners, and none of us is warranted in stopping Wedding Guests . . . unless he has something more unusual to relate than the ordinary experience of every average man and woman. The whole secret of fiction and the drama—in the constructional part—lies in the adjustment of things unusual to things eternal and universal."[2] His stories are

---

[1] F. E. Hardy, *The Life of Thomas Hardy*, II, 7.
[2] *Ibid.*, II, 15.

never static. Plot is always of paramount importance for Hardy. Obviously he read life in terms of things happening—of action and often melodramatic action. His projection of characters, his careful weaving of plots, his ability to concentrate on intense situations would have been effective over the foot-lights. His lifelong interest in the theatre and his natural inclination to the drama would have enabled him to master the inexorable technique necessary for writing actable plays. Henry Arthur Jones said that "had Hardy been born in France, . . . he would have given his time and talent to the stage."[1] Even in England, it was time for him to try the drama.

As a result, no doubt, partly of the enthusiasm for the renaissance of the drama, but more particularly of a suggestion by his friend, James M. Barrie, Hardy dramatized "The Three Strangers" of the *Wessex Tales,* under the title of *The Three Wayfarers.* The play was produced at Terry's Theatre, June 3-9, 1893, with four other short plays: *Bud and Blossom* by Lady Colin Campbell; *An Interlude* by Mrs. W. K. Clifford and Walter H. Pollack; *Foreign Policy* by Conan Doyle; and *Beckie Sharp* by Barrie. The entertainment was disappointing except for the performance of *The Three Wayfarers.* J. T. Grein said, "Mr. Hardy's playlet alone wiped out the bad record of the evening."[2] Hardy himself was so impressed with Charles Charrington's impersonation of the hangman that he wrote to him: "Your performance of the hangman was extraordinarily powerful and took everybody by surprise. You have created quite a character for yourself and quite apart from any interest of another kind I may have in the play, I should like it to be widely seen as evidence of your powers."[3] The success of his "legendary trifle" and the favourable criticisms which followed seem to have helped

[1] Doris Arthur Jones, *Life and Letters of Henry Arthur Jones* (London: Victor Gollancz, 1930), p. 258.

[2] J. T. Grein, "Stage Society: The Three Wayfarers," in *Dramatic Criticism 1900-1901* (London: Greening & Co., 1922), p. 54. The *Theatre* (July-December, 1893, p. 49) supports this view: "The one success of the evening, an unmistakable success, was Mr. Hardy's. . . . Strongly played by Mr. Charrington as the ghoulish hangman, Mr. Waring as the hunted sheep-stealer, Mr. Stewart Dawson and Mr. Fred Thorne as racy rustics of the Hardy breed, it took the fancy of the house and was received with enthusiasm."

[3] This letter is in the collection of Mr. Carroll A. Wilson of New York City.

Hardy overcame his temporary disgust with the theatre.[1] At any rate, he began to heed the many requests for a play based upon *Tess of the D'Urbervilles*.

II. Dramatizing *Tess of the D'Urbervilles*

Even before the success of *The Three Wayfarers* Hardy had been requested to dramatize *Tess of the D'Urbervilles*. In 1892, in a series of letters, George Alexander pressed him for a play founded on "your story." Then when actresses on both sides of the Atlantic implored him for a dramatization, it seems that Hardy was inclined to arrange the stage version himself rather than leave it to perhaps less sensitive and sympathetic hands. In 1894-5 he dramatized *Tess of the D'Urbervilles,* but his version was not presented for thirty years: it was first seen at Dorchester in 1924, and in London in 1925.

The history of this play is curious. Why should Hardy be persuaded to adapt his novel for the stage and yet withhold the adaptation from the theatre for thirty years? The answer would be obvious if no actress wanted to play Tess, or no manager wanted to produce the play. But when many prominent actresses in Europe and America asked for permission to interpret the leading role and when managers in New York and London sought for terms, the problem is tantalizing. The explanation is not so simple as Hardy would indicate in a letter to William Archer, dated February 17, 1909: "P.S. Did I ever tell you the real, secret, reason why Tess was never played on the London stage? Because there was no hero in it, that the manager cd. personate, and bring down the gallery. A manager owned it to me. T. H."[2]

Charles Morgan records a conversation with Hardy in 1922: "He told me, too, that he had written a stage version of *Tess,* and something of its early history; how, after the success of the novel, the great ones of the earth had pressed him to dramatize it; . . . by

---

[1] Cf. Carl J. Weber, *Hardy of Wessex* (New York: Columbia University Press, 1940), p. 222.

[2] This is from one of several original holograph letters which Colonel C. Archer sent me from England from his brother's correspondence.

what mischance the performance of it had been prevented. Where was it now? In a drawer. Would he allow it to be performed? He smiled, gave no answer...."¹ Two years later, however, when Mr. T. H. Tilley, stage manager, coach, and producer of the "Hardy Players," asked for the script of *Tess*, Hardy took it out of the drawer and entrusted it to him. This final and best representation of the amateur company attracted the attention of the professional theatre. It kindled the desire of another generation of actresses to play the role of Tess and rekindled the desire of Forbes-Robertson to produce the play. After *Tess of the D'Urbervilles* appeared in Wessex, it was inevitable that London should at last see Hardy's dramatic version. This it did when Hardy was eighty-five years old.

The Dorchester programme contained these words: "being an adaptation for the stage, by request in 1894-5."² The word "request"³ and the phrase quoted above, "pressed him to dramatize it," are significant. In earlier years, as we have seen, Hardy had wanted to write for the stage, but was discouraged in 1867 by his friends. In 1881-2 he had again taken the initiative in the dramatizing of *Far from the Madding Crowd*. But with *Tess of the D'Urbervilles* the pressure came from the theatrical world, and Hardy seemed reluctant to yield to the insistent requests. Yet, in 1893, the enthusiasm of the advocates of the theatre, and the request of Barrie, had caused Hardy to dramatize his short story, "The Three Strangers." Charrington's success had stimulated Hardy's interest still further. But circumstances had changed in the ten or fifteen years that followed his first attempt at dramaturgy, and Hardy had

---

¹ Charles Morgan included this statement in the account he wrote for Mrs. Hardy of his association with Hardy in the Oxford University production of *The Dynasts* in 1920. It is quoted in F. E. Hardy, *The Life of Thomas Hardy*, II, 208.

² The text was evidently not completed until late in 1895 according to a letter to William Archer, January 2, 1896. See below, p. xxvii.

³ Cf. the *Boston Evening Transcript*, December 11, 1924: "There is a good deal of curiosity (adds the *Manchester Guardian*) about the statement on the program that Mr. Hardy's adaptation from the novel was made thirty years ago 'by request.' It is, of course, a natural speculation that the part of Tess attracted some actress at that time. Some thought that the requester might have been Mrs. Patrick Campbell. Now it is stated that the part is reserved for Miss Sybil Thorndike, which is not to say that her production of the play is settled."

grown away from his first interest in the drama. Established as he was as a leading English novelist, why should he make an experiment with a new medium when there was always his first love, poetry?

It seems perfectly natural, therefore, that Hardy should *not* seek the theatre at this moment of his career, although like other writers he must have felt that the drama was experiencing a renaissance in England. Yet it was likewise natural for him to respond to demands for a work of which he was so genuinely fond. Personal impressions may not count for much, but when I spent days at Max Gate some years ago reading for the first time Hardy's early correspondence with people of the theatre, I felt that the call for his play must have been almost irresistible. He may not have been especially moved by George Alexander's request for *Tess* in 1882, but how could he resist appeals such as Olga Nethersole's, written from Daly's Theatre in New York on November 19, 1894?

> I am writing to implore you to dramatize *Tess of the D'Urbervilles* or to allow it to be dramatized by my friend, Clement Scott, or to collaborate with him and let me have the play. I have dreamed and dreamed of *Tess*, and I should try so hard to do your great creation justice. The character appeals to me beyond my power of expression. It is so human, so pathetic, and so true. Oh, please, give me the chance of doing something really great. I believe I could with such a character to portray. Please answer this letter and tell me my dreams shall be realized. I have just played Marguerite Gautier in "La Dame aux Camélias" for the first time in my life, and every one is good enough to say that it is a creation.[1]

After so much unsympathetic criticism of the novel, Hardy no doubt appreciated this admiration. Tenderly as he had always regarded his heroine, Tess, he would naturally be susceptible to the requests of Olga Nethersole and other actresses, containing such phrases as: "I long to play Tess"; "I am deeply interested in dear Tess. It will be a study I can put my heart in"; and "I should rather play Tess than any other part at the moment."

Mrs. Hardy names a number of the leading actresses of Europe who asked for the role of Tess, including Ellen Terry, Eleanora Duse, Sarah Bernhardt, and Mrs. Patrick Campbell. From my

[1] Max Gate MS.

perusal of the letters I can name others who either asked for it directly or were suggested to Hardy by a manager. To those of the early period, 1895-8, already cited, the names of Elizabeth Robins, Julia Neilson, Helen Blythe, and Mrs. H. B. Irving (Dorothea Baird) should be added. Special mention should be given to Minnie Maddern Fiske, who from all those aspiring to the role was the one chosen to enact Tess in the nineties. Later, in 1910, Lillah McCarthy (Mrs. Granville-Barker) seriously considered interpreting the role at the Kingsway Theatre. And after the success of Gertrude Bugler as Tess in the Dorchester production in 1924, London actresses again became interested. At that time Dame Sybil Thorndike, Lady Forbes-Robertson (Gertrude Elliott), and Gwen Ffrangçon-Davies sought this "most poignant in female parts since Juliet."[1]

Actors as well as actresses asked Hardy for his dramatization. True, Mrs. Hardy records that one prominent actor told Hardy frankly that he could not play such a dubious character as Angel Clare "because I have my name to make, and it would risk my reputation with the public if I played anything but a heroic character. . . ."[2] Yet several of the most prominent actors on the English stage who had already made their names asked to enact the role of Angel, though it was not the perfect masculine lead. William Terriss,[3] H. B. Irving, and Forbes-Robertson negotiated with Hardy for his play.

H. B. Irving wrote to him on August 7, 1896, saying that he, his wife, and his brother were preparing to tour the provinces during the next autumn, and asking whether Hardy could come to a definite arrangement with them about the provincial rights of *Tess*. He expressed the desire for the London rights as well, but thought Hardy might, at any rate, be at liberty to deal with those for the provinces.[4] On June 30, 1897, H. B. Irving wrote again to Hardy, reminding him of their meeting at Lady Jeune's, and stating that

[1] *John o' London's Weekly*, September 5, 1925.

[2] Cf. F. E. Hardy, *The Life of Thomas Hardy*, II, 32.

[3] On June 7, 1897, William Terriss wrote (from the Haymarket) to Hardy asking whether he had made arrangements for *Tess of the D'Urbervilles*, and stating that he would be glad to entertain the matter if agreeable to Hardy (Max Gate MS.). Nothing appears to have come from this offer.

[4] Max Gate MS.

he had been talking to Mr. Legg, George Alexander's secretary, about the version of *Tess* copyrighted at the St. James's. Irving now expressed the desire of his wife, Dorothea Baird, to play the title role.[1] It appears from Irving's next letter that Hardy had replied that he would be pleased to allow Mrs. Irving to play Tess, but at that moment he was evidently expecting Mrs. Fiske to appear in London in Stoddard's version. Apparently for that reason the script was not sent. At any rate, Irving made no mention of receiving it in his reply on July 9. In this letter, Irving asked whether Hardy would let him know *"if the American visit falls through."*[2]

From a number of letters from Forbes-Robertson, it would appear that Hardy may have dramatized his novel with Forbes-Robertson in mind. He may have begun his dramatization at the request of Olga Nethersole (November, 1894), but he seems to have needed the spur of Forbes-Robertson's interest to make him finish it. Obviously, there was no driving force within himself to make Hardy arrange *Tess of the D'Urbervilles* for the stage, or he would not have spread over two years a task which Lorimer Stoddard accomplished in five days.

On March 8, 1895, Forbes-Robertson wrote:

> I should be very glad if there is any chance of your finishing *Tess*. It is very likely I might be in a position to put the play on much earlier than I hinted to you, if it were in my hand soon. I am most anxious to have *Tess*. It is true I do not look on "Clare" as a congenial part; but I think you know I could put my heart into it, and do my best.—We are doing very well with *Romeo and Juliet*, but I am most anxious to have *Tess*, and I think I can promise you an early date.—As time goes on, circumstances change, and ambition alters, and since I saw you, another complication has come upon the programme I mapped out to you at the Lyceum.—One thing is certain, there is no Tess on the English stage but Mrs. Campbell.—You said you saw me as "Clare."[3]

Again Forbes-Robertson wrote, later in 1895: "I am glad you have moved to go on with the play."[4] Still later he wrote: "I am so glad

[1] Max Gate MS.
[2] Max Gate MS. (italics mine).
[3] Max Gate MS.
[4] Max Gate MS.

you have finished the play. . . . Send the play as soon as you can. Having a few hours to myself, I am in the midst of *Jude!*"[1] Forbes-Robertson repeated his request in January, 1896: "I am looking forward to reading *Tess* with the greatest of pleasure. Will you please send us the MS. as soon as possible? If I have to do a play in a hurry, I must do one with comedy, and you must let us open with *Tess* in Sept. . . . , but let me read *Tess* through so that I may see if it could be put in [rehearsal][2] at once."[3]

Hardy must have completed the dramatization late in 1895, for he wrote to William Archer, on January 2, 1896: "I have finished the *Tess* play. But heaven knows what I shall do with it. I have received a large offer for its performance in America, but in my total inexperience I imagine it ought to appear here first."[4] In a letter to Harper, on February 9, 1896, Hardy said: "I hope to send a copy of the play in a few days."[5]

In an undated letter which obviously followed his previous request, Forbes-Robertson wrote:

> I have read *Tess* with the greatest interest, and it seems to me it might be shaped into a fine play—of course the central scene must be the duel between the man and the woman, and very powerful it is as it stands, though no doubt you could add yet another note or two—I am not quite happy about the first and second acts. It seems to me the seduction and the coming child are dwelt on too much. You must not be angry if I speak so bluntly. It is no use, is it, unless one speaks exactly how one is affected? You must let me come and see you at your convenience that we may talk it over.[6]

It seems that Hardy may have taken Forbes-Robertson's advice at least with regard to the first act. He or someone else altered his original text at some time, for there are striking differences between the original version sent to Harper in 1896 and the one played at Dorchester in 1924. We shall note later that Hardy told Henry Arthur Jones he could not get back to rearranging the script when

---

[1] Max Gate MS.
[2] This word was illegible to me but was read thus by Mrs. Hardy.
[3] Max Gate MS.
[4] This letter was among the original letters lent me by Colonel Archer.
[5] This letter was among the files of Harper and Brothers.
[6] Max Gate MS.

he gave it to the players in Dorchester; and since, apparently, the only time he spent much effort on the play was in the nineties, there seems good reason to infer that Hardy tried to please Forbes-Robertson by altering his *Tragedy in Five Acts in the Old English Manner* to a more compact version not dealing at such length with "the seduction and the coming child."[1] At any rate, Forbes-Robertson wanted the play and must have felt satisfied with it to be as insistent as he was. In February, 1896, he asked Hardy for his terms for London, the provinces, and America. "We should pay you royalties in all cases, of course, but should like to control rights. This will in no way hurt your fees." He suggested that the business arrangements be made through Frederic Harrison and Hardy's lawyer. On March 4, 1896, Hardy received a commercial offer from Harrison of the Lyceum.

With the play written, and a definite offer, one would have expected to find *Tess* on the London stage in the nineties. Why did Hardy not accept the offer? A letter to Henry Arthur Jones on March 15, 1896, shows he was considering it:

> Can you tell me if the following are good or bad terms for a play? I am in a hopeless fog on the matter.
>
> In a London theatre, average size:
>
> Houses under £100 .. .. nothing.
> From £100 to £130 .. .. 5 per cent.
> From £130 to £170 .. .. 7½ per cent.
> Over £170 . .. . 10 per cent.
>
> Probably produce play within a year.[2]

Whether it was on Jones's advice that Hardy refused the offer from Harrison, I do not know.

Meanwhile he had disposed of the American rights. The fol-

---

[1] The changes effected between the text acted at Dorchester (1924) and that acted in London (1925) we know to have been the work of A. E. Filmer. See below, p. xcvi.

[2] D. A. Jones, *Life and Letters of Henry Arthur Jones*, p. 171. Hardy showed excellent judgment in consulting Jones. Shaw had done the same thing regarding the terms for the American rights to *Arms and the Man* on April 24, 1894. He wrote: "Can I do better? Am I being had? I have to ask you because you are the only person I know whose business faculty inspires me with the smallest confidence." (*Ibid.*, p. 159.)

lowing letter to Harper and Brothers in New York, on February 9, 1896, explains Hardy's intention of disposing of the American rights separately:

> My first plan was to dispose of the right of acting the play in America to the English company, as they requested. But in view of the uncertainty of the date of their arrival in America, and the length of their stay there, I have decided to refuse this, if I can make an independent contract with an American company, or good terms (for the U. States only).
>
> It seems advisable to open negotiations first with Mr. Harrison Grey Fiske (on the basis of his letter of Dec. 13, 1895, of which you sent me a copy) if his arrangements for the season are not already concluded.
>
> I hope to send a copy of the play in a few days. I should prefer that my version be adhered to, but I would consent to a reasonable modification, if indispensable to its production by a first class company.[1]

On April 28, 1896, Harper received a cablegram from Messrs. Osgood, McIlvaine and Company: "Hardy inclined secure Fiske if terms feasible."[2] Despite his preference that his "version be adhered to," Hardy seems to have given Mrs. Fiske a free hand in both the adaptation and the production of *Tess*, and he was pleased with her success.

The following letter to Henry Arthur Jones (February 16, 1897) suggests mixed feelings, however, with regard to the English stage, and a desire not to be bothered even with copyrighting Stoddard's stage version of *Tess* because of other work, which can only be the composition of *The Dynasts*:

> An American arrangement of *Tess*, based on my draft and suggestions, is to be produced in New York the first week in March, on which production no expense has been spared. Meanwhile my agents over here say I ought to have a copyright performance here on the same day. Now, all this fills me with consternation, for I had secretly hoped that *Tess* was going to fall through altogether, as I have been, and am, more interested in other labours. However, prudence is prudence; and can you tell me how one sets about this sort of thing? Are there people who take it in hand for so much? Some time ago several people well known in London society said they would like to take

[1] Harper MS.
[2] Harper MS.

part in such a performance, and no doubt they would still; "it would be such fun," but fancy me getting up a play. My impression is that it is not necessary, but I am not sure.[1]

Jones must have given Hardy the same advice as his agents, that is, to have the copyright performance. A letter from George Alexander to Hardy indicates that Alexander may have taken the performance at the St. James's in hand "for so much." It informed Hardy that all was arranged and they could await the licence from the Lord Chamberlain; it asked him to bring two or three friends to the St. James's at ten o'clock on Monday, March 2, 1897, and pay two guineas each (to be returned later) to see the performance. Alexander called the procedure one of the farces of copyright. He suggested that the part of Tess was made for Miss Neilson and offered to talk over the murder scene with Hardy when he had finished his present engagement on a play of Pinero's.

It is not easy to explain why Hardy, who had gone so far as to have Stoddard's version copyrighted, did not allow it or his own version to be produced in London, and especially why he did not yield to the widespread demand for the latter. A partial answer may be found (as we have seen) in his growing preoccupation with *The Dynasts*. But his correspondence strongly suggests that the ambition of a number of leading actresses to play Tess was productive of embarrassment from which he could best escape by entirely withdrawing the script. With that "gentle plainness" and "something timid" which (according to Charles Morgan) characterized him, Hardy may have led an actress to believe that he had definitely assented to her playing the role when he had merely meant to be complimentary and kind. The fact that complications arose probably convinced him of his inability to deal with people of the theatre, and made him fear for his time and his tranquillity.

It is impossible to imagine Hardy dealing firmly with Mrs. Patrick Campbell, as, for instance, did Henry Arthur Jones in the affair of *Michael and His Lost Angel*. On December 16, 1895, Jones wrote to Forbes-Robertson: "If Mrs. Campbell is to play the part, she must play it exactly as it is written and upon the lines that I have

---

[1] D. A. Jones, *Life and Letters of Henry Arthur Jones*, p. 355.

laid down. But I feel it will be impossible to go through rehearsals without such constant scenes that it will be better to engage Marion Terry. I am sure you will be wise not to risk it. Please understand I will not have the text altered. . . ."[1] This letter has interest here besides showing the difference of temperament between the practical man of the theatre and the secluded writer of novels. About two weeks after Jones's ultimatum (January 1, 1896), Mrs. Patrick Campbell withdrew from *Michael and His Lost Angel*. She wasted no time in going to Dorchester to see Hardy about *Tess*. Her coming was announced in a letter Forbes-Robertson wrote to Hardy on January 5, 1896: "Mrs. Patrick Campbell is staying at the King's Arms Hotel in Dorchester; and she will be coming over to see you.[2] You and she can go over the play together. Mrs. Campbell found her part in the new play [*Michael and His Lost Angel*] so uncongenial to her that I thought it right to let her resign the part. . . . I am looking forward to reading *Tess* with the greatest pleasure."[3]

After her visit in January, Mrs. Campbell repeatedly wrote to Hardy until August, 1896, imploring him to permit her to enact the role. It appears that Hardy gave her and Forbes-Robertson permission to produce his play within a limited time. But they let the time elapse, and he withdrew his assent. Hardy wrote to Mrs. Campbell on August 7, 1896: "Mr. Buist informs you truly. As it was not

[1] *Ibid.*, p. 173.
[2] Mrs. Hardy told me of the first visit Mrs. Campbell paid to the Hardys in Dorchester. She rode a horse from the King's Arms Hotel out the Wareham road and was conveniently thrown at the entrance of Max Gate. This accident afforded her a dramatic first appearance to Hardy.

Mr. Carl Weber (*Hardy of Wessex*, p. 223) quotes the following statement of Arthur Waugh's: "Thomas Hardy is busily engaged upon the dramatization of *Tess*. It seems that the task is giving him a deal of trouble, and that Mrs. Patrick Campbell is consulted at every turn in the action. The matter arouses a good deal of interest in literary circles, and there are many surmises as to the course the play is likely to follow. It is clear that, for stage purposes, the development must be considerably rearranged. . . . Mrs. Campbell is immensely interested in it." (July 19, 1895.)

Mr. Waugh obviously overstates Hardy's consulting of Mrs. Campbell. Although it is true that Hardy wrote Mrs. Campbell on July 10, 1895, that it would be "a thousand pities" if she did not play Tess, it is very clear that, as negotiations proceeded, Hardy changed his mind.

[3] Max Gate MS.

produced last season, I have dismissed all thought of doing *Tess* in England for some time—if ever. It would be inconvenient to me to have it acted now, and there are reasons other than dramatic why I don't care to go on with it."[1] This escape through delayed production could be explained by Hardy's desire not to be interrupted, but his "reasons other than dramatic" for finding it inconvenient to negotiate further with Mrs. Campbell suggest some underlying complication. It is clear that Hardy felt free to open negotiations with other actresses after the lapse of Mrs. Campbell's rights.

Did Hardy have a Tess in mind? Or was he led on by the many requests? On August 26, 1895, Olga Nethersole had written: "May I ask if it is true that Mr. Forbes-Robertson is to produce your play *Tess*? You know of course how much I have loved your beautiful story, and how I have tried for nearly two years to get the play. If the London rights are disposed of, will you let me know about America? I am sorry to bother you, but I have a longing to *live* that woman's life, if only once. May I ask you to kindly answer this letter. . . ."[2] Olga Nethersole continued to desire the role. On April 30, 1897, almost two months after Mrs. Fiske's creation of Tess in New York, she wrote again from Walsingham House, Piccadilly: "Am sorry that you are not able to arrange with me for the production of *Tess* in London, now, but I sincerely hope you will be able to do so later."[3] Hardy may have regretted his inability to grant Olga Nethersole's wish, but he could feel no responsibility for her disappointment. By Elizabeth Robins' perplexity, however (which she expressed in March, before he gave Mrs. Campbell his decisive answer of August 7, 1896), he was probably embarrassed. Elizabeth Robins wrote on March 18, 1896:

> But it would be a poor compliment to *Tess* if I allowed you to think that I cared not at all about the matter, when sometime ago after your repeated assurances that you were looking to me to interpret the part—and after it being generally announced in the papers (not through me) that I was to play Tess—you entered into negotiations with Mrs. Campbell. I would not for the

[1] Max Gate MS.
[2] Max Gate MS.
[3] Max Gate MS.

world have embarrassed you by the slightest protest and I do not mean to now—but you may judge of my surprise then and my perplexity now.[1]

This letter could scarcely have been written if Elizabeth Robins had not *thought* Hardy had offered her the role. With his keen sense of fairness Hardy could not negotiate further with other actresses. Therefore on August 7, 1896, he answered Mrs. Campbell's next letter with the finality noted above.

But Mrs. Campbell was difficult to discourage, especially since Mrs. Fiske's success on the other side of the Atlantic kept the theatrical world interested. Mrs. Campbell put her pride in her pocket and asked for the part again in July, 1897.[2] Hardy's answer proved final and Mrs. Campbell gracefully withdrew (July 10, 1897). Forbes-Robertson, however, was persistent as late as December 15, 1898: "Would you kindly let me know who has the rights to *Tess*? I understood Mr. Alexander had and sent my messengers to him to ask about it, and he told me he had no rights over the piece. Of course, I refer to the play you and I and Mrs. Patrick Campbell talked about, and not the version done in America. It might be in my power to try it in the country during the next month or two, hence my telegram this morning."[3] Hardy was adamant; yet it is clear he would have liked to see Forbes-Robertson play Angel Clare. Years later, in 1924, we shall find Hardy speaking wistfully on this subject.[4] It is easy to understand why Hardy would not release the play in 1896 to Eleanora Duse, for whom her manager had said it would have to submit to the "inevitable mangling"[5] so that the heroine would be on the scene most of the time, while the hero would be a miserable weakling and "as good as annihilated." With Forbes-Robertson it was different. True, he had suggested some changes in Hardy's text, but he wanted Hardy to make them and was apparently satisfied with the play as revised. By December 15, 1898, however, Mrs. Fiske had had a triumph of almost two years' duration in the United States. And it would be perfectly natural for

[1] Max Gate MS.
[2] Max Gate MS.
[3] Max Gate MS.
[4] Max Gate MS. See below, p. lxxxvi.
[5] Max Gate MS.

Hardy (even for his own interests) to protect her rights, especially as there was the probability of her devoting a season in England to *Tess of the D'Urbervilles*. Her projected visit gave Hardy no other choice in dealing with Forbes-Robertson. To the history of her play we shall now turn.

III. LORIMER STODDARD: THE PLAY FOR MRS. FISKE

Hardy's correspondence shows that Harper and Brothers made contacts with several New York managers in regard to his dramatization of *Tess of the D'Urbervilles*. They found that A. M. Palmer, Augustin Daly, and Henry E. Abbey "were unable to take up the play in this country." Negotiations with Henry C. Miner "led to no result." But Harper received offers from Daniel Frohman, from Messrs. Greenwall and Company, and from J. P. Brian.[1] On April 28, 1896, Hardy decided to accept the offer of Greenwall and Company, who represented Minnie Maddern Fiske. The contract was probably signed some time before September 23, 1896, for when I examined the versions of *Tess* at Harper's, I noted on Hardy's own version these words: "Original MS. of Mr. Hardy's Dramatization of *Tess of the D'Urbervilles*. Duplicate copy of which was made in our office handed to Greenwall and Co. Sept. 23, 96."

Because Hardy followed his novel too closely, managers found his version impracticable for the stage. Despite Hardy's expressed desire that "my version be adhered to," he was willing to sacrifice his preference in order to get a first-class company to present the play. Fortunately, it was to Mrs. Fiske that he sold the American and Canadian rights and it was on her judgment that he relied regarding an actable dramatization. She had read a play by Lorimer Stoddard[2] and thought him capable of dramatizing *Tess*.

---

[1] Max Gate MS.

[2] Lorimer Stoddard (1864-1901) was the son of Richard Henry Stoddard and Elizabeth Barston Stoddard. Lowell said of Stoddard's mother "that she was the best writer of blank verse in America" (*Saturday Evening Herald* (Chicago), May 25, 1888). Young Stoddard was not inexperienced with the stage when Mrs. Fiske asked him to evolve a play from *Tess of the D'Urbervilles*. He had created the role of the British lordling, Arthur Trelawney, in *The Henrietta* with Robson and Crane; he had played "the Prince of Aragon as a fop when Mr.

Stoddard's adapting of the novel was a remarkable feat, for he wrote the entire play between one Friday noon and the following Wednesday night. When asked how he evolved the play, he explained:

[Mrs. Fiske] . . . thought I could take hold of *Tess* and dramatize it, provided the Harpers and Hardy approved it. Well, they did approve, and so I went at it hammer and tongs.

I read *Tess* through very carefully, and turned down a page when I wanted an act to end. For instance, I turned down page 150. Everything before page 150 must be explained or enacted in the first act, and so on all through the five acts.[1] For each act I chose one salient particular point around which the action was grouped and which led up to the climax, always keeping the atmosphere of the thing as much as possible. To start in with, I wrote a scenario of the action, merely the story of the thing without conversation, in order to get the movement of the piece before breaking it up into dialogue. That was the hardest part of the work, choosing what I was going to dramatize.

I had just got this done and written perhaps 50 lines of the first act when I got word that owing to some misunderstanding in the contract the time I was allowed for finishing the work was suddenly curtailed. Mrs. Fiske came to me in all sorts of consternation, quite hopeless as to even producing the piece. "That's all right," said I, "I'll have your play for you," and in five days it was ready.[2]

If Stoddard had been unequal to this extraordinary task, Mrs. Fiske's rights would have expired and *Tess* might have suffered in America an experience similar to that in England when Mrs. Patrick Campbell allowed the stipulated time to expire. Fortunately for Mrs. Fiske she had chosen wisely, and no doubt Stoddard's

Mansfield produced *The Merchant of Venice* at Herrmann's Theatre. He wrote the Napoleon play [*The Emperor Napoleon*—produced at the Herald Square Theatre] for Mansfield, and ought not to be blamed for that, for there was some good writing in the Waterloo and St. Helena scenes, and the thing gave Mansfield a splendid opportunity. He had also written some one act plays of promise." (*New York Times*, February 22, 1897.) He adapted Marion Crawford's *In the Palace of the King* for Viola Allen, and by 1896 had orders from such producers as Goodwin, Daly, and Tabers. Cf. *New York Dramatic Mirror*, September 14, 1901.

[1] A newspaper error. The play has four acts, but the last has two scenes.

[2] Cf. the *Wave*, June 5, 1897. (This interview was reprinted in the *Boston Globe*, September 20, 1905, in an article "*Tess* Out On Time.")

admiration for her spurred him to his strenuous undertaking. This admiration he expressed in the interview from which we have quoted: "And by the way, say right here that Mrs. Fiske is, in my opinion, quite the most wonderful actress we have in America. With her in the title role my work was easy."[1]

The happy combination of the dramatic elements of the novel with expertness of stage technique afforded Mrs. Fiske her vehicle for triumph. Her success was immediate. The *Theatre* said:

> The production of a stage version of Mr. Thomas Hardy's *Tess of the D'Urbervilles* at the Fifth Avenue Theatre is the event of the month in New York, as much by reason of the world-wide renown and popularity of the novel as by the instantaneous success achieved by Mrs. Fiske as the pathetic figure of Tess Durbeyfield. . . . Mrs. Fiske was helped considerably by Mr. Lorimer Stoddard's adaptation. At many points the artistic needs of the story were sacrificed to the more prosaic necessities of the player. The adapter has shown an amount of skill sufficient to make a stirring play. . . .[2]

In considering Mrs. Fiske's performance, it is difficult to apportion the credit as between the dramatic quality of Hardy's work and the technical skill of Stoddard; and it is impossible to determine precisely the contribution of the actress herself. This is especially true if Mrs. Fiske deserves partial credit for fashioning the play. The *New York Sun* said: "That it was her brilliant intellect that devised many of the details of the play Lorimer Stoddard would probably be the first to acknowledge."[3] It was, therefore, more than the summation of these three contributions: it was the fusion, the interweaving—in psychological terms, the *Gestalt*—of the compelling novel, the forceful dramatization, and the inspired acting which made the first performance at the Fifth Avenue Theatre "the most remarkable in its way that has taken place in many a year."[4] The *Brooklyn Daily Eagle* said:

> It is a pleasure to be able to say of the performance that it was great without any qualifying adjectives or clauses. Greatness is rare even in glimpses. Greatness of conception married to power, certainty, and finish of execution is

---

[1] The *Wave*, June 5, 1897.
[2] The *Theatre*, April 1, 1897, p. 231.
[3] *New York Sun*, March 4, 1897.
[4] *Ibid.*

one of those occasions for which the world awaits eagerly. Such a combination does Mrs. Fiske offer. The genius of Thomas Hardy's novel is as incontestable as the pathos and terror of it. These qualities Mr. Lorimer Stoddard has succeeded in a high degree in transferring to his stage version, while at the same time he has eliminated the psychology which would seem to make the book utterly impossible for stage treatment. . . ."[1]

"The vitals of the book are in the play," declared the *Chicago Journal*.[2] And this in large degree is the secret of Stoddard's success and the measure of his skill. "Mr. Stoddard has done as well for Hardy as anyone could who was bent, first of all, upon making an acting play; and he has certainly preserved the tragic tone of the novel, and exhibited Tess as a victim of Fate."[3] His task involved almost insuperable difficulties. As he said in his interview, his first problem was choosing what to dramatize. Unlike Hardy, Stoddard withstood the temptation to crowd his acts and scenes with incidents. He chose only the most striking and subordinated the rest. The condensation and selection necessary make it difficult to translate any novel to the stage, but especially is this true of Hardy's novels, so rich in dramatic and melodramatic action. And the problem is particularly acute in *Tess of the D'Urbervilles*, since it is based on a threadbare theme, "one that has been enacted in every country in all ages,"[4] and depends for its fascination on Hardy's new colouring and atmosphere. It contains, moreover, the subtle, not to say strange, character of Angel Clare, who is made intelligible and acceptable only by Hardy's close and exhaustive psychological analysis.[5] Stoddard handled this theme involving "madness,

---

[1] *Brooklyn Daily Eagle*, October 26, 1897.
[2] *Chicago Journal*, March 8, 1898.
[3] *New York Times*, March 7, 1897.
[4] *Cincinnati Enquirer*, November 30, 1897.
[5] "Hardy devotes 147 pages (nearly 60,000 words) largely to the analysis of motives and exposition of little traits of character (thus accounting naturally and without a hint of theatrical situation, for Tess's failure to confess her sin to Clare before her marriage). . . . Mr. Stoddard must compress all that he uses of this episode, together with dramatic equivalents for much that has gone before, and many needful original devices, in one-quarter of a play containing not more than 15,000 words in all. Naturally many traits of Hardy's heroine have disappeared altogether in the play. Her personal atmosphere has vanished." (*New York Times*, March 7, 1897.) If this last statement is true of Tess, it is equally true of Angel Clare.

murder, and vengeance" and made a "tragedy quite classical in its outlines."[1] He depicted Angel's character almost as satisfactorily as does the novel.

Stoddard did not flinch in presenting the more poignant aspects of the tragedy, "handling these themes, so to speak, without gloves."[2] For this reason he received much harsh criticism, especially outside the metropolitan area. For example, the *Toledo Blade* said: "It is a series of pictures of an imaginary vivisection of a soul, conceived by a morbid mind and thrown, with the delicate cunning of the artist, on a canvas composed of the nerves and emotions of the audience. It is not a great poetic tragedy depicting the sunshine and shadow which into each life must fall. It is only the exploitation of sordid conditions and exceptional infirmities, and its very graphicness makes the poison all the more insidious."[3] Usually, however, even among critics who regard the play as repellent, and as outraging "one's sense of what should be the ethics of the stage,"[4] there are such tempering remarks as: "The unpleasant passages in the story have not been put there merely for the purposes of sensation; they are part and parcel of a curious psychological problem, which is skilfully worked out."[5] In fact, Stoddard does not depict some of the most oppressive scenes, such as "the chill horror of Starve-acre farm."[6] And the sojourn of Tess and Angel "in the uninhabited house, similar in artistic value to the bedchamber scene in *Romeo and Juliet* before Romeo's flight to Mantua,"[7] is not used. Especially are we spared the execution scene—the black flag watched by Angel and Liza-Lu from the distance.

What Stoddard chose can be very briefly stated. In the first act, is the courtship; in the second, the confession after the wedding; in the third, Tess believing Angel is dead yields to Alec; in the fourth, the murder of Alec and the apprehension of Tess at Stonehenge.

---

[1] *Chicago Journal*, March 8, 1898.
[2] *Philadelphia Evening Telegraph*, January 11, 1898.
[3] *Toledo Blade*, November 1, 1898.
[4] *Philadelphia Public Ledger*, January 18, 1898.
[5] *Ibid.*
[6] The *Theatre*, April 1, 1897, p. 231.
[7] *Ibid.*

INTRODUCTION xxxix

That Stoddard chose his material wisely was almost universally agreed. Some critics even preferred the play to the novel:

> Whatever grossness may be discovered in the novel is completely eliminated in the dramatization by Mr. Stoddard. The villainy is there, the over-rush of circumstances, the complete paralysis of free action in the face of forces before which human endurance is as chaff, the mental reaction which logically leads to murder, and its subsequent expiation. The life story of Tess is told with straightforwardness, and with great effect, except as regards the closing scene. . . . Indeed, the play is, to our mind, more impressive than the novel; the pity of it all is impressed in scene after scene, with few digressions and without superfluous exaggeration or malodorous suggestion. . . . One realizes just what certain phases of existence must mean to those who face them, is appalled at the relentless irony of human destiny in some cases, wonders what can be done about it,—and is filled with a great pity, a wider and deeper charity for those who, having stacked cards forced into their hands, play the game of life to the end and lose every trick.[1]

Although a critic for the *Boston Evening Transcript* thought that Stoddard's "matter was too strong for his style,"[2] others praised his play highly. William Dean Howells said: "Mr. Stoddard, whether he has got much or little from Mr. Hardy's novel, has made a play of the sort which will give him the right to be considered hereafter in making up any judgment of the modern drama. He has taken a long step; he has touched a height."[3] Much of Stoddard's success was, no doubt, a result of the fact that he took few liberties with Hardy's novel. As nearly as a representation can, his play preserves the purpose and philosophy of *Tess of the D'Urbervilles*. "He has given the essence and the pith of the story, has not dawdled through the pages, nor tried to keep the book in your mind. Yet he is never untrue to his author."[4]

What additions Stoddard made were for dramatic effect. "His original devices were few but satisfying."[5] He enlarged the charac-

---

[1] *Boston Times*, November 7, 1897.
[2] Undated clipping concerning the Tremont production in Boston (Harvard Theatre Collection).
[3] *Harper's Weekly*, March 20, 1897.
[4] *Chap Book*, April 15, 1897, p. 421.
[5] *New York Times*, March 3, 1897.

ters with whom comedy was possible—the dairymaids, Jonathan, and Tess's parents—and saved the play from lugubriousness. He avoided certain moral issues. For instance, Tess does not know until after her wedding that Angel did not receive her confession. The audience will sympathize more fully with Tess if she is in no wise culpable. To win yet more sympathy, Stoddard has her informed falsely of Angel's death. He deftly employed the dialogue of the novel and skilfully made conversation out of the narrative of the book, the most notable example being found in the confession scene. As was necessary for the theatre, he magnified some of the more important movements for the eye. Naturally the fate of Tess's letter, "my life," had to be put conspicuously before the audience. The *New York Dramatic Mirror* found in the play "a remarkable variety in characterization, a contrast of incident, a blending of motives, and a pictorial diversity, as notable as unusual."[1] Whatever faults the play had, such as a lack of consistency of treatment (in the third act, for example, the eviction scene is melodramatic), they were outweighed, it was agreed, by the fine comedy, the exquisite pathos, the stirring tragedy, and the good literary quality. The critic of the *Brooklyn Daily Eagle* said that the play was "like a symphony played by the Boston orchestra, in which one thinks less of the individual merits than of the harmonious whole."[2] The *Boston Evening Transcript* found the play "of singular power, and the plot is carried through to its logical ending with the directness and intensity of one of the old Greek tragedies. It might well be called 'Fate,' so irresistibly is the heroine hurried to the only conclusion of her life story that the circumstances warrant."[3]

Naturally with difference of motive go differences in characterization, for example in Joan, Alec, and Marian. In the play, Joan Durbeyfield becomes more meddlesome, more actively implicated in the catastrophe. Her standards of morality have been compared to those of the Nurse in *Romeo and Juliet*. The *Boston Daily Advertiser* said that in the novel she was a "mild, slatternly, spirit-

---

[1] *New York Dramatic Mirror*, March 13, 1897.
[2] *Brooklyn Daily Eagle*, October 26, 1897.
[3] *Boston Evening Transcript*, September 19, 1905.

less muddleheaded woman—a mush of whining good nature and shiftlessness. In the play she is a scheming, nagging, persistent creature who deliberately pushes her daughter into wickedness."[1] Alec D'Urberville is also quite differently conceived, with far more subtle villainy and polished brutality. Indeed as Frederick de Belleville played the part, he could even find a defender in one dramatic critic: "[His] air is more manly, generous, and engaging than that of the husband. It is beyond question that *Alec* loves *Tess*. When *Angel* deserts his wife, *Alec* rescues her from poverty, provides liberally for her family, educates and cares for her brother, supplies her with a luxurious home and, so far as the play tells us, is the only genuine friend she has ever known."[2] It is Stoddard's innovation to have Tess employ Marian as a parlour-maid to save Marian from drink. As such she is a useful and even a powerful personage in the episodes of the first scene of the fourth act which show the return of Angel, the murder of Alec, and the flight of Tess.

Of Stoddard's Tess little need be said. He grasped the author's conception of her as a woman all passion and impulse, "in whom," as Hector Charlesworth said, "all the springs of pagan poetry and pagan honour are embodied. . . ."[3] It is true that another critic objected to her as being "expurgated and blood-let . . . in comparison with Mr. Hardy's creation,"[4] but he may have had that impression from Mrs. Fiske's personation. Except for the letter episode, there is slight change in Tess's motivation. Yet Stoddard gives her more dignity. She is less painfully conscious of her "class" as inferior to Clare's.[5] Her self-respect is emphasized by her freedom to refuse the money which her husband offers and commands her to take. And in the final scene at Stonehenge, Stoddard portrays her as self-sacrificing, courageous, and utterly oblivious of death, so that, perhaps even more than in the novel, one is aware of the symbolism of the altar and recognizes that the tragic catharsis

[1] *Boston Daily Advertiser*, November 2, 1897.
[2] *Home Journal*, March 10, 1897 (italics in the original).
[3] *Daily Mail and Empire* (Toronto), February 17, 1899.
[4] *Boston Daily Advertiser*, November 2, 1897.
[5] Stoddard omitted the letter from Clare's father about the incongruity of giving his wife the jewels.

occurs (in Goethe's phrase) "through a kind of human sacrifice."

Critics ranked the play highest among the serious dramas in New York in 1897.[1] The *Chicago Journal* declared that the American stage had risen to certain literary and dramatic opportunities and that the result was a strong, sane play, free from trick devices and steady in movement. It added: "If you felt a gratitude to Thomas Hardy for telling the true truth—truth that is full of beauty and awfulness—you will likewise thank Mr. Stoddard for having used that truth for the purposes of the stage and having kept it unspotted from the banality with which the stage too often smirches things."[2]

"The best of Mr. Stoddard's work, however, is the fact that he has given to Mrs. Fiske in the stage dress of Tess a character of such strength, of such intensity, so virile with life, so vibrant with emotion, that she is able to hold her audience . . . in such rapt attention"[3] from scene to scene. The remark is characteristic both in subordinating the play to the actress and in its enthusiasm for Mrs. Fiske in the title role.[4] What struck dramatic critics most

---

[1] The *New York Herald*, for March 7, 1897, under the caption, "A Dramatic Revelation," quotes expressions of enthusiasm (of varying degrees of percipience) from the New York press: "A great play, the large audience spellbound for nearly three hours." *World*. "It was great. The best play of the season." *Journal*. "The fascinating rural atmosphere well preserved. Boldly and bravely artistic." *Sun*. "A success. Plenty of heart interest." *Morning Advertiser*. "One of the most notable works presented on our stage in recent times." *Press*. "A great play. A superb success." *Evening Sun*. "Marvellously strong—the audience held spellbound." *Evening Journal*. "A great success." *Commercial Advertiser*. "Remarkably good." *Mail and Express*. "Astounding, overwhelming, magnificent!" *Daily*.

[2] *Chicago Journal*, March 8, 1898.

[3] *Cincinnati Commercial Tribune*, November 30, 1897.

[4] This enthusiasm is seen in such headlines as "A Great Actress," "A Wonderful Presentation," and "Mrs. Fiske's Genius Has Full Scope." That the enthusiasm was shared by representative spectators is shown by the following items from the Harvard Theatre Collection (J. A. Waldron, Press Representative):

Robert Ingersoll wrote: "We were all overpowered last night. Mrs. Fiske was marvellous. Her acting was perfect. Every tone, every gesture was pathetic, dramatic, artistic, tragic, and even her laughter was filled with tears."

Ella Wheeler Wilcox said in a letter to Mrs. Fiske: "I had read and lived with 'Tess' so keenly, and dreaded to see it lest it be spoiled to me, but you

forcibly was her complete naturalness. "It is one of those rare instances where the woman is completely merged in the character she is portraying, and her work is far above the mere devices of stage-craft."[1] "As Tess, discarding all known acting traditions except the injunction to hold the mirror up to nature, Mrs. Fiske scores an absolute realization of her ambitions."[2] Repeatedly her realism and her naturalness are remarked in comments on the more intense scenes. Mrs. Fiske did not resort to "a single recognizable stage device," says Edith Wharton, and adds that her chief distinction lay in her sobriety of method and her skill in producing effects with the smallest expenditure of voice and gesture.

In a part like Tess such a capacity for silence and immovability is invaluable. All through the play Mrs. Fiske is the passionate, inarticulate peasant, and not the clever actress in a peasant make-up. Her extraordinary realism deserves special commendation, because it never once oversteps the bounds of stage illusion, because in every detail it is the product, not of haphazard divination, but of a keen sense of stage requirements—the art that conceals art. But no less noteworthy is the skill with which Mrs. Fiske, without sentimentalizing her part, has managed to keep its poetry. Her Tess is a crude, rudimentary creature, but never a vulgar or a brutal one. Mrs. Fiske has heroically eschewed the temptation to take the audience by the two "effects" most certain of success—sentimentality and coarseness. And the result, last night, was a triumph for that much underrated faculty, the intelligence of the theatrical public. The audience vibrated to every one of Mrs. Fiske's touches. A breath of fresh air, an unwonted thrill of reality, permeated the stale atmosphere of the theatre. Every gesture, every intonation of Mrs. Fiske reached its mark.[3]

Of the character of Tess, Mrs. Fiske herself said:

were all the book and more. I never saw such wonderful work on the stage as you did that first night. France may have its Bernhardt and Italy its Duse; but I do not believe either of them ever did such marvellous work as yours in 'Tess.'"

Hamlin Garland also wrote: "There were moments last night of the finest literary feeling, and the whole play lays hold of the most vital and tragic themes of our day. Your work was most original and natural in method."

[1] *Boston Post*, November 2, 1897.
[2] Hector Charlesworth, in the *Daily Mail and Empire* (Toronto), February 17, 1899.
[3] *Commercial Advertiser* (New York), May 7, 1902.

Tess touches sublimity in her sorrows. Her purity is stolen from her. Her child is taken from her. Her husband, whom she loves, forsakes her. She has no friend. She works hard day after day, like a patient, dumb brute, toiling humbly in the fields, sometimes scorched by the sun, again beaten upon by the pitiless rain, but still toiling on humbly, with persistent loyalty and meek devotion to those whose share of food depends upon the labour of her poor scarred hands, and through it all there is no thought of self, but always there is revealed a wondrous, uncomplaining sweetness and humility.[1]

"Every word that Tess utters," wrote one critic, "is fraught with the agony of culminating despair, every utterance is that of a tortured soul."[2]

The appearance of Mrs. Fiske is thus described:

Imagine a tender little woman, with tawny hair, eyes like a summer's night sky, dark but all stars, and a soft intensely feminine voice, who comes up from the meadows with the sweet breath of the kine all about her. She is Tess, Mrs. Fiske's Tess. She is as sweetly pretty as any country lass need be, but with more beauty of soul than of physical feature speaking to you from her face. Sadness broods over it from the very first time we see it. When a smile comes, it is wan and weak and it is as if we had seen death mark her for its own.[3]

Clearly she was not in physical presence or in tone of feeling in the least like Hardy's Tess. The problem which this fact raises was discussed years later in retrospect:

Her problem then, was to make the Tess of the play the kind of a woman she could plausibly impersonate, so that her personality could give life to the part. She had every right to do this—or else acting is not art at all, but a process of mechanical reproduction, like a phonograph. For peasant stupidity she substituted innocence and wistfulness; for the bovine quality she substituted fragility, nervous sensitive trustfulness; for the dumbness of Tess's longings, she substituted a taut-wire emotionalism. Thus in the same set of circumstances the same tragic workings of Fate were plausibly brought about, the same terrible lesson was read. Her Tess was no less a human creature in the fell clutch of circumstances than Hardy's maiden. Here was an almost perfect example of an actor's realization that he cannot get away from his own

---

[1] *Commercial Tribune* (New York), December 5, 1897.
[2] *New York Dramatic Mirror*, March 29, 1898.
[3] *Chicago Chronicle*, March 8, 1898.

personality, and that to succeed greatly in the theatre he must by every device of art use his personality to give life and illusion to his role.[1]

Mrs. Fiske's "conception of the character throughout the play is entirely in keeping with Hardy's theory of Fate, the ironical force of circumstances that determines the destinies of human beings, either for good or evil, for happiness or misfortune, for weal or woe."[2]

On the great scenes two or three representative comments must suffice. At the end of the first act, Mrs. Fiske produced a most revealing effect in one of her consummate silences with almost no expenditure of action or gesture, "when she sits in the garden and imagines Angel Clare is reading her letter telling of her 'fall.' She is absolutely still, and there is no facial contortion, but in her attitude and in her expression is the whole story of her life, past and future—shame, terror, grief, hope, all are expressed with a wonderful and absolutely silent force, which is nothing short of marvellous."[3] Then in the second act, in her confession and appeal to her husband, critics said that she exemplified faithfully Hardy's pure woman. Hector Charlesworth wrote: "With the mute consternation on her face she tells the whole story of what Clare's failure to discover her letter means to her; then follows the confession, made with her hand before her eyes as if to hide her shame. The broken voice, harsh with pain, pleading for forgiveness, and the culmination with its picture of a distrait woman, on her knees, crying in shrill accents for the man who has gone—these could not have been greater achievements than they were."[4] And the *Chap Book* declared:

Only a pure woman would have told the story as this Tess does, and only a great actress would have realized it, and used this simple, subtle means of expression. The ordinary actress would have run through the entire list of emotional gymnastics in face and figure.

Equally fine was the ending of the act where she sank, squatting helplessly and commonly on the floor, repeating her words of entreaty to her husband

---

[1] *Boston Evening Transcript*, July 31, 1916. While the problem raised is a real one, this is scarcely a just description of Hardy's Tess.
[2] *New York Dramatic Mirror*, March 29, 1898.
[3] *Chap Book*, April 15, 1897, p. 421.
[4] *Daily Mail and Empire* (Toronto), February 17, 1899.

not to leave her, in monotone. Réjane plays a scene in *Sappho*, where her lover leaves her, in the same helpless way, and it is interesting to see two such artists unconsciously adopting the same mode and means of expression.[1]

But it was in the murder scene that Mrs. Fiske rose to the heights of her genius as an emotional actress. "Alec's murder is not seen nor heard, yet there is no lack of realistic horror in the scene. As the unhappy woman sways and totters to and fro aimlessly about the room, the thoughts in her blazing brain are right before us. She throws the knife behind the bureau and then not knowing what she is doing tries to pull on her gloves. The pantomimic details of the rest of the scene till Angel returns and she finds refuge at last in his arms, are exquisitely put in."[2] "The femininity of her character, the gentleness of her nature is," according to the *Cincinnati Enquirer,* "even in that awful moment when she revenges cruel wrongs, not obscured. She is not a female fiend, and the audience loves and approves her act."[3] William Dean Howells adds more details of her acting: "Another most poignant effect is that of Tess's bewilderment after the homicide when she comes out of Alec's room with the wild instinct of flight, and half puts on the mantle which she leaves dragging from one shoulder while she stands by the glass trying mechanically to fit on a pair of gloves, and obviously does not know what she is doing. It is a cruel scene, and it is easily the supreme moment of a play which rather abounds in high moments."[4] Edith Wharton expresses the reaction of the audience to this scene: "When after the murder, she stood mechanically brushing her hair—when Angel Clare loosened the brush from her rigid fingers and said, 'Come'—one felt through the whole packed and breathless house the sweep of that mighty force 'which purges the emotions by pity and terror.' The actress had every heart string in her grip."[5]

The role of Tess marked a new era in the career of Mrs. Fiske. "Just previous to her triumph in 'Tess'—Miss [Mildred] Aldrich had written: 'Yet one is, with all this, unable to feel that Minnie

---

[1] *Chap Book*, April 15, 1897, p. 421.
[2] *Chicago Chronicle*, March 8, 1898.
[3] November 30, 1897.
[4] *Harper's Weekly*, March 20, 1897.
[5] *Commercial Advertiser* (New York), May 7, 1902.

Maddern Fiske has yet arrived.'"[1] Obviously in *Tess* she eclipsed her former successes. Whether her Tess was better than her Becky Sharp, which followed, is a matter of opinion, but it was vastly better than her Gilberte Sartory and her Nora Helmer, her finest presentations before Tess. "The nervous haste, the occasional uncertainty and unevenness which marked the work of this actress when she was striving for popular recognition have disappeared. In their place have grown calmness, distinction, and authority; qualities which only come from the assurance that the visions of the artist have found response in the hearts of the audience. . . ."[2] Hector Charlesworth said that *Tess of the D'Urbervilles*

was the foundation of her future fame, because though she did not resemble Hardy's description of Tess physically, she seemed to have gotten into the soul of the character. Previously she had proven her intellectual eminence in Ibsen, but in Tess she showed herself a great emotional actress, though using the subdued methods of Eleanora Duse who had unquestionably influenced her style. The cast . . . was well-nigh perfect, and included two celebrated leading men of that day (1897), John Craig as Angel Clare and Tyrone Power as Alec D'Urberville. Mrs. Fiske was then thirty-two and in the full flush of her powers.[3]

Her triumphant success in the role was commemorated in a bust by Max Bachmann, exhibited in the Fifth Avenue Theatre, which was thus described:

Mr. Bachmann's representation of Mrs. Fiske as Tess is at the final instant of the drama, when, after her stress of existence and her brief moment of happiness, she stands at the ancient altar a victim of circumstances and a sacrifice to the conventions that have made those circumstances fatal. It is at this moment when Tess says, "The sun has come"; and the artist's idea presents a figure in which the woman's sad life is epitomized, yet one in which the glory of her belated felicity shines forth in the face of death.[4]

Nor was Mrs. Fiske's great creation soon forgotten. As late as 1934 the *Boston Post* lauded her performance in an article under the caption of "The Biggest Hits Of The Old Days": "The 'Tess' of

---

[1] Frank Carlos Griffith, *Mrs. Fiske* (New York: Neal Publishing Co., 1912), p. 35.
[2] *Brooklyn Daily Eagle*, October 26, 1897.
[3] Hector Charlesworth's letter to me, December 4, 1942.
[4] *New York Dramatic Mirror*, undated (Harvard Theatre Collection).

Mrs. Fiske glows in the memory of those who saw her at the turn of the century as an experience of first rank. The genius of America's greatest actress fused with that of one of the greatest novelists of all time 'faithfully presented a pure woman.' That was what Thomas Hardy intended to do when he wrote the story of the young English peasant girl and it was what Mrs. Fiske carried over the foot-lights in her simple, natural, and powerful portrayal in the dramatization by Lorimer Stoddard.[1]

It must not be supposed that the audience accepted *Tess of the D'Urbervilles* wholly without protest, or even that the critics were quite unanimous in their approval. One critic, admitting being "belated, provincial, and puritanical," was inclined to "glance a trifle askance at Hardy's ethical signposts," and to resent his presentation of "that malodorous female, the woman with a past" and "an atmosphere redolent ... and vibrant with the shrieks of hysteria."[2] Even those who appreciated what Stoddard and Mrs. Fiske had done doubted that the public would accept *Tess of the D'Urbervilles*. No doubt the fate of Ibsen in New York and the impression of the first-night audience justified the critic of the *New York Times* in his judgment when he said: "... and I do not think that the general effect of his [Stoddard's] play is sadder or more depressing than the effect of the tragic story upon which it is founded. But I am quite certain that *Ghosts, Galeotto,* or *Rosmersholm* could not be more sombre in the acting, and two of these plays are not a bit more frank in dealing with the relations of the sexes than *Tess of the D'Urbervilles*. And that is why I am dubious about the public acceptance of Mr. Stoddard's play."[3]

[1] *Boston Post*, March 20, 1934.
[2] *Boston Journal*, March 14, 1897.
[3] *New York Times*, March 7, 1897. The same article said: "As a 'sensation' it is now uppermost in the minds of those folks who think themselves cognoscenti. As a dramatization of a memorable work of fiction it necessarily receives notice. Mrs. Fiske's artistic reputation helps it, and the fact that the performance is of merit has been noised abroad. But if I believed it would long survive, I should be inclined to believe, also, in the commercial value of the Scandinavian drama. I certainly do not consider either the book or the play immoral, though it is hard to understand how persons who foam at the mouth whenever Ibsen or Sarah Bernhardt is mentioned can go into rhapsodies about Thomas Hardy, who is almost as fond of particulars as Zola and the author of Deuteronomy."

Alan Dale did not think that Mrs. Fiske or anyone else expected the enthusiasm which her work aroused. It was one of those "fag end of the season" experiments that are generally set down with complacent contempt as artistic successes. He imagined Mrs. Fiske saying to herself, "I will do what I honestly believe to be the best, and if they don't like it—well, at any rate, they will have seen it."[1]

It was a very dangerous case. One little slip and the whole cup of merit would have been spilled irrevocably. A lapse for one moment into theatrical self-consciousness would have ruined the play.

Mrs. Fiske, however, scarcely understands the meaning of the word self-conscious. She plays with her artistic temperament carefully wrapped around her. She is Tess—Tess, the luckless; Tess, the simple and ingenuous; Tess, the untrammelled avenger; Tess, the unworldly wise. Rarely has so complete an embodiment of a fictitious character been seen upon our stage. I could detect no flaws. I could see no loophole for complaint in the production. As a rule, I am not fond of dramas that tend toward the midnight hour, but *Tess of the D'Urbervilles* was not long enough.[2]

From such criticism it might appear that Hardy's *Tess* won fame on the stage merely because it was played by Mrs. Fiske, that is to say, that her art made his theme acceptable. But when we remember that Mrs. Fiske had played Ibsen without winning extraordinary success, that can scarcely be the explanation. On the contrary, we must conclude that the play itself was also responsible for Mrs. Fiske's success. Hardy (through Stoddard) contributed the tragic role in which she won her triumph. As Tess of the D'Urbervilles she first achieved fame equal to that of the most celebrated foreign stars. "It is one of the most pregnant happenings of recent years," said Alan Dale. "It is revolutionary."[3]

There can be no doubt that the critic of the *New York Times* soon saw his mistake in predicting that the public would not accept Stoddard's play. Depressing, sad, frank as it was, it ran for eleven weeks at the end of the season in New York in 1897. Then, after Mrs. Fiske presented the play in Boston, Philadelphia, Chicago, and other important theatrical centres, she brought it back to the Fifth

---

[1] *New York Journal*, March 14, 1897.
[2] *Ibid.*
[3] *Ibid.*

Avenue Theatre in New York in March, 1898. The *New York Dramatic Mirror* (which should have known)[1] said: "The public have filled the theatre with encouraging regularity throughout every engagement. Accordingly, it is by no means an exaggeration to say that *Tess of the D'Urbervilles* has not only been the most successful drama from an artistic standpoint, which has been presented to the public this season, but has also proved more remunerative than any other dramatic production that has been presented outside of New York City."[2] Mrs. Fiske kept *Tess of the D'Urbervilles* in her repertoire and for years continued to present it all over the United States and in Canada. Edwin F. Edgett pointed out in the *Boston Evening Transcript* that the credit of the dramatization of *Tess of the D'Urbervilles* was due to American authorship and American acting. And he added: "It is rather noteworthy that it was not seen on the English stage until three seasons after the American production, and then in an unauthorized version over which there was considerable controversy."[3] To this unauthorized adaptation we now briefly turn.

IV. Hugh Arthur Kennedy's Unauthorized Version

It is evident from Hardy's correspondence with H. B. Irving that he was concerned with protecting Mrs. Fiske's rights to produce *Tess* in England if she chose to come.[4] And we recall that Irving

---

[1] Harrison Grey Fiske was the owner of the *Mirror*. According to Hector Charlesworth's letter to me, December 4, 1942, he was also the director of his wife's production.

[2] *New York Dramatic Mirror*, March 29, 1898.

[3] Undated type sheets, identified by Mrs. Lillian Hall, the former curator of the Harvard Theatre Collection (Harvard Theatre Collection).

[4] Cf. p. xxvi. There is also slight evidence in a letter to Miss Charlotte Pendleton, who wrote on June 24, 1900, asking permission to use *Tess* in an opera for which she would write the libretto and Mr. C. Schenk, an assistant to Walter Damrosch, would compose the music. Hardy answered on June 26, 1900: "I should have no objection to this being done, though I can take no responsibility in the matter. It would probably be necessary that you work straight from the novel, and not from any existing dramatization, for instance, Mrs. Fiske's; for though I can imagine an opera would not injure a play on the same subject, the dramatizer might not approve of his work being used as a basis for your libretto." (Max Gate MS.)

had written, "Let me know if the American visit falls through." It may be that the one inconclusive letter from Mrs. Fiske which I found at Max Gate refers to Hardy's voluntary protection of her rights in England. On December 14, 1898, she wrote from New York: "I have received your letter and I thank you most heartily and sincerely for the generous consideration you have shown me in regard to the matter of *Tess of the D'Urbervilles*. Believe me, my dear Sir, with most grateful appreciation. . . ." It is, however, evident that Hardy never parted with his rights over the stage production in his own country,[1] although he did let Mrs. Fiske have the American and Canadian rights. The *New York Dramatic Mirror* was therefore in error (even though edited by Harrison Grey Fiske) when it stated: "The exclusive English dramatic rights to Thomas Hardy's novel are owned by Mrs. Fiske, and Lorimer Stoddard's dramatization, copyrighted in England, is also her sole property."[2] The statement is not only in violation of the property rights of an author,[3] but is also refuted in Hardy's letter to the Reverend Canon Langbridge, on April 25, 1906: "In answer to your inquiry about the dramatization of *Tess* I have to tell you that the rights are still in my hands, but I do not want the story to appear here as a play unless as prepared by myself, and even under such conditions I am not clear that I should be disposed to produce it. The acting version which was presented in America was performed here once, to secure copyright, and to prevent others from doing it without authority, but it was not carried further."[4]

Mrs. Fiske did not visit England, for reasons that do not appear. Frank Carlos Griffith, her manager from 1897 to 1910, was unable to account for her not doing so, and added: "In my humble opinion, and from my experience with London audiences, she would be the

---

[1] The *Stage Cyclopedia*, p. 438 says: "*Tess of the D'Urbervilles*. Adapt. of Thomas Hardy's novel by Lorimer Stoddart [*sic*] St. James, March 2, 1897." Cf. also the *Copyright Register of Dramatic Representations and Performances*: "Thomas Hardy and Lorimer Stoddart [*sic*] . . . . Proprietor of Copyright in Great Britain and Colonies, Thomas Hardy."

[2] *New York Dramatic Mirror*, May 19, 1900.

[3] Cf. Philip Wittenberg, *Protection and Marketing of Literary Property* (New York: Messner Inc., 1937), Article VIII, Subsidiary Rights. Section I, *Title Vested Absolutely in Author*, p. 324.

[4] Colby College MS.

biggest success of the age. English people, however, are indissolubly wedded to tradition, and perhaps would not accept her Tess, as not Hardy's, or that it is not English while in fact it is greater than Hardy's . . . a universal Tess, idealized."[1]

In March, 1900, when Mrs. Lewis Waller enacted in London the unauthorized arrangement by Hugh Arthur Kennedy, one unidentified London newspaper said:

The time has clearly arrived when Mrs. Fiske's patriotism should yield for a little space to her duty toward the writer whose book furnished her with one of the best opportunities she has ever had for the exercise of her genius. *Tess*, indifferently dramatized, has been indifferently acted to an indifferent audience in one of London's second-class theatres.

It has been promised for a long time that the American actress would give *Tess* here, even the theatre in which she should appear has been named, but she did not come and so Mrs. Lewis Waller, an English actress of talent, ordered a dramatization made of *Tess* after having attempted and failed to obtain from Mrs. Fiske the sole English rights of the American version.[2]

But already Mrs. Fiske seems to have postponed or abandoned the idea of a season in London devoted to *Tess*. In Toronto, on February 17, 1899, "chatting with a *Mail and Empire* reporter[3] after the performance last night she spoke of her plans for the future. Next season she intends to play nothing but Becky Sharp in a dramatization of Thackeray's *Vanity Fair* recently completed by Langdon Mitchell. . . . 'I should like to play a different piece every night,' said Mrs. Fiske, 'but there is a strong demand for *Tess* everywhere. Although I will do nothing but Becky Sharp next season, Tess will remain a part of my permanent repertoire.' "[4] Her plan to exclude Tess for the year 1899-1900 obviously also excluded a trip to England.

How long Mrs. Fiske's projected visit and Hardy's desire to protect her rights may have operated as a deterrent, we do not know. When Forbes-Robertson asked for the leading role for his wife in 1924, Hardy said that his manuscript "had been lying in a

[1] F. C. Griffith, *Mrs. Fiske*, p. 141.
[2] Unidentified clipping, March 4, 1900 (Harvard Theatre Collection).
[3] Hector Charlesworth informed me he was that reporter.
[4] *Daily Mail and Empire* (Toronto), February 17, 1899.

cupboard almost forgotten since ever so long, so that she might have had it for the asking any time these last dozen years."[1] We know also that Hardy gave Lillah McCarthy (Mrs. Granville-Barker) the right to produce the play in 1910. By that time Hardy felt relieved of any restriction he may have imposed on his play. It was clear that Mrs. Fiske would never appear in London as Tess. But by 1900 Mrs. Fiske had not given Hardy any indication of her intention not to come to England and Hardy protected her rights.

Mrs. Lewis Waller's[2] production of Hugh Arthur Kennedy's unauthorized version of *Tess of the D'Urbervilles* opened at the Coronet Theatre, Nottinghill Gate, on February 19, 1900, and ran with sufficient success to justify its transfer to the Comedy on April 14. Mrs. Fiske asked the English courts for an injunction restraining Mrs. Waller from further representations and according to the *New York Dramatic Mirror* claimed damages for violation of copyright because Mrs. Waller's play "was based upon the Stoddard dramatization, much of the material of which, invented by Mr. Stoddard, was used, as well as the selection and arrangement of incidents from the novel."[3] Hardy must have supported Mrs. Fiske's claim.[4] The injunction was granted and the play was suspended.

The Kennedy version is evidence of the English demand for *Tess* on the stage. Clement Scott had written repeatedly since 1897: "The play ought to come to England as soon as possible."[5] Mrs. Fiske's failure to come was indirectly responsible for the Waller

---

[1] Max Gate MS.

[2] Mrs. Waller, "formerly known as Florence West . . . sister of Mrs. Clement Scott and Lady Arthur . . . made her first appearance at Toole's in 1883 . . . appeared with Lewis Waller in several plays at principal London theatres . . ." (*The Green Book*, ed. John Parker (London: T. Sealey Clark & Co., 1909), p. 502).

[3] May 19, 1900.

[4] "Thomas Hardy, who rarely permits himself to figure in the newspapers, writes to the *Times* in no uncertain tone about this version of the novel. He says: 'Sir: As I find I am naturally supposed to have something to do with the production of "Tess of the D'Urbervilles" at the Coronet Theatre last night, I shall be glad if you will allow me to state that I have not authorized such a dramatization, and that I am ignorant of the form it has taken, except in so far as I gather from the newspapers.'" Unidentified clipping, March 4, 1900 (Harvard Theatre Collection).

[5] Cf. *Daily Transcript*, March 24, 1897.

production. As the *Observer* said, *Tess of the D'Urbervilles* "was sure to find stage interpreters sooner or later, whether its writer did or did not approve of the dramatization."¹

It will be recalled that on November 19, 1894, Olga Nethersole asked Hardy to dramatize *Tess of the D'Urbervilles* for her or to permit her friend, Clement Scott, to do so. This request implies Scott's willingness, and various criticisms that he wrote of Mrs. Fiske's play reflect more than a critic's passing interest in *Tess* as dramatic material. In 1897, he had gone so far as to visualize a conclusion for it on the boards. In that year he writes:

> I was curious to see how Mr. Lorrimer [*sic*] Stoddard ended his play, and hoped that he would avoid that dreadful last chapter of the novel, with the Winchester Gaol, the black flag, and Angel Clare looking on with his sister-in-law clinging to him. This is how Mr. Stoddard ends the drama. The last the audience sees of Tess is where she stands in the Druidical Temple of Stonehenge, with the first rays of the morning sun bathing her in light, whilst the officers of the law stand ready to take her to the gallows. I own I don't like that; *I had always imagined the concluding scene in this fashion.* Stonehenge, of course; and equally, of course, across the plain the dawn of another accusing day. Tess and Angel Clare have had their last talk, and have slept in each other's arms. Quietly footing the morning dew, the officers of the law are seen dimly in the background silently approaching the weary lovers. Nearer and nearer they come, until their footsteps awaken Angel Clare. With an uplifted hand he warns them off. The law is powerless now. Too late! Tess has paid the penalty. She is dead where she slept. Surely this is better than the gallows. No one wants Tess to be executed. She has suffered enough, and God has allowed her, on account of her many sorrows, to die in her sleep in the chill, dread moment that precedes the dawn. The notion of black flags, ropes, platforms, prison chaplains and tolling bells seems hideous at the end of a romance of love, such a tale of woman's helplessness with fate.²

Clement Scott suggests a sentimental ending to a tragic story and actually forecasts the one to be used in H. A. Kennedy's play.³

---

[1] April 15, 1900.
[2] *Daily Telegraph*, March 24, 1897 (italics mine).
[3] Since it was written for Clement Scott's sister-in-law, Mrs. Waller, one can scarcely assume the identity to be one of coincidence.

Mrs. Fiske's claim that Kennedy used Stoddard's arrangement of scenes was well founded.[1] Besides the selection and arrangement of material, Kennedy borrowed from Stoddard's characterization of Joan Durbeyfield. In both plays, Joan bitterly reproaches Tess for the indiscreet revelation which has ruined Tess's life, and suggests that the only means of repairing their fortune is for Tess to become the mistress of Alec Trantridge.[2] Kennedy also adopted Stoddard's weakest point, that is, the heroine's too ready acceptance of the news of her husband's death, conveyed to her by a man whom she had every reason to distrust, and confirmed by a semi-intoxicated girl. "Not till he had been dead for months and she had grown heartily sick of Trantridge did it occur to her to inquire where he was buried."[3] These are the principal similarities.

Kennedy makes several interesting innovations. In the first act, he has the Reverend Cuthbert Clare in his archaeological researches establish the fact that Tess is of the ancient lineage of the D'Urbervilles. As a result, Angel assures Tess that his family is ready to receive her with open arms. Kennedy handles the letter of confession in a different way from Stoddard. The motivation seems to be equally good. Instead of Tess's mother stealing the letter to Angel, the jealous milkmaid, Marian, intercepts and burns it.

Kennedy's second act appears to have been his best. The confession of Tess's previous liaison with Alec Trantridge is given practically in Hardy's own words. In the third act, Kennedy has Alec appear with a marriage licence before he has heard of Tess's

[1] Witness this comparison:

	Stoddard	*Kennedy*
Act I	Crick's Dairy Farm	Farmyard at Dairyman Crick's, Talbothays
Act II	An Old Manor-House	Wellbridge Manor
Act III	Durbeyfield's Cottage at Marlott	Mr. Durbeyfield's Cottage at Marlott
Act IV	Scene I. Alec's lodging at Sandbourne	Apartments at Sandbourne
	Scene II. Stonehenge, the ruins of the Heathen Temple	Stonehenge

[2] *Morning Post*, April 16, 1900.
[3] *Ibid.*

nuptials with Angel Clare. This is, of course, based on the novel[1] but is absent from the other dramatizations. Then, after Alec finds Tess's marriage an obstacle, he bribes Marian, as in the Stoddard version, to swear that Angel is dead. This deception puts more blame on Alec and makes Marian an accomplice. It motivates the cry "Marian" and the murder of Alec. In the final act, Kennedy made his greatest departure from the American version. The police are on the track of the heroine, but she eludes them. Instead of sending her to die on the scaffold, Kennedy has Tess perish opportunely of mental anguish and exposure at Stonehenge, exactly as in the conclusion proposed by Clement Scott in 1897. The critic for the *Morning Post* said that though the "grip of the play perceptibly relaxed during the last scene—in which Tess has nothing to do but die unarrested—the final reception of the piece was decidedly favourable."[2] This sentimental conclusion substituted for Hardy's pitiless logic was, of course, an attempt to mitigate the tragedy.[3]

[1] At Flintcomb Ash, when Alec does not know Tess is married, he says:

" 'I have already obtained this precious document. It was my old mother's dying wish.' . . .

'What is it?' said she.

'A marriage licence.' "

(*Tess of the D'Urbervilles* (Wessex edition), p. 402.)

[2] *Morning Post*, April 16, 1900.

[3] In all versions, there is some attempt to make the play more acceptable to the Victorian or Edwardian audience. It is interesting to remind ourselves of Hardy's own attitude toward the execution of Tess. It is not too much to say that he shared Clement Scott's feeling that Tess had suffered enough and that, in Kittredge's phrase about Chaucer and his *Troilus*, he ended his tale "under a kind of duress." He would gladly have accepted any mitigation if it had accorded with his standard of truth and honesty.

Mr. Edmund Blunden reveals Hardy's feeling: " 'You must have felt pain to bring her to so fearful an end.' 'Yes. Such dreams are we made of that I often think of the day when, having decided she must die, I went purposely to Stonehenge to study the spot. It was a gloomy lowering day, and the skies almost seemed to touch the pillars of the great heathen temple.' " (*Thomas Hardy* (London: Macmillan & Co., 1941), p. 79.)

Before presenting the final scene in the novel, Hardy broke through his narrative in a paragraph seen at the beginning of "Chapter the Last" in his original manuscript in the British Museum. He vented his feelings, registered his convictions on verity and *vraisemblance* and steeled himself for the logical conclusion: "The humble delineator of human character and human contingencies, whether his narrative deal with the actual or with the typical only, must

INTRODUCTION   lvii

Partly as a result of this attempt, the spirit of the novel is missing from Kennedy's play. It is admitted that Kennedy reproduced accurately the framework of the narrative. He showed some skill in the use of retrospect, and some dramatic resource in fitting together the scenes. The suppression of Tess's letter by the jealous milkmaid is convincing. He preserved the bucolic humours of Jack Durbeyfield and the milkmaids. "But," as the *Observer* says, "although the names are there, the characters are not; and even if the *dramatis personae* were to speak the actual words originally set down for them, their varied accent would betray them."[1] The characters are not of Hardy's village. Their sins and sorrows do not belong to Wessex. The whole is too sophisticated, and the result is the melodrama of convention. The critic of the *Daily Mail* found *Tess* on the stage "unreal, unconvincing, unmoving. The tragic story never once goes to the heart." It loses the atmosphere and "grim inevitableness of the novel" and becomes melodrama of a rather cheap kind. Kennedy, he maintained, fails in what should be the striking moments of the play: "We are not moved by the confession of Tess to her husband on the wedding eve. . . . So also with the scenes between Tess and Trantridge. . . . The murder of Alan [*sic*] Trantridge by Tess did not thrill, the death of Tess in the ruins of Stonehenge did not impress. . . ."[2]

The most interesting criticism of Kennedy's play is Max Beerbohm's:

> Such characters as Angel Clare demand of a dramatist an extraordinary amount of skill. What the novelist may explain at his leisure, the dramatist primarily and above all things be sincere, however terrible sincerity might be. Gladly sometimes would such an one lie for dear civility's sake, but for the ever-haunting afterthought that, 'This work was not honest, and may do harm.' In typical history with all its liberty, there are, as in real history, features which can be distorted with impunity and issues which should never be falsified. And perhaps in glancing at the misfortunes of such people as have or could have lived we may acquire some art in shielding from like misfortunes those who have yet to be born. If truth requires a justification, surely this is an ample one." (Add. MS. 38182, p. 523.) Then with the hand of an artist, he deleted the paragraph as irrelevant to a work of art.

[1] *Observer*, April 15, 1900.
[2] *Daily Mail*, April 26, 1900.

must make clear in a few lines. I do not think that Mr. H. A. Kennedy ... has contrived to prepare the audience for Angel Clare's conduct in the second act. It seems to me that he relied rather on the chance that the part would be interpreted by some actor who, by his manner and appearance, would lead the audience to believe him capable of his abnormal behaviour. But dramatists have no business to be so sanguine. They should make it a rule always to expect the worst of their mimes, not the best. They should, so far as they can, contrive every part so that it will carry conviction despite the worst performance imaginable. I do not say that Mr. Kittredge's performance of Angel Clare was the worst imaginable, but it was certainly bad enough to make one regret that Mr. Kennedy had not taken very much more care in writing the part.[1]

He admits Kennedy's ingenuity; but continues:

"Tess," more than most books, should have been saved from the stage. Some novels as being merely melodramatic deserve no better fate than being foisted on the stage. Others, in containing no melodrama at all, and being, therefore, unlikely to attract the public, are allowed to rest within their covers; if they were dramatized, at any rate they would not be degraded so unspeakably as "Tess." For "Tess" as a book is full of melodrama. The melodrama in it is made beautiful by the charm of Mr. Hardy's temperament. One sees it softened and ennobled through a haze of poetry. One would vow in reading it, that it was sublime tragedy. But come the adapter, however reverent, and how fearfully one's eyes are opened! A seduction, a deception, an intercepted letter, a confession, a parting, a broker in the house, a relapse into impropriety, a taunt, a murder, a reunion, a death scene—that is all that "Tess" is when translated to the stage. A wronged heroine, a villain, a prig, some comic rustics—these and nothing more![2]

Of Mrs. Waller's acting Max Beerbohm says:

[1] Max Beerbohm, "Tess," in *Around Theatres*, March 3, 1900, p. 88.
  The critic of the *Stage*, while not disposed to cavil at Tess's natural death at Stonehenge, disapproved of Kennedy's diction: "For a man of such practical experience in writing, as the dramatic critic of the *Sunday Times*, the dialogue of *Tess* is by no means brilliant, and the dissolute recklessness of Alec need not be vulgarized by the introduction of such phrases as 'Not a bad sort,' 'Old Girl,' 'Boss,' and 'I can't face that this morning,' this last remark being made when an egg is offered him for breakfast." Undated, but follows the Saturday, April 14, 1900 production (Harvard Theatre Collection).
[2] Beerbohm, "Tess," pp. 88-9.

Nor can I think at this moment of any actress less like my own idea of Tess ... than Mrs. Lewis Waller.... Mrs. Waller is an accomplished actress. She is always intelligent, often powerful. In the third act (the scene of the murder), she acted very powerfully indeed; and throughout the play she gave proof of her natural intelligence. But her face has not, I think, one feature in common with the face of Tess; and, as far as her voice and manner—well! Tess was a simple, romantic girl, sprung from the soil of Wessex. Mrs. Waller's voice and manner on the stage are always exceedingly sophisticated and metropolitan. She might go on trying to act Tess till doomsday, yet would never for one moment succeed in demonstrating anything but the impossibility of her task.[1]

Before the play was taken to the Comedy Theatre, Kennedy overhauled it "thoroughly, and generally to its advantage."[2] The cast was strengthened by Oswald Yorke's replacing William Kittredge as Angel Clare and by Fred Terry's succeeding Whitworth Jones as Alec. Mrs. Waller herself received better criticisms. The *Stage* conceded that Kennedy's version "(whether authorized or unauthorized ...) certainly provides Mrs. Lewis Waller with a fine acting role, out of which she makes nearly the very utmost possible."[3] And the *Daily Mail* said: "Mrs. Waller did all that was possible with Tess. She has intensity, perception, strength. Once, the moment after she has stabbed Trantridge to death, Mrs. Waller showed us the horror and the terror of it."[4] Had the court not sustained Mrs. Fiske's injunction restraining Mrs. Waller from further representations, this revised Kennedy version might have had a fairly long run. If London accepted (with some enthusiasm) this *Tess of the D'Urbervilles,* one may imagine the triumph Mrs. Fiske could have had in England.

V. Baron Frederic d'Erlanger's Opera

On February 2, 1902—almost two years after Mrs. Waller with-

---

[1] *Ibid.*, pp. 87-8.
[2] The *Stage* on the April 14, 1900 production (Harvard Theatre Collection).
[3] *Ibid.*
[4] *Daily Mail*, April 26, 1900.

drew her play—Baron Frederic d'Erlanger[1] wrote to Hardy from Park House, Rutland Gate:

You have no doubt heard of the well known Italian librettist, L[uigi] Illica, to whom the world owes the adaptation for the musical stage of *La Vie de Bohème, La Tosca,* and the libretti of many other celebrated operas.[2]—It is on his behalf and my own, as a composer, that I wish to speak to you.—We think that *Tess* would make a wonderful book for an opera, and are anxious not only to obtain your kind permission to use the novel for the purpose but also to submit to you our ideas and intentions. The matter is one of art and of business. I shall be very grateful if you will grant me an interview to discuss it from both points of view.[3]

Hardy agreed to d'Erlanger's suggestion for turning *Tess* into an Italian opera, but four years elapsed before the opera was ready for production. On February 8, 1906, Baron d'Erlanger wrote hopefully to Hardy:

I am glad to inform you that my opera has been accepted for performance at the San Carlo Theatre, Naples, and that the production is to take place at the end of March or the first week in April.

Nothing has been neglected that could contribute to giving the opera a truly English character, and I have gone to the expense of having costumes designed by Percy Anderson, who is considered to be an artist in the line. The models of the scenery have also been made in London, as well as dresses of the principal artists. As regards the cast, I trust that it will be highly

---

[1] The name of Frederic d'Erlanger was well known in metropolitan musical centres in 1902. He belonged to the famous family of international bankers who were noted for their interest in music and painting. Baron d'Erlanger's father had been one of the earliest patrons of Wagner and had been largely responsible for the production of *Tannhaeuser*. And while Frederic d'Erlanger was a member of a foreign banking house in London and a director of the New Cape Railway, he was also a director of the Grand Opera Syndicate. As a student of Anselm Ehmant in Paris, he had published an album of songs before he was twenty-one, but most of his composition had been for orchestra. His *Suite Symphonique* had been produced at Covent Garden Promenade concerts in 1895, and his Pianoforte Quintet for piano and strings was played at St. James's Hall in 1902. In the same year Kreisler first performed his violin concerto at a Philharmonic concert. In addition to string quartets, a sonata for violin and piano, and numerous songs, Frederic d'Erlanger had written before 1902 two operas: *Jehan de Saintré* (produced in Hamburg in 1894, and at Covent Garden in 1897); and *Inez Mendo* (produced in London, 1897). Cf. *Manchester Guardian*, July 15, 1909; and *Daily Express*, July 15, 1909.

[2] *Iris* (1898); *Rosabla* (1902); and later (with Giacosa) *Madama Butterfly* (1906).   [3] Max Gate MS. (second paragraph).

satisfactory, at least as far as the principal characters are concerned, most of my interpreters being those who have sung with marked success during the Italian autumn season at Covent Garden.

I need hardly tell you that my librettist, Signor Illica, has complied with all your wishes which you expressed to me some three years ago and which were also my own.

The names of the characters are the same as those of the novel and only two new characters, both of minor importance, have been introduced, viz;— those of a money lender [Toronto, substituted for Parson Tringham] and a servant [Nancy]....[1]

In this act [3rd] we have tried to describe the struggle in Tess's heart between love and conscience, and it ends with a love duet between our heroine and Angel.

The 4th act, which is of course the most dramatic, is that in which Tess confesses her past and the lovers part.

In your letter to me of October, 1902, you reserved to yourself the right to say whether and in what way you desired your name to appear on the libretto; it is not yet published, but I have at least received the proof copies required for rehearsals, and steps will be taken to insure the copyright in America before the production of the opera.[2]

Unfortunately, I am not in a position to give you an English translation of the libretto and, if I remember right, you told me you do not understand Italian. I should, therefore, be very grateful if you would kindly let me know as soon as possible whether you would like me to call on you in order to give you a more detailed account of the way in which Illica has treated the subject. I shall be leaving London on Saturday the 17th instant, but I am at your disposal any day next week.[3]

The production in Naples on which Baron d'Erlanger had spared no expense proved disappointing. A fatality more surprising and disastrous than any of the coincidences in Hardy's novels ruined the opera. It is described in d'Erlanger's letter to Hardy from Milan, on April 21, 1906:

Mount Vesuvius behaved most unkindly to me and upset all my calculations.—I had spent a month in Naples working like a slave to ensure a fine performance of my opera when the terrible eruption took place. Owing to

[1] He gives a brief summary here. I omit it and his comments on the first and second acts.
[2] *Tess* was not copyrighted in England until June 24, 1909. In the meantime Claude Aveling made an English translation of Illica's libretto.
[3] Max Gate MS.

circumstances which it would take pages to report to you, the opera was given on the very night of the worst catastrophe and consequently before a small audience the state of mind of which it is hardly necessary to describe.—Notwithstanding all the adverse factors *Tess* met with a most hearty reception and was favourably reported upon by the press.

Unfortunately the theatre had to be closed the following day by order of the municipality. Though the result of my efforts has been most disappointing, I cannot say that I have worked in vain.—The impression created by the reception granted the opera is distinctly favourable and I shall now be able to alter those portions of the score which require to be shortened or strengthened so that I no longer run the risk of having to revise it after publication as is generally the case when operas are printed before having seen the footlights.[1]

Of the single performance of the opera in Naples the *Manchester Guardian* said: "Both performers and the audience were half choked with lava dust, and the noise of the falling masonry all round the theatre was an unrehearsed accompaniment to the music."[2]

The disaster impressed Hardy as an incident in keeping with the career of Tess. He answered d'Erlanger's letter on April 28, 1906:

I was sorry to hear from you that the production of the Opera should have so strangely coincided with the eruption—was there ever such a coincidence before! It may, however, be a blessing in disguise, if the changes it permits you to make turn out to be improvements.

I cannot help feeling that, for an opera to have won any sort of approval in such circumstances, it must have been an unusually strong one, and really one to build high hopes on. I wish it could be brought to London.

The volcano was all one of a piece with Tess's catastrophic career.[3]

As Hardy wished, d'Erlanger brought the opera to London, where it was presented on July 14, 1909, as the last of the season's novelties. (This was after an attempted presentation at Milan which was thwarted by a general strike of orchestral musicians.[4]) At the Covent Garden *première,* it had a "most enthusiastic reception from

[1] Max Gate MS.
[2] July 15, 1909.
[3] This letter was among the copies of Hardy's letters to Baron d'Erlanger which the latter kindly sent to me.
[4] This was described in d'Erlanger's letter to Hardy, July 8, 1909 (Max Gate MS.).

INTRODUCTION   lxiii

one of the largest and most fashionable audiences of the season."¹

After attending rehearsals the preceding week, Hardy was interested enough to be there, although he considered first nights insincere, meretricious, and stagey. And there is little doubt that he was pleased with the reception. While he sat unobserved and unrecognized in the stalls with Mrs. Hardy, the librettist, the composer, and conductor were called before the curtain several times. *Tess* was a success "bordering on a triumph that it richly deserved."²

Critics were fairly well agreed that Baron d'Erlanger had written a charming, though not very distinctive or original, score. *The Times* said that the music had the charm and organic beauty of the best modern Italian school.

> The numerous choruses have an English colouring which the music for the principal artists lacks; in the first scene is a charming part song in quintuple time; and the dance of the "club walking girls" is suitably simple, the chorus sung in the dairy scene is very bright, and in the last scene besides the epithalamium there is at the very close a very pretty serenade sung outside, while Tess is making up her mind to drown herself. The most charming section of a work which is, if anything, almost too full of suavity, is the prelude to the third act, a piece of pastoral character, owing a little to the *Waldweben* [sic] of *Siegfried*. The whole is admirably scored. There are "leading motives" and that which signifies the love of Tess and Angel, is carried on and cleverly developed in the several scenes, to which it gives an agreeable unity.³

¹ *Daily Express*, July 15, 1909.
² *Daily Telegraph*, July 15, 1909. In the royal box were Queen Alexandra, Princess Victoria, and Prince Charles of Denmark. The Duchess of Rutland and Lord and Lady Innes, Lord Esher, Baron and Baroness de Meyer, Signora Tetrazzini were also among the many prominent people present. "There has rarely been even during this most flourishing season so representative a gathering as was assembled to welcome the first performance of *Tess*" (*Sphere*, July 24, 1909).
³ *The Times*, July 15, 1909. Cf. the *Daily Express* (July 15, 1909) which praised the great beauty of the love themes of the introduction and declared that the symphonic prelude to the third act "which indicates the awakening of nature to the influence of spring, after the devastation of winter thus typifying Tess's reawakening to the love of Angel Clare after her betrayal" was a "really noble piece of music."

The Times added that "this is not one of the operas in which music is sacrificed to drama or forced into a subordinate position."[1] Baughan of the *Daily News* criticized the score as lacking dramatic emotion and originality,[2] and found its merit mainly negative: the avoidance of anything vulgar or hysterical or too heavy for its subject. But among the more positive qualities, there was some attempt at freshness and simplicity in the first act with the picture of the Durbeyfields on May Day, and some emotional tension and strength in the duet between Angel and Tess in the last act.

In general, too, the vocal writing is effective, and the scoring is always picturesque and pleasing. I am not at all sure that Mr. d'Erlanger has any real talent for dramatic music. The best parts of *Tess* are precisely those in which no strong emotion has to be expressed. . . . The composer often obtains a pleasing effect from the solo voices, chorus and orchestra as a whole, but when it comes to hitting off the character of the *dramatis personae* or expressing the depths of the emotions which move them to action Mr. d'Erlanger shows the limitations of his talents . . . an opera must contain music which expresses the emotion of the drama. . . .

In this opera Tess, finding that Angel cannot face the idea that she belonged to another man even against her will, quietly gathers an armful of the garlands which decorate the bridal bed and creeps out of the house to put an end to her stricken life. A dramatic composer of any real talent would have invented something poignant and haunting to express the deep grief of Tess. Remember what Puccini has done in his simple way in *Madama Butterfly*. Mr. d'Erlanger does not rise above ordinary "effective" operaticism. . . . The best pages in the score are those which describe the "atmosphere" of the story, and not those which attempt to realize its drama. . . . That the opera will have a *succès d'estime* is certain but whatever its fate may be, *Tess* is not an opera of any strength or originality. . . . Mr. d'Erlanger is too polite to make us acquainted with any music we do not know or might not like.[3]

[1] July 15, 1909.
[2] Filson Young (*Saturday Review*, July 17, 1909) noticed the repeated, if unconscious, imitation of Wagner, "the long-drawn Italianized Wagnerian melodies," but found something more potent in the "sequence of admirable orchestral utterances which serves to represent the great talking voice of destiny muttering its majestic monologue throughout the drama."
[3] *Daily News*, July 15, 1909.

INTRODUCTION lxv

Of the music of the individual roles the *Boston Evening Transcript* quoted the following criticism from *The Times*:

Neither the tenor nor the baritone music is very individual, and the tenor song in the first act is the least English thing in the whole score. . . . One of the most effective parts is that of Aby, Tess's little brother, with whom she has a pretty duet in the second act, and who has a solo in the final serenade.

The music for Tess herself is admirably expressive and suits Mlle. Destinn to perfection. What realization of the character there is is almost entirely due to the artist, who in appearance, gestures, and everything else shows us the "pure woman" whom Hardy drew. But though she made the deepest impression, it must be recorded that all parts were capitally sung, and the standard of performance was as high as has been the rule this year at Covent Garden.[1]

While the critics considered the music by far the best half of the opera, they conceded that Signor Illica had written an interesting and effective little drama though (as we cannot fail to see) it contains little of Thomas Hardy's work. The synopsis of his libretto as published in the *Boston Evening Transcript* is as follows:

The first act takes place at Jack Durbeyfield's cottage, the home of Tess, on May Day; the family circumstances are in a very bad way, the old horse Prince being the chief mainstay of the domestic resources. Toronton, a dealer, brings to Durbeyfield and his wife an agreeable surprise in the shape of an old pedigree. From this it appears that the Durbeyfields are descended, are "worn away" from the great family of the D'Urbervilles, a representative of which dwells in the neighborhood. The parents hope to improve their circumstances by claiming kinship with these great people of the neighborhood, and endeavor to persuade Tess to go to see them, hoping that her beauty will induce the head of the family, Alec D'Urberville, to propose a "family" alliance. Tess refuses, having already an admirer, Angel Clare, who, however, is too diffident to speak. But a terrible calamity that falls on the Durbeyfields turns the tide of affairs. Aby, the little brother of Tess (a delightful, childish character, straight from the book), brings the news that Prince has been killed in a collision with the morning mail-cart. Their breadwinner gone, ruin stares them in the face, and Tess resolves to go as "maid" to the rich old lady at D'Urberville House.

[1] July 31, 1909.

The second act (the garden of D'Urberville House, toward the close of a July day) sees Tess installed, and marked down by Alec D'Urberville for his prey. Her beauty has roused the jealousy of her fellow servants, Dark-Car and Nancy. These characters are transplanted from the village to D'Urberville House in order to introduce Hardy's scene in the village on market day, where Alec rescues Tess from the onslaughts of infuriated women. Unhappy in her surroundings, Tess then resolves to go home. But Aby's arrival, with appeals for help and a distressing account of the family circumstances, decides Tess to stay and earn money to send to her stricken mother. This resolve brings about Tess's undoing, for Dark-Car locks her out of the house as night closes in; Alec appears, and Tess turns to him for assistance; he persuades her to remain in the garden with him, and so the tragedy begins.

The third act takes place at the Talbothays Dairy. Much has happened to Tess since the tragedy of that night at D'Urberville House. A child has been born to her, but has died, leaving Tess free to begin a new life. Here in the Talbothays Dairy, all is happiness and sunshine. On Tess has fallen the greatest of all human blessings, for she loves, and is loved in return; and so deep is her love for Angel Clare that she vows to make confession to him before yielding to his wooing. But faltering in her resolve she exacts a promise from her father to take on himself the task of confession, and at the end of a scene with Angel her love conquers her doubts and fears, and, believing that all will be well, she suffers Angel to win her.

The fourth and last act brings us to the evening of the wedding day. Tess, not knowing that her father has shirked his task of enlightening Angel, is supremely happy, and pours out her gratitude to her husband for his generous forgiveness. Angel cannot understand her meaning, and Tess then realizes that her father has broken his promise. In a few disjointed but telling, words, the pitiful truth is made clear, and Tess realizes that Angel is lost to her forever. In vain she pleads that the sin was not hers, but another's, and implores him to take her away to some remote land, where they can live out their lives alone. Severed from the one and only good influence of her life, Tess knows that her dream is ended, and with a hurried farewell to the little bridal chamber, she disappears from Angel's horizon forever.[1]

Though the summary omits the fact, Tess drowns herself while her lover cries in despair, "Tess! Tess! Tess!"

Illica took great liberties with Hardy's novel. Naturally, he had to choose incidents from the novel, for, as the *Daily Telegraph* says,

[1] July 31, 1909.

"Hardy's romance is so abundant in incident that a trilogy after the fashion of *The Niblung's Ring* would have been required to contain it all, and trilogies are a little out of date now."[1] Illica, like Stoddard, resisted the temptation to crowd his acts with incidents, but unlike Stoddard he emphasized the beginning instead of the end of the novel. The confession scene of the fourth act, for example, corresponds to the second act of Stoddard's play. By bringing the libretto to a close after Tess's confession to Angel, Illica tells only half the story. Hardy realized that it would take at least two operas to tell the complete story. He confessed to the critic of the *Daily Chronicle* that he was quite satisfied with the manner in which the book had been converted by the librettist. "And what has been left out of the original story," he added, "might one day form the basis for another opera."[2]

More questionable are Illica's liberties with the characters. Tess, for instance, becomes the typical operatic heroine. Could we imagine Hardy's Tess turning to Alec for help when Dark-Car locked the door? Or trusting her bibulous father to make her confession to Angel? Or even drowning herself in the operatic manner? *The Times* says:

Of all Mr. Hardy's creations Tess is surely the most individual; her mixed ancestry, her strong native impulses, her country shyness make up not merely one of the most vivid figures in fiction, but one of the most lovable in spite of all her transgressions of law. In the opera she is presented by librettist and composer as a peasant of an ordinary type, with whom, were it not for Mlle. Destinn's wonderful acting and magically beautiful singing, we should feel uncommonly little sympathy. And, if Tess's individuality has not been conveyed, still less is there in the opera any of the scent of the good clean earth that is the distinctive feature of the book as it is of so much of the author's work.[3]

It seems a pity to transplant Hardy's simple Wessex villagers to the conventional grand opera stage where "they become possessed of the noblest passions, the keenest intelligence, and utter their

[1] July 16, 1909.
[2] *Daily Chronicle*, July 15, 1909.
[3] *The Times*, July 15, 1909.

emotions in the most impassioned Italian."[1] Baughan said: "The passionate and sensual Alec D'Urberville is musically a mild philanderer, and Angel Clare only an operatic tenor. Among other things he sings of 'wild and craven fears that wreck and torture,' but the music insists on being amiable and colourless."[2] As Angel Clare, Signor Zenatello "was Italian to the core. No such strange figure of an Italian bandit in holiday attire could ever have entered the imaginations of Mr. Hardy's dwellers in Wessex."[3] Mrs. Hardy told me that Angel in the opera looked like an Italian organ-grinder. She also objected to having Prince on the stage, where the Durbeyfields feed him hay. She wrote that the opera was "Italianized to such an extent that Hardy scarcely recognized it as his own novel."[4] But Hardy accepted the operatic conventions. He told the critic of the *Daily Chronicle* that d'Erlanger's *Tess* had greatly interested him as a work of art. "It was somewhat curious to hear the Italian dialogue," he said, "but after all one must remember that opera is a convention. The music seems to me to be quite suitable for the dramatic situations and I most sincerely hope that Baron d'Erlanger's work will meet with the appreciation of the public which I think it deserves. . . . I have congratulated him on the result of his artistic labour."[5]

Tess was produced during each of the three following seasons: 1910, 1911, and 1912.[6] One infers that it must have had some financial success to have been thus revived. Baron d'Erlanger sent Hardy a cheque on October 8, 1912. In his reply (October 10, 1912) Hardy expressed his appreciation of the music of the opera:

The music grew upon one very distinctly, especially in the second year, as many musical people told me; and judging from my own experience in the sale of books, the British public nibbles a long time before it takes hold. In

[1] *Daily Express*, July 15, 1909.
[2] *Daily News*, July 15, 1909.
[3] *Ibid.*
[4] F. E. Hardy, *The Life of Thomas Hardy*, II, 139.
[5] *Daily Chronicle*, July 15, 1909.
[6] Cf. F. E. Hardy, *The Life of Thomas Hardy*, II, 143 for 1910 production; *Who's Who in Music and Drama* (New York, 1914), p. 84 for 1911; and d'Erlanger's letter to me (March 16, 1935) for 1912 production.

the case of the other new operas, I have often thought that the Covent Garden Management (not realizing this sufficiently) drops an opera too soon. And in the present case the *subject* is coming more and more to the fore. Another trial or two therefore would be an interesting experiment.

The death of King Edward[1] at the beginning of the season that was the crucial one, served to check the opera at the moment when it might have caught on, I think.

However, I leave that in your hands. Do you ever compose songs? I get many requests from composers known and unknown for permission to put my lyrics to music.[2]

I find no evidence that the Covent Garden management considered further trial of *Tess*. Evidently the opera did not take hold. Hardy's desire to have it revived, however, is significant of his interest in the theatre from the time he finished *The Dynasts*. Thirteen years later when Gwen Ffrangçon-Davies played in Hardy's own version of *Tess of the D'Urbervilles*, Baron d'Erlanger sent his congratulations. Hardy answered from Max Gate (September 13, 1925) as follows:

Dear Baron Frederic d'Erlanger:

So far from having forgotten you I can say we were talking of you and your beautiful Opera within the last few days and wondering whether it would ever be revived, accidental circumstances having cut its career at its first appearance in London. The music was very haunting and I for one should like to hear it again.

Many thanks for your congratulations on the present production of "Tess"—though as you probably may know that play is one I wrote a long time back.

Yours very sincerely,
Thomas Hardy[3]

It will now be our concern to trace the history of Hardy's resumed contact with the theatre between 1908 and 1925, as it bears on the fortunes of the play which he "wrote a long time back."

[1] Cf. Laurence Housman, *The Unexpected Years* (London: Jonathan Cape, 1937), p. 230: "the death of King Edward brought the theatrical season to an untimely end."
[2] D'Erlanger MS.
[3] D'Erlanger MS.

VI. Hardy's Contact with the Theatre: 1908-1925

After Hardy withdrew his script of *Tess of the D'Urbervilles* in the nineties, the world heard nothing more of it until 1924. Yet the fact that he had made his dramatic version was not forgotten. His friend, Mrs. B. A. Crackenthorpe, wrote to Mrs. Granville-Barker (Lillah McCarthy): "He is keen, keen on the theatre and everything connected with it.... I believe the secret wish of his heart is to see scenes from 'The Dynasts' staged before he 'passes on.' But *that's* not what I wanted to tell you! This is it. He has got, actually finished, ready, *his own dramatized version of Tess*. (Not the American version, which is still being played all over the States, he told me, but his own.) He has promised to send me this, his own *Drama of Tess*, as quick as he can...."[1] Lillah McCarthy places this letter "a little time after my meeting with Hardy,"[2] which occurred after a performance of Masefield's *Nan*,[3] and which she thus describes: "One night, just after I arrived in my dressing-room, the manager, A. E. Drinkwater, the father of John Drinkwater the poet, followed at my heels and said, 'Mr. Thomas Hardy would like to see you.' I was breathless, but not more so than Thomas Hardy when he appeared at the door, shaking. He did not pause; he came in and said: 'You must play my Tessy, you *must* play my Tessy. I shall send you the play I have made from my book; and you *will* play my Tessy, won't you?' "[4]

If this experience had taken place before Mrs. Crackenthorpe's letter, one would not think that Lillah McCarthy needed Mrs. Crackenthorpe's aid to get the role of Tess. And if Mrs. Crackenthorpe had known that Hardy insisted on Lillah McCarthy's playing Tess, she would not have felt it necessary to interest her in the drama. But at any rate, whether Hardy changed his mind or whether Lillah McCarthy failed to follow up the offer soon enough, it took the intercession of Mrs. Crackenthorpe to bring the two together to discuss Miss McCarthy's representation of Tess.

---

[1] Lillah McCarthy, *Myself and My Friends* (London: Thornton Butterworth, 1934), p. 102.
[2] *Ibid.*, p. 101.
[3] *Nan* opened at the Haymarket, June 2, 1908.
[4] Lillah McCarthy, *Myself and My Friends*, p. 101.

On June 1, 1910, Mrs. Crackenthorpe wrote to Hardy:

I have just written a line to Mrs. Hardy praying her permission to bring with me tomorrow Mrs. Granville-Barker (Lillah McCarthy) who will be driving with me tomorrow afternoon.

Now behind this simple request is a deep-laid plot and I'd better "own up" at once—I always do better when I play the "Bold bad villain."— Diplomacy is a coat that never fitted me.

Lillah McCarthy wants exceedingly much to meet you. She and Granville-Barker should have come in on Monday last when you were here, but they were detained at the Galsworthys . . . too late. . . .

She is keen, keen, keen to play Tess—your Tess—the Tess you keep in that drawer. . . . Somehow it's her part. She feels it and I know it.—So we're coming tomorrow unless forbidden—and—pray forgive me.[1]

When we remember Hardy's breathless enthusiasm for Miss McCarthy's Nan, it would be indeed surprising if he had not handed the script over to her. Evidently all that was needed was Mrs. Crackenthorpe's proposal to each of them. Lillah McCarthy took the manuscript with her to London. She wrote to Hardy two weeks later (June 15, 1910):

I should have written to you before to thank you for letting me read "Tess," but I gave it to my husband to read and he gave it to Mr. J. M. Barrie and I was waiting for their final decision on it before writing to you.

My husband says the 1st and 2nd acts are just perfect as they are, but the III will want a little working over, but he wanted Mr. Barrie's opinion before making any suggestions.

I telephoned Mr. Barrie tonight and he told me he had not yet read the III act, but he promised to read it at once. He agrees with my husband about acts I and II.

I love the play entire just as it is, and would not alter a thing, but these expert dramatists are useful people and you know how wonderfully kind Mr. Barrie always is. I am hoping to get a production of "Tess" the 2nd week in July if you would allow it to be done for three matinée performances at the Haymarket Theatre. Or would you prefer that we keep it till next autumn and produce it in the evening bill? Nothing is definitely settled yet. . . . I shall be ever grateful to dear Mrs. Crackenthorpe for taking me to meet you and Mrs. Hardy. It was the great moment of my life to shake hands with you both. . . .

[1] Max Gate MS.

I hope to be able to make a definite proposal to you for "Tess" in a very few days.[1]

Hardy answered on June 17, from 4 Bloomfield Court:

Dear Mrs. Granville Barker,

I am glad to get your letter about *Tess* and I think I had better leave the whole matter in your hands. If you would like to produce it at those three matinées, please do. . . .

I suppose the suggested changes in the 3rd act would not be too heavy and would be mainly in the nature of omissions? The only stipulation I should make on that point would be that whenever any arrangement we may enter into comes to an end, and right of performance lapses into my hands, I should not be compelled to omit the modifications if I wish to retain them.

On the other hand, as a matter of policy, it might be wise for you to play the tragedy exactly as it stands, and allow me to be the scapegoat for its imperfections. I could take these defects upon my shoulders by writing a prefatory note to the playbill to that effect. Experts often, by eliminating crudeness, destroy the crispness and naïveté of a play. However do as you like.

What I should like to stipulate is (I suppose) that in the event of the play promising a commercial success, some guarantee of its continuance should be given. Otherwise when you had "created" the part, no other leading actress might care to take it up. I am not keen on making money out of it, but, not being a rich man, I naturally should like to get what may be got, if anything.

You are probably aware that no authorized version of the novel for the stage has ever been performed in England (except of course the Italian opera, which is certainly different from the play and ends at the parting after the confession). All other versions have been piracies.

Very sincerely,
Thomas Hardy

P.S. Cannot you come and see us again next Monday and bring Mr. Barker?[2]
T. H.

This letter is perhaps the most definite expression we have of Hardy's interest in seeing *Tess* on the London stage. And while he is conscious of the drama's imperfections, he seems to have pre-

---

[1] Max Gate MS.
[2] Max Gate MS. First draft of the letter.

ferred it just as it was. This is one of those rare instances where he betrays some hope of making some money from a production. But we must remember of course that he had been encouraged by the tremendous financial success of Mrs. Fiske's creation in America and by the welcome given Baron d'Erlanger's opera at Covent Garden in the preceding season. In fact, this correspondence was taking place when the opera was again being played. By this time, too, the last volume of *The Dynasts* was finished and the "Hardy Players" had produced with surprising success *The Trumpet-Major* and *Far from the Madding Crowd*. There were no complications to hinder the production of *Tess* in 1910 and Hardy had found an actress whom he considered suitable for the title role—hence his eagerness to see the play on the London stage. And no doubt he was disappointed when he received a note from Lillah McCarthy from the Kingsway Theatre, dated June 21, 1912, saying: "It is a great regret to us that we are not able to produce it [*Tess*] as *Fanny's First Play* has had such a long run, it has put back our arrangements for a whole year. . . . We are due to do my husband's play, the *Voysey Inheritance*, after that a revival of a play of Shaw's so I am afraid this will put back the time for your play longer than you would care to wait."[1]

Another thirteen years were to elapse before *Tess of the D'Urbervilles* was to be seen in London! By that time Hardy could take little interest in its production. It was far too late for its success to influence his career. He wrote to Forbes-Robertson on November 27, 1924, "I have no desire at my time of life to see the play, *Tess*, acted in London."[2] Yet the next year a London actress played *Tess*.

The Hardy Players

While these fruitless negotiations with Mrs. Granville-Barker were proceeding, Hardy's contact with the stage was re-established by his interest in the "Hardy Players." This group was a characteristic product of its time. In the early years of the twentieth century and up to the outbreak of war in 1914, there was, says William Archer, an

[1] Max Gate MS. [2] Max Gate MS.

extraordinary efflorescence of dramatic ardour and assiduity. The first unmistakable symptom was the series of local pageants, which combined the gentry and commonalty of quite a number of towns in open-air celebrations of municipal history. The earliest and best of the pageant-masters was Mr. Louis N. Parker, who organised admirable shows at Sherborne in 1905, Warwick in 1906, Bury St. Edmunds in 1907, Dover in 1908, Colchester in 1909. . . . [These pageants] were only the most conspicuous sign of a general hankering after dramatic expression. Village players and community players sprang up on every hand. Folk-dancing was revived along with folk-song. And in these little local enterprises there was a strong tendency to include all the arts of the theatre. The amateur companies not only made their own dresses and painted their own scenes, but often wrote their own plays.[1]

In 1904, Mr. Parker wrote to Hardy asking him to write a folk-play to be given with the Sherborne pageants; but Hardy, who cared little for pageants,[2] excused himself on the grounds of preoccupation with other work.[3]

Dorchester at the time had a flourishing dramatic and debating society, which began by giving public readings of Shakespeare, Goldsmith, and Sheridan. On February 8, 1908, Mr. A. M. Broadley was scheduled to lecture on "Napoleon's Threatened Invasion of England"; and Mr. Alfred H. Evans (father of Maurice Evans), a member of the committee, suggested that to illustrate the lecture an interlude might be arranged based on Hardy's *The Trumpet-Major*. With Hardy's consent, Mr. Evans adapted the supper scene in the miller's house, which was put on with the soldiers in uniform and the rustics in fustian. London papers reported its success; and Hardy was so pleased by the performance that, with *The Dynasts* finished, and prepared to resume other interests, he urged Mr. Evans to attempt a dramatization of the whole novel: "You must certainly make a play from my story," he said.[4] Thus originated the idea

---

[1] William Archer, *The Old Drama and the New* (London: William Heinemann, 1923), pp. 368-9.

[2] Information given to me by Mrs. Hardy.

[3] In August, 1934, I saw his letter to Mr. Parker in the shop of Bickers, a London bookseller, in the Haymarket.

[4] Information from a letter to me from Mr. Alfred H. Evans, February 22, 1937.

that was to convert the Dorchester Dramatic and Debating Society into the "Hardy Players."

Further encouraged by the successful production of three rustic scenes from *The Dynasts,* under the title of *Ye Merrie Maie Fayre,* on May 6 and 7, 1908,[1] Mr. Evans went forward with his full-length play. On the following November 18 and 19, the Dorchester Dramatic and Debating Society presented in the Corn Exchange, Dorchester, Mr. Evans's version of *The Trumpet-Major.* The *Daily Chronicle* reported:

> The quaint old town of Dorchester, outwardly still sleeping in its ageless sleep amidst the broad Wessex pastures, is really all agog within-doors over nothing less than a genuine Dorset dramatization, acted by genuine Dorset folks, of Mr. Hardy's ever-endeared story, *The Trumpet-Major*!
>
> The affair, however, is of much more than local interest. In some respects it is quite unprecedented. Never before, for instance—not even in the pageants—has the work of a famous writer been dramatized in his own native town during his life-time amidst the very scenes that he portrays, and by the descendants of the very types whom he has immortalized. . . .[2]

The local character of the production is emphasized in the letter inserted in the programme by Mr. H. A. Martin, secretary of the Dramatic and Debating Society, which contains one very significant phrase:

> I beg to hand you herewith a Programme of the play practically written by Mr. Thomas Hardy, to be presented for the first time by members of the Dorchester Dramatic and Debating Society on Wednesday, November 18. . . . It is full of local colour and the spirit of the period, when Dorset folk were daily expecting a landing of Napoleon's Troops. The production will be amateur throughout, the adaptor, the stage manager, who is preparing the scenery from sketches by local artists, the performers, and the tailor making the uniforms all being inhabitants of Dorchester.[3]

The significant phrase is, of course, *practically written by Mr. Thomas Hardy.* It is evident that Hardy was willing that those

---

[1] Produced by the Reverend Roland Hill for the benefit of the Church schools. The scenes selected were 1.5.7 (Old Rooms Inn, Budmouth); 1.2.5 (Rainbarrows' Beacon, Egdon Heath); 3.5.6 (Durnover Green, Casterbridge).

[2] November 19, 1908.

[3] Carroll A. Wilson MS.

words should appear on the programme or they would not have been there. Mr. Evans's introductory note (November 30, 1908) to a collection of criticisms gives more evidence of Hardy's part in the play:

The outline of the play was decided by the Author, both as to the necessary variation in the story and as to the finale. Mr. Hardy was strongly in favour of cutting out the Oxwell Hall scenes, as being unnecessary to the story; but on my pointing out the excellent character study afforded by old Squire Derriman, and the opportunity for an effective curtain at the end of the scene, he yielded. I fear that the play was unduly lengthened by this introduction. It was not the Author's wish that broad Dorset be spoken by either John or Bob Loveday; but possibly Festus Derriman should have shown more acquaintance with the vernacular.[1]

No Hardy play except *Tess* caused so much interest in the outside world as did *The Trumpet-Major*. The *Dorset County Chronicle* remarked that in the front seats were "a *posse* of leading dramatic critics who had come down from London especially for the occasion. . . . Seldom in a provincial town, and certainly never before in Dorchester, has such attention been given by the London daily and weekly papers to an amateur local production. . . ."[2] Hardy was prevented by illness from seeing the performance, but he wrote to a friend: "It is exciting such keen interest everywhere that I shall no doubt have an opportunity of doing so at Weymouth or Bournemouth. The only criticisms I have read are those in *The Times* today, the *Daily News,* and the *Daily Chronicle* preliminary one yesterday. . . ."[3]

The Trumpet-Major was played again at the Harrison in Dorchester on December 31, 1908, and in Weymouth on February 8, 1910. Mr. Evans revised the script and revived the play at the Corn Exchange in Dorchester on November 27 and 28, 1912. On December 5, the production was taken to London and performed at Cripplegate.

In the sixteen years following the first success of *The Trumpet-*

---

[1] Carroll A. Wilson MS.
[2] November 26, 1908.
[3] See Maggs Bros., London, catalogue no. 611, October, 1935, p. 54, item no. 654. The letter was priced £10. 10s. (Italics mine.)

INTRODUCTION lxxvii

Major, the Hardy Players presented thirteen other plays (seventy-two performances in all). They fall into three divisions: those adapted by Mr. Evans, those adapted by Mr. Tilley, and those written by Hardy himself. To Mr. Evans belong: *Far from the Madding Crowd* (November, 1908)[1]; *The Mellstock Quire,* from *Under the Greenwood Tree* (November, 1910); *The Distracted Preacher* (November, 1911); and *The Woodlanders* (November, 1913). To Mr. Tilley belong: *The Return of the Native* (November, 1920); *A Desperate Remedy,* from *Desperate Remedies* (November, 1922); *A Rustic Wedding Scene,* from *Under the Greenwood Tree* (February, 1924); and the expansion of *The Mumming Play of St. George* (November, 1923). And to Hardy himself belong: *The Three Wayfarers* (November, 1911); *Wessex Scenes from "The Dynasts"* (June, 1916); *O Jan! O Jan! O Jan!* (November, 1923); *The Famous Tragedy of the Queen of Cornwall* (November, 1923); *The Mumming Play of St. George,* expanded by Mr. Tilley (November, 1923); and *Tess of the D'Urbervilles* (1924).

Mr. Evans chose *Far from the Madding Crowd* for the second production of the Hardy Players. He tried to pack into the play as much as possible of the novel, including Hardy's dialogue, and with some success.[2] *The Times* found it "a more satisfactory play than the version which was played at the old Globe Theatre in 1882, and dramatically, of course, better suited to the stage than Mr. Evans's first adaptation, *The Trumpet-Major*."[3] The former opinion was shared by Hardy. He "had nothing to do with the adaptation," says Mrs. Hardy, "but thought it a neater achievement than the London version of 1882 by Mr. Comyns Carr."[4]

The proposed revival of a play written by Hardy himself, which had first been produced on the professional stage in 1893, naturally aroused curiosity. "The most interesting dramatic news of the moment," said the *Pall Mall Gazette,* "is that on November 15 and 16, [1911,] a new play by Mr. Thomas Hardy, to be called *The*

---

[1] The dates in brackets refer to the productions by the Hardy Players. For complete list, provided by Mr. Tilley, see Appendix.
[2] The exclusion of Fanny Robin from the stage, his principal omission, *The Times* approved: ". . . she is always in the background of the book itself, and the adaptor has done wisely in leaving her there" (November 18, 1909).
[3] *Ibid.* [4] F. E. Hardy, *The Life of Thomas Hardy,* II, 140.

Three Wayfarers, and based on one of the *Wessex Tales,* published first in 1888, will be acted at the Dorchester Corn Exchange by a company recruited from the Dorchester Dramatic and Debating Society, and will probably afterward be given in London under the auspices of the Society of Dorset Men." And the article goes on to revive the discussion of 1892:

In common with most of our great novelists, Mr. Hardy has done very little work for the stage—much to the loss of that institution, for a man who knows life and character so intimately, and is so sincere a writer, could not fail to be interesting ... and it is absurd to imagine that a man who has mastered the art of the novelist could not also, if he pleased, master that of the dramatist. Indeed, on the continent nearly all the great novelists have also been dramatists; and our own novelists are at last beginning to bridge the gulf between the two branches of literature, novels and plays. With such men as Mr. Barrie, Mr. Masefield, Mr. Galsworthy, and Mr. Arnold Bennett among our dramatists, there was evidently a place for Mr. Hardy had he cared to take it.[1]

We hear, in another advance notice from a special correspondent in Dorchester, of Hardy's "attending the final rehearsals every evening. He has entered into the whole thing with the kindliest zest, and has expressed himself as delighted with the efforts of his good neighbours."[2] *The Three Wayfarers,* with *The Distracted Preacher,* was given in London, at Cripplegate, on November 27, 1911, and there were numerous other amateur performances of Hardy's script.[3]

After achieving some success with *The Mellstock Quire,* Mr. Evans turned for his last adaptation from comedy to tragedy. *The Woodlanders,* says *The Times,*

---

[1] Copied in an unidentified Boston paper, October 29, 1911 (Harvard Theatre Collection).

[2] Unidentified clipping (Harvard Theatre Collection).

[3] Weymouth, December 15, 1911 (Hardy Players); Radcliffe Idler (dramatic club), December, 1913 (cf. *Boston Evening Transcript,* December 9, 1913); Kelninside Academy, Glasgow, permission given to adapt, April 1, 1921 (Max Gate MS.); Marling School, Strand, Christmas, 1921 (*ibid.*); Keeble College, Oxford, June 21, 1926; Bournemouth, a broadcast on December 30, 1926 (Tilley MS.). The Carl Rosa Opera Company asked permission on February 23, 1924, to make an opera from the play (Max Gate MS.); the project, as I was informed by Mrs. Hardy, was not carried out.

differs from all its predecessors in that the element of rustic humour is less conspicuous, and as the story advances it resolves itself unmistakably into a tragedy, and ends on a sombre tragic note. . . . Mr. Evans has eliminated from the play the tardy reconciliation of Grace Melbury and her erring and repentant husband, which lightens the shadows of the ending of the story. Thus the play ends in unrelieved gloom, and the audience went home in a repressed and chastened mood.[1]

Though written by Mr. Evans, *The Woodlanders* was produced by Mr. Tilley,[2] who from 1913 to 1924 was the guiding spirit of the Hardy Players. It saw the *début* of Gertrude Bugler, then seventeen (and "a fortunate find," said Mrs. Hardy), in the role of Marty South.

Before the next dramatization of a Hardy novel, Hardy had followed the success of Granville-Barker's arrangement of *The Dynasts* (at the Kingsway in London in 1914) with his own acting version of the drama, which was first presented by the Hardy Players at Weymouth on June 2, 1916.[3] Mrs. Hardy describes the play as "more limited in scope" than the Granville-Barker version, but "picturesque and effective." It embraced "scenes of a local character only, from which could be gathered in echoes of drum and trumpet and alarming rumours, the great events going on elsewhere."[4] Hardy utilized five scenes from *The Dynasts*.[5] While drawing on the dialogue, he treated it freely. He broke up long speeches into short ones, put words into the mouths of different characters, and made some important additions to the play. He added a love element by writing the part of the waiting maid for Gertrude Bugler, elaborating it from one line in *The Dynasts* into

---

[1] *The Times*, November 20, 1913.
[2] Mr. Evans wrote to me on February 22, 1937: "I made the adaptation, but had nothing to do with the production."
[3] Its success drew a request for a performance from the Countess of Shaftesbury, president of the Red Cross in the county of Dorset (Max Gate MS.), which was given on December 6 and 7, 1916.
[4] F. E. Hardy, *The Life of Thomas Hardy*, II, 172.
[5] The scenes were: 1.1.1 (England. A Ridge in Wessex); 1.2.4 (South Wessex. A Ridge-like Down near the Coast); 1.5.5 (London. The Guildhall); 1.5.7 (King George's Watering-Place, South Wessex); and 3.5.6 (Wessex. Durnover Green, Casterbridge).

the romance of this young girl and a soldier (a stranger to the printed play) who brings the news from Waterloo. Hardy's rustic humour never appeared to better advantage than in some scenes of this adaptation. Mr. Tilley's efforts as producer won the commendation of the London critics.[1] Barrie (now Sir James) congratulated him and the cast on their achievement: he had been utterly unprepared, he said, for such delight as he had experienced in "the Nazareth of Dorchester."[2]

In *The Return of the Native,* his first dramatization for the Hardy Players, Mr. Tilley (says a contemporary critic) "has simply transcribed the dialogue of the chief scenes of the novel and only added a few sentences of his own where it was necessary to link the dialogue together. The result is not a finished drama, but a vivid series of living illustrations to the novel. He gives just what such a native company as his can render better than any other, the general appearance of the characters, their manners, and accents and dialect, their gestures and clothes, in short all the local colour. . . ."[3] The play won a local success, with Gertrude Bugler receiving lavish praise. Hardy wrote of the production: "More interested than I expected to be. The dancing was just as it used to be at Higher Bockhampton in my childhood."[4] A month before *The Return of the Native* was taken to London, Mrs. Hardy wrote (December 26, 1920) to Sir Sydney Cockerell:

Yesterday the Mummers (under our beloved Mr. Tilley) came and performed in the drawing room here, to the intense joy of T. H., his brother and sister (whom I had here) and the rest of the household. And friends who accompanied them fiddled to us and sang carols outside—the real old Bockhampton carols. Then they came in, had refreshments in the dining room and we had a very delightful time with them, Miss Bugler looking prettier than ever in her mumming dress. But the other members of the company are being a little upset by all the applause being given to her. . . .[5]

It can be easily imagined that Mr. Tilley could make little from

---

[1] Cf. F. E. Hardy, *The Life of Thomas Hardy*, II, 172.
[2] Information from Mr. Tilley.
[3] *Christian Science Monitor*, December 14, 1920.
[4] F. E. Hardy, *The Life of Thomas Hardy*, II, 215.
[5] *Friends of a Lifetime: Letters to Sydney Carlyle Cockerell*, ed. Viola Meynell (London: Jonathan Cape, 1940), p. 307.

INTRODUCTION lxxxi

Hardy's *Desperate Remedies* but melodrama and, as Charles Morgan said, at times "desperate melodrama." Yet he conceded that the result had its own quality and merit and was redolent of Dorsetshire. "It is not Mr. Hardy's play, nor need professional actors fear for their laurels when the Hardy Players bring it to King's Hall, Covent Garden, on Tuesday night, but it is altogether charming and vastly amusing. It is proof, too, that, if a writer be great enough and well-beloved by his own people, he can afford to let them use his work as a basis for their own. The result may not be his, but his generosity does him honour."[1] It is not surprising, however, that Hardy decided after the production of this play not to allow any more of his novels to be dramatized in Dorchester. For the next two years (to the end of their existence), the Hardy Players gave, with the exception of Mr. Tilley's expanded version of *The Mumming Play of St. George,* only Hardy's own dramatic versions of his work. With *The Mumming Play* appeared *O Jan! O Jan! O Jan!*[2] a slight dramatic poem interspersed with folk-song and dancing, which Hardy called an operetta, and the one-act play, *The Famous Tragedy of the Queen of Cornwall.* Hardy wrote the latter especially for the Hardy Players and added the role of Merlin in the prologue and epilogue just for Mr. Tilley. Hardy invited Sir James Barrie and Harley Granville-Barker down to Dorchester to attend a rehearsal three weeks before the performance. It was probably the technical problems which their criticism provoked that caused Mrs. Hardy to record that "the performance, and particularly the rehearsals, gave Hardy considerable pleasure."[3] The Players acted *The Queen of Cornwall* in a pleasant hearty way. Mrs. Hardy says: "The great difficulties which the play presented to amateur actors, unaccustomed to reciting blank verse, who were at their best in rustic comedy, were more or less overcome. . . ."[4] Edmund Gosse wrote, "His new play is a wonderful performance."[5] And a special cable to the *New York Herald* recorded: "Critics present said that in *The*

[1] *The Times*, November 17, 1922.
[2] Cf. Ernest Brennecke Jr., *The Life of Thomas Hardy* (New York: Greenberg, 1925), p. 20.
[3] F. E. Hardy, *The Life of Thomas Hardy*, II, 236.
[4] *Ibid.*
[5] *Sunday Times and Sunday Special*, November 18, 1923.

Queen of Cornwall Hardy proved he could have been a great dramatist."[1] But the final and most successful production of the Hardy Players was *Tess of the D'Urbervilles*.

The Dorchester Tess

In 1922, Mr. Tilley had read Hardy's script of *Tess,* but did not feel that the Dorchester players could attempt its production at that time. In 1924, however, Mr. Tilley considered that Gertrude Bugler, who had played Marty South (1913), Fancy Day (1918), and Eustacia Vye (1920), could take the leading role. He, therefore, asked for the play.

Mrs. Hardy's letter of August 24, 1924, states the conditions on which Hardy would agree to the presentation:

> We have thought that in meeting the company of players on Monday evening it might be advisable for you to let them know the conditions on which Mr. Hardy agrees to their performing of "Tess," so that if they demur to them on your reading them over the idea of their doing the play can be abandoned, and he will not send copy.
>
> 1. That performance in Dorchester only be conceded at present, any question of performance elsewhere being left to be agreed on in the future.
>
> 2. Every announcement of the play is to include the statement that it was dramatized from the novel in 1894-5 (without stating by whom).
>
> 3. The cast decided on is to have Mr. Hardy's sanction, who is to be entitled to reject any actor that in his opinion is unfitted for the part, though this is not likely.
>
> 4. Nothing is to be mentioned publicly or allowed to get into the press of its intended production till discussion of "The Queen of Cornwall" opera has died down—say the end of September.
>
> 5. No more dialect or local accent than is written in the play is to be introduced by the performers, each part being spoken exactly as set down.
>
> Of course, Mr. Hardy does not suppose there will be any objection at all to the above, as it is merely what any author expects, and he is reading through the play to see that it is all right for your putting it in hand.[2]

The conditions were accepted, and Mr. A. J. Gillam, the secretary of the Dorchester Dramatic and Debating Society, thanked

---

[1] November 28, 1923.
[2] Max Gate MS., first draft of Mrs. Hardy's letter.

Hardy in a letter of October 2, 1924, for his interest in the activities of the Society and for his special favour in according them *Tess*.[1] But despite Mrs. Hardy's letter, the programme carried Hardy's name. Hardy may have changed his mind on Barrie's advice or more likely because of his approval of the production.

The Hardy Players reached the height of their achievement in *Tess*, on November 26-9, 1924. With this play their productions came to an end, for Hardy suggested that they produce something else for a while. He had no more plays to give them and evidently wished to see no more dramatizations of his work in Dorchester. And any production after *Tess*, he realized, would be an anticlimax. Gertrude Bugler in the title role received more extravagant praise than ever before. The critic for *The Times* saw in her performance "the right sort of simplicity and breadth" and "a most moving sincerity and beauty—more beauty, one imagines, than could have been achieved by one or two of the most eminent professional actresses who have longed to play the part."[2] Sir James Barrie was so much impressed with her acting that he told the Hardys, "The girl should go on the London stage at once."[3]

Revived Interest in Hardy's Play

When Hardy decided to release his play for the local amateur production, he inevitably directed the attention of professional actresses again to *Tess of the D'Urbervilles*. Dame Sybil Thorndike must have inquired about the play at the end of October, for Hardy wrote to her on November 2, 1924:

As you are probably aware the performance here by the Dorchester

[1] Max Gate MS.
[2] *The Times*, November 27, 1924; quoted in the *Boston Evening Transcript*, December 11, 1924.
[3] Mrs. Hardy reported this remark.
  Hardy's lively interest in the Society's success with *Tess* is apparent in a letter to the Mayor of Bournemouth in December, 1924 (Max Gate MS.), which refers to a charity performance to be given at Weymouth. This performance was given on December 11. At it a sixpenny programme autographed by Hardy was auctioned, and rivalry between a Hardy enthusiast and a sporting gentleman brought up the price to twenty-seven pounds. (This information was supplied by Mr. Tilley.)

amateurs is for our local entertainment only, and has nothing to do with the question whether it is a good play or a bad one. . . . It would certainly be desirable that Mr. Casson . . . should see one of the performances, as I daresay that a practical eye could gather from the inexperienced acting an idea whether the adaptation was successful as a turning of the tragedy from narrative to dramatic form. . . . Please don't mind sending the play back when you have read it, if you are not quite sure you wish to take it up, as you will guess from what I have told you that I am very vague about its practicability. I was not, of course, aware that you had been impressed by the story, or I would have hunted up the play for you to read a long time ago. . . .[1]

On November 5, Sybil Thorndike answered: "I feel so overjoyed that you have considered my doing the play. It's one of the things I've really wanted to do in my life, and one ought to do what one wants—one seems to give more then."[2] After the play arrived, she thanked Hardy (on November 11) and asked him to have tea with her husband on the following Sunday to discuss it. Then she and her husband, Mr. Lewis Casson, went to Dorchester for one of the performances. They wanted to produce *Tess* in London.[3]

On February 11, 1925, Sybil Thorndike asked Hardy about some changes which she thought advisable and suggested referring the play to St. John Ervine. It is from Ervine that I have the explanation for the failure of the proposed performance:

Mr. Lewis Casson and his wife, Dame Sybil Thorndike, went to see it and were anxious to produce it in London. They told Hardy, however, that it had various faults and asked him if he would be willing to collaborate with a dramatist. He said he would. Casson then suggested two names to him: those of Harley Granville-Barker and myself. Hardy did me the great honour of choosing me. At the time, I was living in the south of France and working on my book about Parnell. Casson wrote to me and asked me if I would be willing to work on the play and I replied that I should be delighted to do so,

[1] Max Gate MS., first draft of Hardy's letter.
[2] Max Gate MS.
[3] In fact the *Boston Evening Transcript* of December 11, 1924, had these headlines: "In Old Age Hardy/ Gives the Theatre/ His Famous Novel/ 'Tess of the D'Urbervilles' now acted/ His Own Play, Hidden for Thirty Years/ Emerges in England—A Remarkable/ Piece, Written in His Prime and Well/ Preserving His Tragedy of Destiny/ Characters and Incidents in the New/ Medium Miss Thorndike as Heir."

but that I must first finish the Parnell book. This was agreed to, and Hardy's script was sent to me. Just as I reached the end of my book and was about to begin the play, I received a letter from Hardy, telling me that Sir James Barrie had been staying with him and had told him that the play as he had written it was faultless, and had advised him not to let anybody touch it. He, therefore, asked me to return the script, which I did. Dame Sybil Thorndike then withdrew her offer to produce the play, which was subsequently produced at Barnes with Miss Gwen Ffrangçon-Davies in the eponymous part. ... Mrs. Hardy told me afterwards that her husband greatly regretted that he had taken Barrie's advice.[1]

Sybil Thorndike was not the only London actress interested in *Tess*. The day after the first performance of the Hardy Players, November 27, 1924, Sir J. Forbes-Robertson wrote again, this time for his wife: "Suffer me to put in a plea for my wife who has just returned from a triumphant tour of Australia and South Africa. Personally I think she could do your great creation justice, for she is an actress of the very highest calibre, and if the play were placed in her hands, it would be produced with the greatest care, and properly cast."[2] Hardy replied on November 29, 1924:

I am flattered by the wish of Lady Forbes-Robertson. As you may guess I have no great desire at my time of life to see the play, *Tess*, acted in London; and the fact is that it has been lying in a cupboard almost forgotten since ever so long, so that she might have had it for the asking any time these last dozen years. It happens, however, that now it has come to life it may be out of my power to hand it over to her. The matter stands thus: that if any manager wishes our girl here—Mrs. Gertrude Bugler—to do the part in London with a professional company that he would provide, I am morally bound to let her do it, seeing how well she has served us. Should that not come off, there is an understanding with Sybil Thorndike (who asked to read the play 2 or 3 weeks ago) that she may have it, though I have not definitely assented; and some managers and critics who have been down here think that the part would not suit her. If she should be of the same opinion, and Mrs. Bugler should not be able to go to London, the play would be free, and I should entertain with great pleasure the question of Lady Forbes-Robertson presenting the character as I am already aware of her great abilities.

[1] Letter from St. John Ervine to me, dated from Honey Ditches, Seaton, Devon, October 2, 1937.
[2] Max Gate MS.

Alas; years and years ago, you ought to have been Angel Clare, and she Tess! How well you would have carried the thing off.[1]

On February 4, 1925, Gertrude Bugler finally told Hardy that for domestic reasons she could not go to London. We know, too, that on February 11, Sybil Thorndike suggested referring the play to St. John Ervine; but we do not know when Sybil Thorndike withdrew her offer, nor why Lady Forbes-Robertson was not given a chance to play the part. Evidently there were disturbing complications once more. Probably Hardy could not please Barrie and the producers at the same time. At any rate, he wrote to his theatrical agent on June 12, 1925: "I have decided to withdraw the play *Tess of the D'Urbervilles* from offers to managers if not for good, at any rate for the present. I therefore ask you to return the script to me. I hope making inquiries about it gave you no trouble."[2] It is indeed surprising that, after this sudden withdrawal in June, the play was produced at Barnes by a professional cast on September 7, 1925.

VII. Hardy's *Tess* on the London Stage: 1925

There is nothing in the correspondence to show how *Tess* reached the London stage. Hardy himself could have known little of the matter, for he wrote to Mr. (afterwards Sir) J. C. Squire: "It has got upon the stage in such an unexpected manner, & almost against my wish, for I no longer believe in dramatizing novels, & have no dramatic ambitions."[3] Even Miss Gwen Ffrangçon-Davies, who received the role, hardly knew what happened. She said in *John o' London's Weekly,* on September 5, 1925, two days before the performance: "It is only now when the fog of events has cleared and the actual production is at hand that I can think clearly of those tremendous days that followed the altogether unexpected announcement that I was to play the part of Tess in the dramatic version of Mr. Hardy's great novel." Mrs. Hardy told me that Mr. Phillip Ridgeway, the producer, arranged everything; yet I infer that

[1] Max Gate MS., first draft of Hardy's letter.
[2] Max Gate MS., first draft.
[3] Colby College MS., original holograph letter, September 29, 1925.

INTRODUCTION   lxxxvii

Hardy must have approved. *The Times,* of August 9, 1925, said: "Mr. Thomas Hardy has just approved Mr. Phillip Ridgeway's choice of Mr. Ion Swinley to play the part of Angel Clare, Mr. Hardy's hero." One would suppose that his approval must also have been asked for the selection of Miss Ffrangçon-Davies as heroine. And we know Hardy allowed alterations in the text.[1]

Gwen Ffrangçon-Davies had had a brilliant career as a singer and actress before 1925. She had sung the leading soprano role in Rutland Boughton's music dramas produced by him at the Glastonbury Festival in 1919-20. ("We kept Gwen," he told me, "until she became too famous and too expensive.") From 1920 to 1925 she sang various roles, including Etain in *The Immortal Hour,* at the Old Vic in London (1923), and she played the parts of Lady Mary in *The Admirable Crichton* (1923), Queen Mary in *Mary Stuart* (1923), Cordelia in *King Lear* (1924), Juliet in *Romeo and Juliet* (1924), Hilda Wanger in *The Master Builder* (1924), and Cleopatra in *Caesar and Cleopatra* (1925).[2] With this experience in acting Shakespeare, Ibsen, Barrie, and Shaw, Gwen Ffrangçon-Davies approached *Tess of the D'Urbervilles.* As a gifted actress and melodious singer she had been highly praised. Her Etain had been described as fragile and ethereal; her Juliet, as exquisite and charming; her Titania, as sweet and gracious. Yet there is nothing in all this to suggest that she could easily assume the role of Hardy's Tess. Her art (as one critic observed) was "neither simple nor elemental but sophisticated, subtle, and 'fey.'"[3]

It is not surprising, therefore, that she had mixed feelings in undertaking Tess. Naturally she was flattered by the honour, but quite naturally, too, she was overwhelmed by the responsibility. She said in *John o' London's Weekly,* on September 5, 1925:

To read again the novel of *Tess* was my first task—joyfully undertaken. As, bit by bit, the story returned I realized that here was a novelist whose sense of the drama was such that whole passages of his work could be extracted

---

[1] See below, p. xcvi.
[2] Cf. *Who's Who in the Theatre,* 8th edition, ed. John Parker (London: Pitman & Sons, 1936), p. 595.
[3] *Christian Science Monitor,* October 6, 1925.

entire for stage production. But as I read the novel, and then, later, the play, it came to me above my jubilation how colossal was the task I had before me. . . . I consider that though the part calls for exceptional histrionic talent and really requires a genius to do it justice, on the other hand no other actress has been so aided in her part as I have in mine. Every movement, thought, and emotion of the girl receives its space in the novel, so that when rehearsing a scene in the play I had merely to read the similar passage in the novel to gain all the material I needed for the proper revealing of the character. But despite this assistance the part is frightening in its potentialities. To my mind Duse is the only actress who could have fulfilled Mr. Hardy's creation in the flesh. But she is gone, and my greatest ambition is only to prove not unworthy of the honour.

Besides having the aid of the novel in her interpretation, Gwen Ffrangçon-Davies had the help of Hardy at Max Gate. There can be no question that her association with him inspired her representation of Tess. She said in the same article: "The days spent in Dorchester discussing the play with the author were among the most vivid of my life. And when we visited the scenes described in the book and saw the actual homesteads and farms of Tess's village, she became to me no longer a creature of printed words, the dream girl of a writer, but rather a living and breathing person with whose every thought and action I was in harmony." No other actress, except, of course, Gertrude Bugler of the Hardy Players, had such help from Hardy. It is clear that he enjoyed Miss Ffrangçon-Davies' visit, and we shall see later that he commented on her intelligence to Henry Arthur Jones. He persuaded himself and her that she looked like Tess—or rather Herkomer's drawing of Tess which had appeared in the *Graphic*.[1]

[1] Gwen Ffrangçon-Davies said (*John o' London's Weekly*, September 5, 1925): "When the book first appeared, Professor H. Herkomer, R.A., a friend of Mr. Hardy, drew an imaginative sketch of the scene where Tess returns home after the dance to find her mother at the wash-tub. She is pictured framed in the doorway, slightly catching up her dress. I had never seen this picture before Mr. Hardy had shown it to me, yet at once we both saw how similar were my features to those of the Tess shown in the picture. It will need very little make-up for me to personify the artist's impression. . . . I asked Mr. Hardy if Tess ever had a human likeness or was she entirely his own creation. He told me that first Tess was suggested to him by a girl he saw driving a milk-cart in a Dorsetshire lane. Some months later, by which time his memory had

TESS RETURNING FROM THE DANCE (HERKOMER)
Photograph by W. H. Cumming, Dorchester

As was to be expected there was a difference of opinion among critics about Miss Ffrangçon-Davies' success in her role. One said: "*Tess,* though a very imperfect play, is worth seeing, if only for the acting of the name-part. . . ."[1] Another wrote: "I have praised her previous performances—even parts of her Juliet and certainly her sweet and gracious Titania. But alas! I regret I cannot praise her Tess. The brilliant little lady seems to me to be totally unfitted for the character, which I note . . . she has been describing in interviews as 'my immortal part.' . . . [She] is plaintive rather than pathetic and 'soulful' rather than strong."[2] The *Daily News* remarked: "The book states explicitly that there was nothing ethereal about Tess, and those who have seen this actress in *The Immortal Hour* must know that her work can have this quality in delicate abundance. With her fragile grace she might seem a creature too remote and too exquisite for the Tess in whose hardy, toiling body paganism fought a losing battle against a bitter creed. . . ."[3]

We have seen that in physical presence and personality Mrs. Fiske was recognized by the critics to be very remote from Hardy's Tess.[4] Wisely she did not try to bridge the gulf, but gave her own representation of Hardy's tragic story. Gwen Ffrangçon-Davies was not less remote from the heroine of the novel, but she lacked the absolute freedom on which Mrs. Fiske insisted when she refused Hardy's play, drafted an expert dramatist to arrange the play according to her own ideas, and even wrote some of the lines to suit her personality. Miss Ffrangçon-Davies, on the other hand, took the role after Barrie had warned Hardy not to let any expert dramatist touch it. And while she drew inspiration from her discussions with Hardy about the representation, she was restricted

assumed the form of Tess, he saw the milkmaid again. Whether she had greatly changed in appearance or whether the author had created Tess above and beyond her, he never knew. At least the milkmaid bore no resemblance to the Tess of the novel."

[1] *Monitor Bureau,* September 11, 1925, in *Christian Science Monitor,* October 6, 1925.
[2] Unidentified clipping of September 13, 1925, under the heading "Dramatic Gossip" (Harvard Theatre Collection).
[3] Quoted from the *Daily News* in *Public Opinion,* September 11, 1925.
[4] Cf. p. xliv.

from freely expressing her personality as an actress. We shall see later that she had made very good suggestions about lines and a necessary scene but was not allowed to carry them out.

St. John Ervine summed up the difficulties that Gwen Ffrangçon-Davies or any other actress must face in Tess where the majority of the audience will have their individual preconceptions of the character:

No one comes between us and Tess in the novel, but several persons, all of them different in mood, come between us and her on the stage. Her author brings her to us at a time when the fervour of creating her has, perhaps, abated. An actress endeavours to adapt herself to the imagined woman. A producer adapts her adaptation to his, or she adapts his adaptation to hers. A dozen different obstacles are raised between us and our Tess, and so, no matter how finely the actress does her work, there must be some disappointment.

I thought Miss Gwen Ffrangçon-Davies gave a very beautiful and moving performance of the part, and one which will not be easily excelled, if it ever is excelled. . . .[1]

James Agate was less sympathetic:

The ardours of summer passion and the rigours of bleak days in wind-swept fields should be implicit in the bodily presence of this woman; more can be conveyed to us by what she *is* than by what she must say or do. . . . Miss Gwen Ffrangçon-Davies, though her intellectual mastery of the part was never to seek, has insufficient physical presence, and her acting lacked wealth of accomplishment. This Tess was little almost to insignificance, her deepest note being that of the plaintive. It has often been noted that effects which are good in the novel are poor on the stage. Mr. Hardy tells us of a pouted, deep-red mouth, and the way the lower lip had of thrusting the middle of the top one upward. Curiously enough, Miss Ffrangçon-Davies has always had this little trick, which, on the stage, has the effect of reducing woe to peevishness. It should be understood that the actress did nothing wrong, and achieved many perfect things in a little scale.[2]

[1] "At the Play," *Observer*, September 13, 1925.
[2] *Sunday Times and Sunday Special*, September 13, 1925. Mr. Agate continued: "One actress long unfamiliar to the stage—I mean Miss Mona Limerick—could have looked and played the part ideally. So, too, could Mrs. Patrick Campbell before her art took drawing-room ways. And today perhaps only Miss Sybil Thorndike has the technical resource and sweep of emotion which are needed to deal with the great third act."

Four years later, however, when criticizing the London presentation by Mrs. Bugler, Hardy's ideal Tess, who was supposed to have Tess's bodily presence, Mr. Agate praised Miss Ffrangçon-Davies more highly: "Nobody could ever in body or mind have been less like Hardy's full-blown peony than Miss Gwen Ffrangçon-Davies. Yet Miss Ffrangçon-Davies gave an exquisite performance owing to the fact that she is an artist of very great accomplishment. To play Tess properly it is not necessary to know the workings of a dairy; probably the less the actress knows about dairies the better. But it is necessary to know a good deal about the workings of the stage."[1]

Other critics were even readier to accept Miss Ffrangçon-Davies' natural limitations and to judge her presentation on its intrinsic merits. The *Christian Science Monitor* said: "[Gwen Ffrangçon-Davies] played it with a touching earnestness, a tender pathos, and a subdued emotional power that were most appealing. Admirable, too—apart from the occasional inaudibility, due to excess of tenderness—was the technical finish of her work; her silent exit, after the tragedy, with her frightened glance rivetted on the door, being perfectly done, and a lesson to all young actresses, in the conveyance of wordless effect."[2] J. T. Grein said: "Her rendering, sensitive and intelligent, was moved by a genuine sincerity. Her eyes, wide open, were filled with sadness and her gestures were always eloquent of simple nature—a beautiful creation and not less beautiful because it over-brimmed with an exquisite pain."[3] Barrie telegraphed to Hardy, at the time of the hundredth performance, that Miss Ffrangçon-Davies was splendid. Among other expressions of appreciation, none carries more weight than that of Henry Arthur Jones, in a letter to Hardy to be quoted later.[4] From them all, we gather that Gwen Ffrangçon-Davies gave a beautiful and self-consistent interpretation of Tess. "Undoubtedly the large audience was stirred by her performance," said St. John Ervine. "The applause she received was not the languid, almost affected, applause of the average first night, but applause which had sincerity in every beat."[5]

[1] *Ibid.*, July 28, 1929.
[2] October 6, 1925.
[3] *Theatre*, December, 1925.
[4] See below, p. ciii.
[5] *Observer*, September 13, 1925.

Interpreting Angel Clare was probably more difficult in 1925 than it had been in 1897. The Victorian psychology of his character tried the skill of both dramatists and actors. Mr. Agate contends that Angel's mentality dates the tragedy:

Is it wrong to see in Mr. Hardy the first realist to cast the sombre mantle over the facts of life which the Victorians saw sentimentally, and the preceding age had viewed with gusto? Times change, and it is possible that Mr. Hardy's book dates. The novelist found tragedy in a situation which would not be tragic today, for the reason that the situation would not be there, the mentality of Angel Clare being definitely of a past age. But if the book may be said to date, at least it dates nobly. It was the production of a lofty mind, and as such it is immune from the assault of Time. Tragedy once great, can suffer no decrease.[1]

Critics disagree about Mr. Ion Swinley's portrayal of Angel. Mr. Agate says: "If I read Angel Clare aright, he should have great charm, overlaid by an inheritance of moral convention. Mr. Ion Swinley gave us the convention without the charm...."[2] Yet St. John Ervine gives Mr. Swinley high praise:

Tess inevitably takes the first place in any consideration of her story, but it was fortunate for the audience that Mr. Ion Swinley was able to play the part of Angel Clare. Angel is an irritating character in the novel, lamentably priggish and unforgivably indifferent to what becomes of Tess after she has made her confession to him. Mr. Swinley removed the priggishness and left us with a tormented man whose behaviour could be understood. The love passages between Angel and Tess are finely done. For me there was not a moment's doubt that these two unhappy creatures supremely loved each other. Miss Ffrangçon-Davies and Mr. Swinley rose to the great level of their author, and did not fall from it.[3]

Both critics agreed that Mr. Austin Trevor was not very successful as Alec D'Urberville, though St. John Ervine thought that the dramatist and the producer must share the blame: "The least happy part of the play was that of Alec D'Urberville, for whom too little provision was made by the dramatist. Mr. Austin Trevor was very skilfully made up to look like a bounder, but he did not successfully

---

[1] *Sunday Times and Sunday Special*, September 7, 1925.
[2] *Ibid.*
[3] *Observer*, September 13, 1925.

cope with his part. I suspect, however, that the blame for this lies not with Mr. Trevor, but with Mr. Filmer, the producer, whose hand fumbled very badly over the 'foreshow' and the first and second acts. There was no fumbling in the third and fourth acts or the after-scene."[1]

It would be surprising, indeed, if London had not shown intense interest in the play. "The production of *Tess of the D'Urbervilles* as a play is an event which sets our thoughts flowing down different channels," says the *Daily News*.[2] "The novel has for various reasons become the most famous English novel of its day, and it is natural that our interest in its dramatization should overflow the bounds of our ordinary curiosity about a new play. . . . But, every stream of speculation which flows away from this event must eventually lead us to the ocean—to the fame and achievement of Thomas Hardy."[3]

But the interest in the play, if intense, gave signs of being shortlived. One rather cynical critic advised Mr. Ridgeway "to utilize this 'Tess' boom in every way as speedily and in as far-flung a manner as possible. That is to say, in the provinces, America, Australia, Canada, etc. For even a Hardy boom like this may not

[1] *Ibid.* St. John Ervine's comments on Joan Durbeyfield are also interesting: "Tess's mother . . . was richly done by Miss Margaret Carter. I see that Mr. Charles Morgan, of *The Times*, regarded Miss Carter's performance as a 'hard, cruel' one, but I did not feel that myself. This was a kindly enough woman— it was to her that Tess instinctively went for comfort—who lacked imagination, but had the fortitude which carries such people through great tribulation and leaves them unsoured at the end of it."

[2] Reprinted in *Public Opinion*, September 11, 1925.

[3] *Ibid.* An Associated Press despatch from London to the *New York Times*, on September 7, comments on the first night: "The event had caused tremendous interest, and thousands of persons were disappointed when they were unable to obtain seats. Among those was the Marchioness Curzon of Kedleston. The play was considered a great success. The audience included many prominent persons, among them Lord Beaverbrook; Henry Arthur Jones, the dramatist; Sir Barry Jackson, director of the Birmingham Repertory Theatre; and Nigel Playfair, manager of the Regent Theatre, King's Cross." (Harvard Theatre Collection.) Nor was interest in the play restricted to England. Alfred Zeiten inquired about the possibility of presentation in America (August 11). Permission was sought to translate into Spanish by M. C. Fernandez-Burges, Barcelona (August 19), into Italian by Valentina Capocii, Naples (December 23), and into French by Roger Ferdinand (November 25), this version to be presented at the Théâtre de l' Atelier. (Max Gate MSS.)

have a very long life."[1] It would seem that in regard to part of this advice Mr. Ridgeway did not have a free hand. A letter from Barrie, of August 15, 1925, advised Hardy to deal directly with the American managers and with provincial and colonial companies.[2] For the rest, Mr. Ridgeway failed to take the play to the West End in the first flush of its success and excitement. When he finally transferred it to the Garrick, after two months at Barnes, interest was cooling, and as Miss Ffrangçon-Davies said in a letter to me, "the slump that followed [Queen] Alexandra's death killed it."[3] Thus Hardy's *Tess of the D'Urbervilles*—the play which actresses had coveted for thirty years—ran for only four months in London.

On March 29, 1926, Miss Christine Silver appeared in the same version of *Tess of the D'Urbervilles* at the King's Theatre Hammersmith. The *Daily Telegraph* said:

To compare her with Miss Gwen Ffrangçon-Davies . . . would be little more than to contrast one rose in the Durbeyfield cottage garden with another. In some respects it was a slightly older and even more piteous Tess; that is all. From the moment of her first appearance, and her confession to her mother of the injury done to her, to the still more bitter confession to the man she loves, and the final scene of remorseless tragedy, the acting of this Tess was perfect in its simplicity, its tenderness and pathos, and had a startled tremulous beauty that was all Miss Silver's own. The audience showed its enthusiasm in no half-hearted fashion. Most capable support was given her by Mr. Frank Freeman as Angel Clare.[4]

It was a mistake in judgment on the part of the producer when Mr. Ridgway persuaded Gertrude Bugler to change her mind and play Tess in London in 1929, with a professional cast. The audience on occasion responded, but more it would seem to her sincerity and intrepidity than to her acting, and the critics hardly knew how to judge her out of her native surroundings.[5] Her inexperience on the

[1] Unidentified clipping, "Dramatic Gossip," September 13, 1925 (Harvard Theatre Collection).
[2] Max Gate MS.
[3] September 15, 1935.
[4] March 30, 1926.
[5] The *New York Sun* (August 6, 1929) reported that "Hardy's ideal Tess" was "a puzzle"; London could not decide "whether she was a great actress or a very competent amateur"; "she walks, she talks like an amateur, but she has great sincerity and a gift of repose."

stage was all too evident. Nor could her approximation in presence and feeling to the Tess of the novel compensate for what was lacking. To the more critical, nature was no adequate substitute for art. St. John Ervine noticed that her "artless sincerity" was "moderately attractive to jaded play-goers," but that what was certainly her "natural manner" often gave the effect of being "stilted and unnatural."[1]

James Agate, deploring the mistaken generosity of the audience, went further and traced her failure to the fact that she felt the part of Tess so passionately. "Drama," he said, quoting William Archer, "consists of imitation and passion." Passion Mrs. Bugler certainly had. "When she wept her body shook, and one knew that she had not ordered its shaking. She was 'feeling her part,' and those storms of weeping caused the spectator more distress than delight." As to imitation, it had been sufficiently advertised that there would be none. "It has not been claimed that Mrs. Bugler is an actress," but "that she is like Hardy's Tess"; but here one encounters the difficulty (already noticed in connection with more artistic portrayers of the role) that "each of us has his own Tess." Even the greatest actress "cannot give us our own Tess. What she can do is build up out of her own feeling for beauty another portrait which we can hang without too much disparity upon the wall of our own mind."[2]

Another critic, Con O'Leary, emphasized Gertrude Bugler's fidelity to Hardy's Tess, that is to Wessex life and feeling as Hardy saw and realistically presented them, but he recognized that "One of the greatest traps of the theatre is too great fidelity to life."

Amid a crowd of brilliant actors she is the imperfect one,[3] because she is herself a Wessex country girl, and with all her anxiety she is playing out the Wessex heart in travail. Amid the babel of assumed rural accents hers rings out confidently native to Hardy's heart and intention. Her fault is that she is

[1] *Observer*, July 28, 1929.
[2] *Sunday Times and Sunday Special*, July 28, 1929.
[3] Professor George Herbert Clarke, who saw her in the part, makes a shrewd comment in a letter which he was good enough to write to me on January 10, 1938: "Mrs. Bugler . . . was surrounded—I cannot say, supported—by a group of professionals who were helping themselves along by means of the usual actors' tricks. The two types of acting did not coalesce in the interest of the performance as a whole."

too true to Tess. She was the actual Tess . . . because she brought the heart and emotion of her native Wessex into the West End and was the Tess of the fields and the cottage and the dairy—the actual Tess of Hardy and the D'Urbervilles—rather than the Tess of the Duke of York's Theatre. . . .[1]

The text of Hardy's play which is included in this volume is the one Mrs. Hardy procured for me by a letter to Hardy's London theatrical agent. It is referred to as the London version, since it was played in London by Gwen Ffrangçon-Davies, Christine Silver, and Gertrude Bugler. The differences between it and the play acted in Dorchester are indicated in the foot-notes. The reader will notice that the material of the two plays, with the exception of the Foreshow, is essentially the same. There are, however, numerous changes of phrasing, and many transpositions of lines in order to point a scene or effect a better curtain. About these alterations there is no mystery. They were made by A. E. Filmer, who wrote to Edmund Blunden:

> I had some interviews with Mr. Hardy and my shyness and trepidation at the contemplation of the first, were grotesque. (Unfortunately I am a born respecter of persons.) But T. H. was sweetness incarnate, his whole personality emanated gentleness. I do not remember any other so unlike the portraits of him—drawings, photographs, and so on. Well, when I had screwed up my courage to the point of making, with sincere humility, certain suggestions, he literally gave me *carte blanche*. He said, "Do exactly as you think fit," and when I left him, "I am very happy, sir, that the play is in your hands."
>
> I took scissors, cut up the script and rebuilt the play. So far as my memory serves me I made no cuts, and I need hardly say that I made no alterations in the text; it was a matter of rebuilding (mainly to give each scene an effective curtain) and readjustment of speaking cues . . . all that sounds—and I hope is—very theatrical. For if a play is not to be made effective and attractive, why produce it?[2]

Since A. E. Filmer's alterations are retained in the text, we infer that Hardy approved of them and had made some arrangement about keeping them just as he had formerly suggested to Lillah

---

[1] Con O'Leary, August 1, 1929; unidentified clipping (Harvard Theatre Collection).

[2] Edmund Blunden, *Thomas Hardy*, pp. 170-1.

McCarthy on proposed changes to be made by Granville-Barker and Barrie.[1] He had evidently come to the conclusion that modifications by a professional playwright would improve his play.

One of the correspondents sent to Dorchester had pointed out that the novel was too complicated for the type of adapting Hardy had used:

> The greatness of the book consists in the grandeur of the scale to which it is constructed, the slow but inevitable march of its events, the minuteness of its character-drawing and dissection of motives, the utter simplicity and truth of its atmosphere. Every one of these qualities demands elbow-room and leisurely writing, such as the three hours' traffic of the stage will only allow to those who understand by instinct or by long experience how to work easily within the limits imposed by the economy of the theatre . . . and in the telescoping process which has taken place many of the motives and much of the atmosphere of the original disappear. It is impossible to doubt that *Tess* would have been a great play if its author had conceived it first in dramatic form and had simplified its structure accordingly.[2]

It is, of course, asking too much of Hardy or any other adaptor to expect him to capture for the stage those elements obtained through description, as, for example, the beauty of those rare stretches of happiness in Tess's life—the summer months at Talbothays Dairy or the short spell of bliss which she and Angel shared after the murder. We are, however, aware (as Hardy obviously was) that there are faults in the structure of the play. Probably the worst is that he tries to cram too much into his acts and scenes. He did not pretend to simplify the plot by selecting the most salient incidents and subordinating the unimportant details. Naturally he wanted to tell the whole story; likewise it was impossible. As we have seen, Illica told the first half of Tess's story; Stoddard and Kennedy the last. Hardy alone tried to tell it all. In doing so, he took two acts in the Dorchester version to arrive at Talbothays, the point where Stoddard raised his curtain.

Mr. Filmer did not improve the play in this point to the satis-

---

[1] See p. lxxii: ". . . I should not be compelled to omit the modifications if I wish to retain them."
[2] Unidentified clipping, November 27, 1924 (Harvard Theatre Collection).

faction of the critics. The *Morning Post* said: "What was lacking was the immense mood of the novel. Only so much of that enveloped the piece as one brought to it from one's own store of the printed story's impression."[1] The *Daily Herald* said: "You cannot cut up a great work of fiction after this fashion into a 'fore-show, four acts, and an after-scene'—without losing the very essence of its power. A series of portraits of Tess 'at different stages of her life' tells but a commonplace story. It is Hardy brooding over her tragedy that makes her immortal; and the stage cannot give us that."[2] And the *Manchester Guardian* said: "The play is a shadow of the book. It cannot be anything else. Sometimes the shadow is faint, sometimes it is distorted."[3] The *Morning Post,* however, acknowledged that every criticism of Hardy the dramatist was in reality a tribute to Hardy the novelist;[4] and *The Times* confessed that the story as Hardy tells it on the stage is no arraignment of convention or of anything else. It is the tragic tale "of a beautiful soul in a beautiful body, of a woman who loved and suffered."[5]

Apart from overcrowding his play, Hardy failed most in his dialogue. Sometimes he transplanted speeches that in the novel were spoken in a country lane or on a threshing floor to another place where they were not so appropriate. One feels that Hardy did not give enough consideration to the dialogue. In taking it almost wholly from the novel, he did not provide sufficient connecting links. And nothing can save a play whose dialogue is weak or stilted. Mr. St. John Ervine said, "The chief defect in Hardy, as a potential dramatist, was his inability to write natural, fluent dialogue, except when he had to put words into the mouths of rustics."[6] One other technical weakness Hardy betrayed in his use of the letter. He had the excellent opportunity of presenting this important symbol (which Tess calls "my life") dramatically before

[1] Reprinted in *Public Opinion*, September 11, 1925 (Harvard Theatre Collection).
[2] *Ibid.*
[3] *Ibid.*
[4] *Ibid.*
[5] *The Times,* November 27, 1924; quoted in the *Boston Evening Transcript,* December 11, 1924.
[6] *Observer,* July 28, 1929.

the eyes of the audience; yet, strange to say, he was the only adaptor who let the opportunity slip. Instead of magnifying the incident for the eye, he simply has Tess narrate in her confession the mishap of the letter's going under the carpet.

The flaws of the play, however, did not shake St. John Ervine's confidence in Hardy's dramatic powers: "They are the flaws, not of a man working in a medium which he has no right to use, but of a man working in a medium with which he is not fully familiar."[1] He felt that only a great dramatist could have conceived the scene where Tess dresses and departs in silence, whereas only "a potentially-great dramatist could have provided the anticlimax [the landlady's discovery of the murder]. It was excess of matter, not lack of it, that brought the landlady on to the scene. It was excess of dramatic imagination, not an insufficiency of it, which prevented Mr. Hardy from dropping his curtain a moment or two after Tess had flown."[2] That Hardy was aware of the play's structural deficiencies is evident not only in his correspondence with Lillah McCarthy and Sybil Thorndike, but in his attempts in the different versions to meet perplexing problems. Sometimes he sacrificed a beautiful scene, such as the jewel scene, and marked it "omit or not at option" because it demanded too many entrances and exits; or again he left action insufficiently motivated because to supply the deficiency would require additional changes of scenery. Yet curiously enough the two weaknesses of the play which worried Gwen Ffrangçon-Davies most, the rapid transition from Act III to Act IV, and the entrance of Alec on the wedding night, are not in Hardy's original version. (Instead, of course, there is the melodramatic eviction scene, similar to one in Jerrold's *Rent-Day*.)

Hardy's correspondence with Miss Ffrangçon-Davies is significant, revealing as it does his recognition of the faults of construction and, even more, his readiness to accept ideas for the improvement of the play. After forty performances of *Tess* at Barnes, Mr. Phillip Ridgeway took it to the Garrick Theatre in the West End. Before the move, Miss Ffrangçon-Davies (in a letter of October 14, 1925)

[1] *Ibid.*, September 13, 1925.
[2] *Ibid.*

asked Hardy's permission to make some changes in the script. She objected to the abruptness of transition between the confession scene and that in the luxurious apartment at Sandbourne. What she especially wanted was *some* scene showing Tess "poor and troubled," so that those in the audience unfamiliar with the novel would not feel that Tess went too rapidly from one man to another. She noticed that occasionally someone tittered at the beginning of the fourth act, thinking Tess a "light woman," but added that the scene always gripped the audience as it proceeded. She wisely suggested dividing the third act into two scenes, in the second of which Tess's struggle and despair would reveal her reason for returning to Alec. If she were allowed to add the scene she had written, she thought that they might eliminate Alec's entrance into the Wellbridge Manor scene, "which," she said, "I remember you saying you didn't like— I always find it difficult to avoid the suggestion of melodrama which it does seem to involve." She also requested the restoring of the scene with the diamonds, which had been cut because it caused too many entrances and exits. She repeated: "And if you *could* remove Alec from the wedding night scene, my joy would be complete."

Hardy's reply on October 17, 1925, said that in an earlier version he had shown a scene combining the swede-hacking with the bailiff's coming for the furniture of Tess's mother, but this he had omitted because it made the play too long. He had endeavoured to get the same effect by substituting Alec's call on the evening of the marriage. He thought that this call and the discussion of the family's poverty by Joan made the situation sufficiently clear. Since he could not find the old version, he gave Miss Ffrangçon-Davies permission to adopt her additional scene in consultation with Mr. Filmer if Mr. Ridgeway approved. He recognized that her version would not require more scenery while his would.[1]

When Gwen Ffrangçon-Davies asked Hardy's permission to add some lines she had written about Tess's new clothes which Angel had bought her for the wedding (so that the audience would not think she was over-dressed) Hardy liked her suggestion and granted

---

[1] Max Gate MS., Hardy's first draft.

the permission. When she asked for some reference in the last scene to the fact that Stonehenge was older than the D'Urbervilles, he sent her some lines of his own. It is significant of her knowledge of stage requirements that Miss Ffrangçon-Davies made these suggestions for a whole scene and bits of others to make the play more convincing. And it is, of course, significant of Hardy's approval of the actress and his wish to improve the play that he was willing to accede to her requests. He must have been pleased when Miss Ffrangçon-Davies added in one of her letters that many Hardy lovers told her that for them Tess had taken visible shape.[1]

Although the suggestions of Miss Ffrangçon-Davies are not incorporated in the revised version of Hardy's script, and although they were tried only once at the Garrick Theatre,[2] they are important as showing Hardy's co-operation with an intelligent and sensitive artist, and as revealing his own perplexities about his play. It seems clear from his earlier correspondence that while he was fully conscious of the technical faults of his play, they did not worry him very much. As he had said in "Why I Don't Write Plays," he did not believe in subordinating "the presentation of human passions" to the exigencies or the arbitrary fashions of the stage, or in letting anything interfere with "the high relief of the action and the emotions." All he seemed really to care about was keeping the pathos of Tess's tragedy. In that he was successful. While his play cannot claim equality with Stoddard's for craftsmanship, there is power in the characterization. His Tess is as piteous, indeed if anything more heart-rending than Stoddard's. She remains a great steadfast, tragic creature. To condemn the play for faults of construction is, as J. T. Grein says, to take too narrow a view. "To me

---

[1] Max Gate MS.
[2] When I asked Gwen Ffrangçon-Davies whether she carried out her suggestions at the Garrick, she replied: "I was most anxious to put the alterations in when we moved to the Garrick—and we did put in the jewel scene and the scene I wrote between Acts III and IV for one matinée—but the management were afraid of any change and would not let me keep it, to my great disappointment, as it much improved the play. Alec was removed from the wedding-night and the face-slapping incident put into the intermediate scene of the moving of Tess and her mother and the children. It was only played at the one matinée I spoke of. . . ." (Letter to me, September 15, 1935.)

it is more than enough that here we have the stuff of drama, a tragedy all pity and pain, with an Ariadne thread of purity and heroism woven into it, that gives the dignity and the intensity of a Greek play and reveals the workings of a great mind." "We forget," he continues, "the moment of anti-climax after Tess's haunted departure when the murder was done ... in the shaking tremulous beauty of the closing scenes on Stonehenge. The simplicity, the pathos, the infinite yearning and the poetry of that reunion and that parting clutched the heart strings. 'I am ready.' The story is done, the play is ended, the Katharsis of suffering has been fulfilled."[1]

We have seen the criticisms of the production in the press, some of which were written by Hardy's friends, J. T. Grein, St. John Ervine, and Charles Morgan. There is still another, however, which should be considered, that of Henry Arthur Jones. His criticism was not written for the public, but for Hardy himself. Its interest is enhanced when we remember that in the nineties Henry Arthur Jones had tried to persuade Hardy to write for the theatre.

In the *Life and Letters of Henry Arthur Jones,* his daughter records:

Of all the plays we saw in 1925, Hardy's *Tess of the D'Urbervilles* interested my father more deeply than any other. He loved the book, which he had read more than once—a thing he very rarely did with a novel. . . .

We were at the first night at the Barnes Theatre, and, although H. A. J. was seventy-four, he made the long journey to Barnes a few weeks later to see the play a second time, and when the production came to Golders Green he saw it again. My father was deeply moved by the play and the fine acting, and he wrote the following letter to Hardy:

"8th September, 1925

"Dear Thomas Hardy,

"You may like to know what I felt and thought at the first performance of *Tess.* All through, it was an evening of great emotion and deep interest to me. The massive quality of your noble work in the novel stood plainly out in the play like one of the pillars of Stonehenge. There were no grave faults of technique, and there were some excellencies, due, I daresay, to the fact that you are not a professional playwright. I challenged the appearance of

[1] *Theatre,* December, 1925.

Alec on the bridal night immediately before the confession. It disturbed the unity of the impression that the scene in the novel had left in my mind. It makes a double distraction in Tess's already too distracted heart, and it divides the volume of interest and movement towards the dreadful moment of the confession. However, Alec had to be thereabouts brought into the play, and I do not pretend to tell you how you ought to have done it. The confession remains one of the most poignant and absorbing scenes in all the range of the drama. It shows what great fame you would have won as a dramatist, if you had given yourself to the theatre—which luckily for English literature you did not. The last act was also most deeply moving, and the end had large solemn tragic beauty and impressiveness. I found it true to Arnold's favourite word—'Fortifying.' The play fulfils the purpose of tragedy and purges the mind by moving us to pity and terror—oh, the deepest, deepest pity.

"It was beautifully and appropriately played throughout. Miss Gwen Ffrangçon-Davies wrung my heart in the third and fourth acts. My daughter and I found ourselves with streaming cheeks. Miss Davies was so unforced, so sincere and restrained. There was not one wrong note in her performance. I cannot remember when I have been so much touched. She must not be judged because she did not render those aspects of the character which are in the novel and not in the play. She played unerringly those scenes which you gave her to play. I am sure the play would have lost immensely its beauty and pathos if Tess had been acted by a robust wench in a robust way. That character is not in the play you have written.

"Ion Swinley, in the measure that his part gave him the opportunity, is equally deserving of praise. Angel Clare is a difficult part to render on the stage in a way that will send it home to the average spectator. Ion Swinley's performance showed careful study and insight, and was of great value to the play. His fine voice and presence helped to make the part attractive. The most thankless part of Alec was also capitally played. The peasants were credible and veritable rustics. The Dorset dialect was well sustained. Our stage peasants are generally accomplished linguists, and speak a polyglot blend of Yorkshire, Norfolk and Somerset, with marked preference for 'Zummerset.'

"The difficulties of adapting a novel to the stage are rarely understood and never appreciated. Aristotle has illuminated them in the distinction he draws between the play and the epic. There can be no true or quite satisfactory adaptation of a novel to the stage. To the extent that a play is a consistent organic whole it must differ widely from the novel from which it is quarried, not only in the course of its action, but also in the necessary adjustment of each character to the action. Again, the novelist in writing a play is largely deprived of his chief tool—his style. De Maupassant, whose style is the perfection of delicate jewellery in story-telling, emerged as a crude vulgar melodramatist when he was not at all unskilfully adapted at our favourite St. James's Theatre. . . .

"I offer you my warmest and most sympathetic congratulations on *Tess*. I felt that I must put down these thoughts while they were fresh in my mind. . . . I regret that I have seen nothing of you these last tremendous years. Our last two meetings were in the theatre, when you came with Professor Bradley and me to see *Othello*, and when you had a seat in my box on the first night of *The Case of Rebellious Susan*. If you come to London you will give me a chance to shake hands with you, will you not?

"Faithfully yours,
"Henry Arthur Jones."[1]

Mrs. Hardy told me that her husband was greatly pleased to receive this letter. *Tess* in the theatre had revived in these two writers expressions of friendship. Hardy answered on September 13, 1925:

Dear H. Arthur Jones,

It was with much pleasure that I received your letter telling me of your visit to the Barnes Theatre for the performance of the *Tess* play. An experienced judgment like your own has a settling effect upon the chaos of opinions I have read in the newspapers as to the general effect of the production, though of course I make allowance for your indulgence towards the manifold defects in the construction of the play. As you probably know, it was written thirty years ago, when both you and I were younger, and our views of the theatre—at any rate mine—were not quite the same as they are now. If I had adapted the novel in those [*sic*] days, I daresay I should have done the job differently; but when, quite by accident, and at the request of the amateur players here, I looked it up, I found I could not get back to the subject closely enough to handle it anew. However, all independent observers agree with you in saying that it did not fail to move the emotions, which is quite as much as one could expect, though one critic, by the way, said that the audience "all went to be moved, but none were moved"—a puzzling statement which I pass over in the face of the other testimony. I am quite of your opinion in respect to Miss Ffrangçon-Davies. She has been down

---

[1] D. A. Jones, *Life and Letters of Henry Arthur Jones*, pp. 354-8.

here, and we liked her very much; her great intelligence, too, was striking, while she was free from the vanities one too often finds among the stage people.

It is a long time since we met. I well remember your *Case of Rebellious Susan*, and, of course, several of your other plays. I sometimes wonder that new plays from your hand do not appear oftener now that the terrible Victorian restrictions are removed, and events can be allowed to develop on the stage as they would in real life. . . .[1]

Two remarks stand out as significant. Hardy says that his views on the theatre have changed since the days when he wrote the play thirty years before. It is interesting to speculate what kind of play he would have made in 1925. The other important remark includes "now that the terrible Victorian restrictions are removed." Was Hardy thinking of himself as well as Henry Arthur Jones? If he could have developed events for the stage in 1895 as they develop in real life, might Hardy have written social drama? Or as the critic for *John o' London's Weekly* said, "If he had been born fifty years later, and were starting life by expressing himself as a dramatist now, what a difference there might have been."[2]

Hardy did not see *Tess* at Barnes or at the Garrick in London. A wireless to the *New York Times* on September 7, 1925, said: "He was advised by his physicians not to attend the première. . . ."[3] A letter of Hardy's to Sir Sydney C. Cockerell, on September 28, 1925, suggests that he was not very much interested in going to see it: "I have not seen the play *Tess of the D'Urbervilles* and don't suppose I shall. It is very odd that I should have drifted into a job which I quite disbelieve in—a dramatized novel—and did not at all foresee when I gave way to the request of the local players that I would let them have something."[4]

Yet Hardy did see the play—and evidently enjoyed it. The cast of the Garrick Theatre went to Max Gate. Gwen Ffrangçon-Davies wrote to me: "The most perfect performance, and incident-

[1] Quoted *ibid.*, pp. 358-9.
[2] August 24, 1925.
[3] Unidentified clipping (Harvard Theatre Collection).
[4] Colby College MS.

ally *my* best one, was in the drawing-room at Max Gate—an unforgettable experience."[1] Mrs. Hardy includes a letter of a member of the cast in her biography. Miss Margaret Carter, who played Joan Durbeyfield in the Garrick troop, described the occasion to a friend in America:

"Mr. and Mrs. Hardy behaved as if it were a most usual occurrence for a party of West-End actors to arrive laden with huge theatrical baskets of clothes and props.

"They met us in the hall and entertained us with tea, cakes and sandwiches, and Mr. Hardy made a point of chatting with everyone.

"The drawing-room was rather a fortunate shape—the door facing an alcove at one end of the room, and we used these to make our exits and entrances, either exiting into the hall or sitting quietly in the alcove.

"Mr. and Mrs. Hardy, a friend of the Hardys [Mr. T. H. Tilley, who also gave me an account of the performance], and two maids who, in cap and apron, sat on the floor—made up our audience. I think I am correct in saying there was no one else. The room was shaded—lamps and firelight throwing the necessary light on our faces.

"We played the scenes of Tess's home with chairs and a tiny drawing-room table to represent farm furniture—tea-cups for drinking mugs—when the chairs and tables were removed the corner of the drawing-room became Stonehenge, and yet in some strange way those present said the play gained from the simplicity.

"It had seemed as if it would be a paralysingly difficult thing to do, to get the atmosphere at all within a few feet of the author himself and without any of the usual theatrical illusion, but speaking for myself, after the first few seconds it was perfectly easy, and Miss Ffrangçon-Davies's beautiful voice and exquisite playing of the Stonehenge scene in the shadows thrown by the firelight was a thing that I shall never forget. It was beautiful.

"Mr. Hardy insisted on talking to us until the last minute. He talked of Tess as if she was someone real whom he had known and liked tremendously. I think he enjoyed the evening. I may be quite wrong, but I got the impression that to him it seemed quite a proper and usual way to give a play—probably as good if not better than any other—and he seemed to have very little conception of the unusualness and difficulties it might present to us."[2]

These last productions of *Tess* in London and at Max Gate

[1] September 15, 1935.
[2] F. E. Hardy, *The Life of Thomas Hardy*, II, 243-4.

directed a flood of publicity on Hardy. The criticisms, the telegrams of congratulations, the reception of the Garrick cast and the performance in his drawing-room were undoubtedly too exciting for him. Mrs. Hardy even expressed the opinion that if it had not been for the "fuss" about *Tess,* he would have lived to be ninety. When asked whether he enjoyed having his works on the stage, she said he loved it. No doubt he shared Laurence Housman's feeling, expressed in *The Unexpected Years:* "In my experience, the production of plays can provide an author with livelier satisfaction than the writing of books. It is pleasant to be told that one's books are appreciated; but it is not merely pleasant, it is thrilling, to see one's play, or its characters, brought to life by good production or good acting."[1]

Such is the history of Hardy's *Tess of the D'Urbervilles* on the stage. Its dramatization was begun at the request of George Alexander and Olga Nethersole, finished for Forbes-Robertson, sought by Bernhardt, Duse, and Mrs. Patrick Campbell, offered to, but rejected by, Minnie Maddern Fiske, and finally withdrawn by Hardy for thirty years. Then it emerged in the sleepy little town of Dorchester and found its way at last to London, almost against Hardy's desire, when he was eighty-five years old. Meanwhile in Stoddard's version *Tess* had made its place in the annals of the commercial stage. And besides the play by Kennedy and the Italian opera, discussed above, there were other dramatic versions of the novel including two films and two farces.[2]

Nor is there any reason to suppose that the last dramatization of *Tess* has been written or staged. In the week of November 26 to 30, 1946, an adaptation by Ronald Gow was played at the New Theatre in London. While Laurence Olivier and his Old Vic company played *Lear* in Paris, the Bristol Old Vic company filled the breach in London by presenting Wendy Hiller in *Tess of the D'Urbervilles.* The text of Gow's play was called by the *Daily Herald* "the best dramatic version yet of Hardy's tragic novel."

[1] Laurence Housman, *The Unexpected Years*, p. 205.
[2] See Appendix.

By beginning on the wedding night of Tess and Angel Clare, it reveals an original stroke of genius on the part of the author. Lionel Hale wrote: "This marked feat of self-denial gives us time for a completely faithful Tess, an adequate Clare, and all you want of Alec D'Urberville" (*Daily Mail,* November 28, 1946). He added: "This acting version, however, has, in general, the great virtue of being faithful to the original. Passing over the awful truth that all stage versions must be inadequate when it comes to the masterpieces of fiction, this somehow combines the spirit of Hardy with the letter of the theatre." Of Wendy Hiller's role, he said: "This was, all things considered, about as honest, patient, lovable, truthful, moving a performance as the London stage has seen for 12 months. The part is generously written, but it was generously played." Mr. F. E. Hansford, in a letter to me on December 12, 1946, said of the production: "I thought highly of it. Wendy Hiller did not quite touch the heights of Gwen Ffrangçon-Davies' impersonation—the latter, indeed, was an ideal Tess. . . . Wendy Hiller's was of a slighter build—but she was decidedly *spirituelle,* especially in the closing scenes which were impressive."[1] The appearance of this prominent actress in an apparently good contemporary acting version showed that there is still interest in *Tess of the D'Urbervilles* as material for the theatre.

[1] The scenes of the play:

Act I

The Manor-House at Wellbridge.   New Year's Eve, 1880.

Act II

Scene 1. Tess's Home at Marlott.   Sixteen months later.
Scene 2. The Herons, Sandbourne.   Two months later.
Scene 3. A Railway Station.   One month later.

Act III

Scene 1. The House in the Forest.   A week later.
Scene 2. Stonehenge.   Two days later.

I. HARDY'S ORIGINAL VERSION (1894-5)

TESS
of the D'Urbervilles

A TRAGEDY
IN FIVE ACTS
In the Old English Manner

PERSONS

ANGEL CLARE, *aged* 28
ALEC D'URBERVILLE, *aged* 28
JOHN DURBEYFIELD, *aged* 50
FELIX CLARE, *aged* 29
JONATHAN KAIL, *aged* 60
ABRAHAM, *aged* 10

TESS, *aged* 18
JOAN DURBEYFIELD, *aged* 40
LIZA-LU, *aged* 12
SARAH, *a club girl, aged* 16
MARIAN, *aged* 25
IZZ, *aged* 20

OTHER CLUB GIRLS; TWO FIDDLERS; MILKMAIDS AND MEN; AN OLD LABOURER AND HIS WIFE; A MANSERVANT; A FARM BAILIFF; A LODGING-HOUSE KEEPER; HER SERVANT; STREET PASSENGERS; &C.

ACT I

THE MAIDEN

SCENE: Marlott Village, Vale of Blackmoor

On the right is the exterior of the Durbeyfield's cottage, with open shed attached, forming entrance to dwelling. Within the shed are chairs, a table, etc. A green lawn in the centre towards back. A highway on the left runs down to the front, and is screened from the cottage and green by a tall hedge. In the background stretches the beautiful Vale of Blackmoor: woodlands and pastures, to a distance of many miles.

SEASON: *early summer.* TIME: *morning.*

JOAN DURBEYFIELD, *with a letter in her hand, is standing in front of the cottage with* SARAH. JOHN DURBEYFIELD *is sitting in the shed. The boy* ABRAHAM *and the girl* LIZA-LU *are playing near.*

SARAH: Has this notion of Tess's going away anything to do with your husband finding out that he is descended from the old ancient family of D'Urberville?

JOAN: Why yes! As soon as Pa'son Tringham the antiqueerian told us that my husband is Sir John D'Urberville by right I thought of the rich lady and her son of that name, living out at Trantridge, and I packed off Tess to claim kin, as of course he's a sort of cousin of hers; and the long and the short of it is that they want her to come and stay with them.

SARAH: What is she going to do with herself in such a grand house?

JOAN: Manage the chicken farm.

SARAH: That's not much, considering you be people of blood, and kin to the lady.

JOHN: That's what I da say. Surely they ought to honour us more.

JOAN: Pooh. 'Tis only just to occupy her. Mr. Alec D'Urberville, the old lady's son, is a very handsome gentleman, and 'tis my belief our relation to en mid be closer some day. (*Nods knowingly.*) That he's much struck wi' Tess I know.

JOHN: I don't like my daughter going there to work. We be the oldest branch o' the family, owning the title and they ought to come to us—particular if the young gent wants to marry her.

JOAN: True, Sir John. But they won't.

JOHN: They be nothing beside us—a junior branch of us, no doubt, hailing long since King Norman's day—perhaps about Oliver Grumble's time.

JOAN: Well—they be rich; and the young man likes our maid. Anyhow, two branches of a family can be on visiting terms.

ABRAHAM: Yes. And we'll all claim kin! And we'll go to see 'em when Tess is gone to live with 'em.

LIZA-LU: And we'll ride in their coach, and wear fine clothes!

JOAN: Well, Tess ought to go. 'Twas through her bad driving that the shaft of the mail-cart ran into our horse and killed the poor thing. We have not known what in the world to do to get another and if she goes to them she'll get their help to buy one. She'll be sure to please the lady's son, Tess will; and like enough 'twill lead to his marrying her. In short, I know it!

SARAH: How?

JOAN (*speaking mysteriously*): I've tried her fate in the fortune-telling book, and it brought out that very thing.

JOHN: H'm. But the maid herself don't seem to care about going.

JOAN: She won't say no long.

JOHN: Tess is queer.

JOAN: But she's tractable at bottom. Here she is coming. Don't tease her. Leave her to me.

TESS enters blithely from cottage.

JOAN: Now, Tess, I've had another letter, as I told you, and you mustn't back out of going now. You can win the lady round to do anything. She says she wants you to look after them pet chickens of hers; but that's only her artful way of getting 'ee there without raising your hopes. She's going to own 'ee as kin—that's the meaning of it.

Tess: She didn't even see me.

Joan: Well somebody saw you for her—her son.

Tess: Yes, mother. He saw me.

Joan: And he owned you very nicely.

Tess: H'm. He called me coz.

Joan: Ah—I knew it, Jacky, he called her coz. And of course he and she want you very much to come.

Tess: I don't altogether think I ought to go. Who wrote that letter saying I must come? Will you let me see it?

Joan: Mrs. D'Urberville wrote it, of course.

She *hands letter.*

Tess: It is a man's writing—his—the son's—in his mother's name.

Joan: Is it? Well, so much the better. He is very much interested in you. He's going to call for an answer this morning, as you see.

Tess: I would rather stay with father and you. I don't care about him.

Joan: But why? He's a mighty handsome young man.

Tess (*coldly*): I don't think so. . . . And he didn't talk to me at all—nicely.—I mean in a way he ought.

Joan: Oh—you chaw too high. There's your chance, whether or no.

Tess: I'll think it over.

She *goes out meditating.*

Joan: She's made a conquest. And she's a fool if she don't follow it up.

John: I don't quite like my girl going away, if she don't wish to.

Joan: But do make her go, Jacky! He's struck with her. You can see that from his coming, and writing. He'll marry her and make a lady of her; and then she'll be what her forefathers were.

John: Well, perhaps that's what Mr. D'Urberville means—it is possible! Sure enough, he *mid* have serious thoughts about improving his blood by linking on to the old line. (*Looks off stage.*) Perhaps this is he coming? I'll be off. I'm too shaky to see him just now. Tess—the little rogue!—if she should bring about that—ha-ha!

Takes stick and enters cottage.

ALEC D'URBERVILLE *enters from highway, in driving costume, with a cigarette, and a little basket of strawberries.* JOAN *curtsies.* SARAH *and the children go out.*

ALEC: Is your daughter at home?

JOAN: I think she's in the garden, sir.

ALEC: Now, Mrs. Durbeyfield, we must have her. We like her much, and I am sure my mother will not consent to give her up.

JOAN: I am sure I want her to go to you, sir. But she must please herself. I'll call her. (*Goes to corner of cottage.*) Tess!

ALEC: I've brought a little basket of early strawberries for her.

JOAN: Oh—thank you, sir! I think she's coming.

JOAN *goes out.*

ALEC (*placing strawberries on the table*): Well—I'm damned. Ha-ha! What a funny thing! . . . This family first to have invented me as their rich cousin, on the strength of the ornamental new name taken by my father, dear old Simon Stokes! and then my finding such a crumby girl to be the daughter! I'd be cousin to half a hundred such any day with pleasure!

TESS *enters round corner of cottage; starts.*

TESS: Oh—I didn't know it was you, sir. (*Retreats.*)

ALEC: Stop, stop, Tess! It isn't a brave bouncing girl like you who are afraid of me! Now, my dear girl, you are coming on a visit to us, as relations. Though my mother, who is a curious woman, calls it coming to look after her poultry farm.

TESS: I don't know that I am coming.

ALEC: Why, you talk as if there were harm in it. And look here—I've brought you—I mean my mother has sent you—a basket of strawberries. They are early ones. I thought—she thought—you'd like them. Try one, dear.

TESS (*dubiously*): I don't think your mother knows anything about them.

ALEC: Well, never mind. Try one, dear. (HE *takes a strawberry from the basket and holds it by the stem to her mouth.* TESS *covers her mouth.*)

TESS: No, no. I would rather take it in my own hand.

ALEC: Nonsense! (HE *persists;* SHE *retreats till she is against wall; laughs distressfully, and takes it with her lips as offered.*)

ALEC: There's a darling.

TESS: Don't call me darling. I don't like it!

ALEC: But you will like it some day. Now, my mother's message by letter this morning was that you were to come to her. And I am sent to fetch you.

TESS (*suspiciously*): Not *sent*? It is your own doing I expect!

ALEC: Well—you must come. It will be helping your family, and your duty to them is not to refuse. Discourtesy to us means poverty to you.

TESS (*sadly*): Yes: I see that it will be helping father and mother. And—if it is true that Mrs. D'Urberville really does want me—I suppose I must go.

ALEC: That's sensible of you. Now, get your things together, please, whilst I go to the inn and tell them to put the horse in. Then I'll call for you. But, Tess—one little kiss on those cherry lips—in my mother's name, of course—just to seal the agreement.

TESS (*drawing back*): No, sir: certainly not. I've not agreed to anything with you. It is Mrs. D'Urberville who wants me, unless you have told me untruly.

ALEC: I mean—as her agent. Come now!

Moves towards her.

TESS: I don't agree—I won't have anybody kiss me!

HE *endeavours to catch her—*SHE *dodges round the table in the shed, and overturns it to check him.*

ALEC: Fie—that's temper! ... Very well—I won't give your father the cob I promised him in place of his old horse. So you'll suffer for your unkindness that way.

TESS: I didn't know you were going to give him one.

ALEC: I was.

TESS (*resignedly*): Oh very well—I suppose I must give in! Only I wish you wouldn't ask me! Very well—I won't mind. It means nothing!

HE *attempts the kiss.* SHE *eludes him again.*

ALEC (*losing his temper*): So you can go from your word like that, you young witch, can you!

TESS: Oh—take it then, since you be so determined! But I thought you would be kind to us, and protect us as your kinsfolk—without wanting me to do this!

ALEC: Kinsfolk be hanged! Now!

TESS (*tearfully: her breast heaving*): But I don't want anybody to kiss me, sir! And I wouldn't have agreed to go with you if I had known!

HE *attempts to kiss again—*SHE *slips her handkerchief between her cheek and his lips.*

ALEC (*nettled*): Oh! You are rather sensitive for a cottage girl. You shall be made sorry for that some day!

TESS: For what?

ALEC: You know very well. Insulting me by using your handkerchief like that. You may live to regret it—unless you agree willingly to let me do it again, and no handkerchief.

TESS (*warily*): Wait just a moment, then, while I get my hat in case I should catch cold out here.

SHE *slips into the cottage, and is heard bolting the door.*

ALEC D'URBERVILLE *goes to the window.*

ALEC: What—you are not coming out again?

TESS: Certainly not, sir.

ALEC: You artful hussy! You said you wanted your hat on purpose to get away from me! I'll swear you did.

TESS: Perhaps I don't deny it.

ALEC: Damned if I'll be beaten! (HE *tries to get in at the window.* SHE *pulls to the casement, and hurts his arm.*)

ALEC: You devil! You confounded, artful, impertinent, damned—

TESS (*within the window*): You ought to be ashamed of yourself for using such wicked words! I don't like you at all! I hate and detest you! I'll never come to your mother's house at all!

ALEC (*rubbing his arm, and laughing carelessly*): Well—I like you better for this skittishness, upon my soul. Come—let there be peace. I'll never again do such a thing against your will. My life upon it, now! . . . Now look here. Wait and cool down a bit. Remember you are to come to my mother. She will be much disappointed and annoyed if you don't. I've got the gig here, and will call for you in half an hour, just as was planned. Pack up your things, and forget this. Remember, I shall come back in half an hour, to fetch you. Your things can be sent afterwards. (*Aside.*) A damned hussy, pretty as she is! . . . Her spirit wants breaking a bit. And I'll do it before I've done!

Enter JOAN *followed by* ABRAHAM *and* LIZA-LU.

JOAN: Was anything the matter? I thought I heard—I hope, sir, you've been able to persuade her that she owes it to your mother to go, after your kindness to us all?

ALEC: Well—I don't know. She's a little ungrateful. But I am coming back to fetch her in half an hour.

HE *goes out by highway.*

JOHN DURBEYFIELD *enters from garden and sits down.*

JOAN: Where is Tess? The gentleman seemed ruffled a bit.

TESS *is heard unbolting door. She enters.*

What's this, Tess? You haven't been such a simpleton as to offend the gentleman? He's coming in half an hour, you know, and you must pack, if you be going.

TESS (*after a pause*): I think I've changed my mind about going. I've never seen a Mrs. D'Urberville at all. He seems to be master there.

JOAN: And suppose he is?

TESS: I don't care about him. I'd rather not go.

JOAN: What—after all? You ought to be ashamed of this, you ought! (*To the boy and girl.*) There's a sister you've got, who'll do nothing for her family!

ABRAHAM & LIZA (*plaintively*): Tess won't go and be made a lady of—she won't! And we shan't have no nice new horse to drive and lots of money to buy fairings! And Tess won't be dressed up and look pretty in fine clothes, and we shan't be happy never no more! (*They weep.*)

TESS: He tried to kiss me: and I didn't like it at all.

JOAN: It was early for that, certainly. But, Lord, a kiss is not much to make a fuss about, if 'tis well meant. I didn't make such ados in my time! Your father little knows—ah, well—he was all the better for his ignorance, dear man.... Well, if you mean to ruin us, Tess, do it and make an end o't.

TESS (*restlessly*): Oh, I don't know what to say! It is for you to decide, mother, after all—I don't want to be an obstinate girl! It was certainly through me that we lost our old horse; and I suppose I ought to do something to get this fresh one he promises! ... But I don't like Mr. D'Urberville being at the house I'm going to!

ABRAHAM & LIZA: Tess won't go to our gentleman cousin's, and we shall be ruined and die!

JOHN (*coughs in chair*): What's this bother about? Whatever any of ye do or don't do, 'twill make no difference to me—I shan't be head of the old D'Urberville family much longer. I'm ticketed Underground.

TESS (*moved, after a pause*): I will go.

JOAN (*exultantly*): Ha—that's right, dear! Now you'll make your fortune. What a chance for a pretty girl!

TESS: I hope it is a chance. But oh—not in the way you mean, mother! Now, put my things together. Since it has to be done, let's do it soon.... Get my hat and jacket, Liza-Lu.

JOAN: But you'll never set out to see your grand kin without dressing up a bit?

TESS (*impatiently*): But I am going there to work!

Enter LIZA-LU *with old hat and jacket.*

JOAN: Well, yes. (*Aside.*) At first there may be a little pretence of it, but that won't be for long! (*To* TESS *who has put on old hat and jacket*.) But I do entreat 'ee to put your best side outward, and wear your Sunday clothes!

TESS (*indifferently*): Very well. I suppose you know best!

Enters cottage.

JOAN: I tell 'ee what it is, Sir John. He'll never have the heart not to love her. She gets prettier every day, and her skin is as sumple as a duchess's. But whatever you do, don't say any more to her of his fancy for her, and her chance of catching him. She's such an odd maid that it may set her against going there even now. . . . If all goes well, I shall certainly be for making some return to that antiqueerian for telling us of our connection with this great family—dear, good man!

TESS *re-enters, dressed in her best jacket, her hair elaborated; and bringing her best hat, white cotton gloves, and cotton sunshade, in her hand.*

JOAN: That's more sense! Now let me finish you off. (*She puts on* TESS's *hat, ties it, etc.*) Now, children, get a tutty for her. (LIZA-LU *brings a flower, and* JOAN *pins it on* TESS's *bosom.*) Now your gloves. (*She pulls* TESS's *gloves on.*) There—look at her, Jacky. You ought to see yourself, Tess. He'll fall like a nine-pin before 'ee.

ABRAHAM: Now she's going to marry the gentleman cousin, and be a lady complete!

TESS (*impetuously to her mother*): I won't go, if I hear any more of that! How can you put such stuff into their heads, mother!

JOAN: Hush, children. Going to work, my dears, to get enough money to buy another horse. . . . Ah—there's Mr. D'Urberville! (*Holds up her hand, and calls out.*) She's ready, sir.

ALEC (*from side*): That's right. Punctual to the minute. I won't bring the gig further down. Her box can be sent. Come along!

JOAN (*to* JOHN DURBEYFIELD): You see it is a gig, and not a common cart.

TESS: Good-bye, father.

JOHN: Good-bye, my maid. . . . Well—I hope your young kinsman will like such a comely sample of his own blood. Tell him,

Tess, that being sunk, quite, from our former grandeur, I'll sell him the title—yes, sell it—such is poverty—at no onreasonable figure.

JOAN: Not for less than a thousand pound!

JOHN: Tell'm I'll take a thousand pound. Well, I'll take less, when I come to think on't. He'll adorn it better than a poor rickety feller like me can. Tell'm he shall have it for a hundred. But I won't stand upon a trifle—tell'm he shall have it for fifty—for twenty pound. That's the lowest. Dammy, family honour is family honour, and I won't take a penny less!

TESS: O father!

> SHE *wipes her eyes, and goes out by highway slowly. They all look after her off stage.*

JOAN: Don't they look handsome together! His cigar, and his dandy cap, and natty jacket, and breeches and all!

ABRAHAM: And his white neckcloth, and stick-up collar, and brown gloves, and diamond pin a-twinkling!

LIZA: Why—Tess won't get up into the gig with him! Now he's jumped down. That's to coax her up.

JOAN: She's looking back at us, poor little thing! (*Sighs.*) Ah! now she's jumped up and he beside her. Off they go! What a glorious couple for a wedding!

LIZA (*beginning to cry*): I almost wish Tess wasn't gone away!

> ABRAHAM *also begins to cry.*

JOAN (*wiping her eyes*): Well, I hope 'tis for the best.

JOHN (*arousing himself*): What's the matter?

> ABRAHAM *and* LIZA-LU *retreat.*

JOAN: Oh, I don't know exactly. I was thinking that perhaps it would have been better if we'd waited a bit, and learnt a little more about the family.

JOHN: Oughtn't ye to have thought of that before?

JOAN: Well, yes. But it is a chance for the maid. Still, if it were the doing again, I wouldn't let her go till I had found out whether the gentleman is really a good-hearted young man, and choice over her as his kinswoman.

JOHN: Yes, you ought perhaps to have done that.

JOAN: As one of the genuine stock she ought to make her way with him, if she plays her trump card aright. And if he don't marry her afore he will after. That he's all afire with love for her any eye can see.

JOHN: What is her trump card? Her D'Urberville blood, and my old ancient family you mean?

JOAN: No, stupid. Her face, as 'twas mine. . . . Ah, there they be again! (*All look off stage.*) Good-bye, Tess dear!

TESS (*from the distance, off stage*): Good-bye!

JOAN, ABRAHAM, LIZA-LU *wave handkerchiefs.*

END OF ACT I

ACT II

MAIDEN NO MORE

SCENE: The same.   *A few weeks later.   Evening.*

JOAN DURBEYFIELD *in a holiday gown,* SARAH, *and several other village girls in white, members of the Girls' Benefit Club, are standing outside the cottage under the shed. Two fiddlers stand near, violoncello player, etc.*

JOAN: Well, now she's coming home for her holiday we shall hear all particulars. The fortune-telling book that prophesied marriage won't be so far wrong, take my word for it.

SARAH: It's been wrong sometimes.

JOAN: Then 'twasn't worked right. I thought that day she went away with Mr. Alec, now more than three months ago, how well she would ornament a carriage alongside him. How she will take the shine out o' the folk here when she becomes his wife. . . . But what time is it? (*She puts her head inside the window to look at the clock.*) She'll be here before you've had another dance, if the carrier is up to his time.

FIDDLES. *The* GIRLS *form a figure, and dance, without male partners.*

TESS *enters by the highway from the back, in a different frock and hat from those of last scene. She carries a bundle, and sits down behind the hedge, resting with her head on her hand. The* DANCERS *recede and music softens.* JOAN *and* JOHN DURBEYFIELD *enter their dwelling.*

TESS (*looking around*): This is home! . . . Oh how shall I tell 'em—how *shall* I! (*She again rests her head on her hand.*)

ALEC D'URBERVILLE *enters by highway, breathless and in riding costume.* TESS *looks up, and starts to her feet. During following duologue the* GIRLS *try dance figures in dumb-show at back, without music.*

ALEC: Why did you slip away by stealth like this? I only discovered by accident to-day that you were gone, and I have been riding like the very devil to overtake you! How unnecessary it has been for you to toil home like this! Do have a little sense and come back!

TESS: I shan't come back.

ALEC: I thought you wouldn't—I said so! It's like you. (*He lights cigar.* TESS *weeps.*) What are you crying for?

TESS: I was thinking I was born here, and how different it was when I went away!

ALEC: Well, we must all be born somewhere.

TESS: I wish I had never been born—here or anywhere else.

ALEC: Pooh! Well, if you didn't wish to come to our house why did you come? . . . Not for love of me, I'll swear.

TESS: 'Tis quite true. If I had gone for love o' you, if I had ever sincerely loved 'ee, if I loved you still, I should not so loathe and hate myself for my weakness as I do now. My eyes were dazzled by you a little while; that was all. (ALEC *shrugs shoulders.*) I didn't understand what you meant till it was too late.

ALEC: That's what every woman says.

TESS (*passionately*): How can you dare to use such words! My God, I could knock you! . . . Did it never strike your mind that what every woman says some women may feel?

ALEC (*laughing*): Fie, dear! That's temper! But I am sorry to wound you. I did wrong—I admit it. . . . Only you needn't be so everlastingly flinging it in my face. I am ready to pay to the uttermost farthing. You know you need not work in the fields or the dairies again. You know you may clothe yourself with the best, if you'll come back, instead of in the simple way you have lately affected, as if you couldn't get a ribbon more than you earn.

TESS (*her voice quivering*): I have said I will not take anything more from you, and I will not—I cannot! I *should* be your creature to go on doing that, and I won't!

ALEC: One would think you were a princess from your manner, in addition to a true and original D'Urberville, which I am not—ha-ha! Fancy your not knowing that one may assume any old name one pleases.

He walks to and fro with his hands in his pockets.
Well, Tess, dear, I can say no more. I was born bad, and I have lived bad, and I shall die bad, in all probability. But upon my lost soul I won't be bad towards you again, Tess. And if certain circumstances should arise out of our intimacy, which may put you in difficulty, send me one line, and you shall have what you require. I may not be at Trantridge—I am going to London for a time. But all letters will be forwarded.

TESS *withdraws coldly, and takes up bundle to depart.*
You are not going away like that, dear? Come.
Removes cigar and bends to her face.
TESS (*indifferently*): If you wish. See how you've mastered me!
Lifts her cheek and he kisses her.
ALEC: Now the other side, for old acquaintance' sake! (*Kisses her again.*) You don't give me your mouth, and kiss me back. You never willingly do that. You'll never love me now, I fear?

TESS: Ah—true! I have never really loved you, and I think I never can. Perhaps, of all things, a lie on this point would do me the most good now, for I may have the best of reasons for getting you to stick to me. But I have honour enough left not to tell that lie!

ALEC (*after a pause*): Well, you are absurdly melancholy, Tess. As you know, I have no reason for flattering you, *now*; but I can say plainly that you can hold your own for beauty against any woman of these parts, gentle or simple. If you are wise you will go into the world, and show it before it fades. . . . And yet, Tess, will you come back to me? Upon my soul I don't like to let you go like this!

TESS: Never, never! I made up my mind as soon as I saw—what I ought to have seen sooner! and I won't come.

ALEC: Then good-bye, my four months' cousin. Good-bye. Perhaps some day you'll be glad to come back to me.

>ALEC *retreats and disappears.*

>SHE *advances down the highway, and comes round to the cottage door. The* CLUB GIRLS *at back see her and crowd round her.*

GIRLS: She's come—she's come.

TESS: Yes. I have come.

A GIRL: What a conquest you've made, dear! We were just talking about it. I wish I had a rich cousin to fall in love with me! Is he fair?

ANOTHER GIRL: No. He's dark, I've heard.

TESS: He's not really my cousin—only of the same name! And I don't know that he's in love with me—please don't say it!

GIRLS (*severally*): She's shy—she's shy! He's going to marry her, only she won't admit it. (TESS *shakes her head sadly.*) Oh yes he is— we know what we know! . . . And he's been such a splendid heart-breaker—so we've heard. My—what a conquest!

>TESS, *distressed, turns away.*

How pretty she is! And how that best frock and hat do set her off. I believe that they cost an immense deal and that they are a gift from him.

>JOAN *enters from cottage.*

JOAN: My dear Tess!—why didn't you come in! I didn't know you were here. So you've paid us a visit. How be ye? I'll call your father. John!

> *Enter* JOHN DURBEYFIELD *from cottage. Welcomes her.*

JOAN (*aside to* TESS): Have you come home to be married?
TESS: No. I've not come home for that, mother.
JOAN: Only for a holiday?
TESS: Only for a—holiday; a long holiday!
JOAN: What—isn't your rich cousin going to do the handsome thing?
TESS: How could you think he was my cousin, mother. He's not my cousin—no relation to us at all. They are not real D'Urbervilles—they only took the name when they had made their money.
JOAN: Oh?—that's news to me. (*She turns to* JOHN.) Hear that, Sir John?
JOHN: Ah—these upstarts! Heaving out we old nobles o' the land!
JOAN: Well—is he going to marry 'ee?
TESS: No—he is not!
GIRL (*to* JOAN): She won't tell! She's as close as wax. I expect they mean to do it privately.
JOAN: I can't say. It depends upon her entirely.
JOHN: You mean, she being the real stock has more reason to be ashamed o' such an alliance than he.
JOAN: Don't 'ee be so stupid, Sir John. Your brains do not reach the level o' your blood, that I must say.

> JOHN *turns to go indoors.*

GIRLS: But you'll come and have a dance with us, Tess?
TESS: No thank you, dears. I'd rather not this evening.
JOAN: Nonsense, Tess. Just to keep up your return! If you wish, I will. Here, Sir John—come along! Fiddlers, "Haste to the Wedding."

> *Fiddlers play "Haste to the Wedding."* SHE *drags out* JOHN DURBEYFIELD *and makes him dance as her partner in the figure of "Haste to the Wedding" which he does unwillingly, using his stick to support himself as he dances.*

JOAN (*as she dances*): I feel for all the world as if I was but just married to-day! . . . (*Dance ceases.*) She seems tired. You must be, Tess. And you must want some supper. (*To* GIRLS.) You must excuse her.

> GIRLS *retreat to green, back of stage, and exeunt.* JOHN DURBEYFIELD *goes into cottage.*

JOAN: But, Tess—bain't you really going to marry him?
TESS: It is as I say— there is no thought of marriage between us.
JOAN: . . . But he's fond of 'ee—so it must be your own fault.
> *Pause—she regards* TESS *closely up and down.*

Come—you've not told me all. What's the matter?
> TESS *puts her face upon her mother's neck and whispers something.*

JOAN (*dumbfounded*): Tess, Tess!—Can it be. . . . And yet th'st not got him to marry 'ee! Any woman would have done it, except you, before she'd let him go so far!

TESS: Perhaps any woman would except me!

JOAN: It *would* have been something like a story to come back with if you had! After all the talk about you and him which have reached us here, who would have expected it to end like this! (*Wipes eyes with apron.*) Why didn't 'ee think of doing some good for your family, instead of getting yourself into a mess like this! See how I've got to teave and slave, and your poor weak father with his heart clogged like a dripping-pan. I *did* hope for something to come out o' this! To see what a pretty pair you and the young gentleman made that day you drove away together four months ago! See what things he's given us—all, as we thought, because we were his kin. But if he's not, it must have been done because of his love for you. And yet you've not got him to marry!

TESS: Marry me! He's never once said a word about making me his wife. He wants me to go back to him—that's all. If he had wished to marry me I might have agreed, to save myself from what may be a-coming. But, mother, you don't understand my feeling towards this man! Perhaps it is unusual, unnatural; but there it is; and it is this that makes me detest myself! I have never cared deeply for him, and I don't now. I have dreaded him. I winced before him when I found I was in his power, and I broke down when he took advantage of my silly helplessness. I was, I suppose, blinded by his flash manners, for he, in a way, dazzled me. But I soon despised him, and now I've run away from him. Go back to him as before I will not! I hardly wish even to marry him if I could, for my name's sake.

JOAN: Then you ought to have been more careful, if you didn't mean to get him to make you his wife!

TESS (*weeping passionately*): O mother, my mother! How could I be expected to know? I was not much more than a child when I left this house four months ago. Why didn't you tell me there was danger in such men? Why didn't you warn me? I never had any chances of learning, and you did not help me!

JOAN: I thought if I cautioned you against his fond feelings and what they might lead to, you would keep him off, and so lose your chance of a more proper connection with him. . . .

Enter JOHN DURBEYFIELD.

Well, we must make the best of it, I suppose. 'Tis nater, after all, and what do please God.

JOHN: What's that you must make the best of?

JOAN (*sighs*): Oh—something Tess has been telling. . . .

TESS *retires*.

Tess has been telling me—a very unexpected thing.

JOHN (*sitting down*): Oh? Well—

JOAN (*hesitating*): A dreadful thing has happened to her. I wish I had never let her go to the place. You ought to have looked into the matter more before she went.

JOHN: I did. I said I didn't like my children going and making themselves beholden to strange kin. I'm the head of the noblest branch of the family, and we ought to live up to it.

JOAN: He's no kin to us—you ought to have known that.

JOHN: Well, what has happened? Have they been snubbing her?

JOAN: Worse than that! And how we hoped it would be for her good to go there. . . . John, Tess has got into trouble with that young man!

JOHN: What?—You don't mean—

JOAN (*wiping her eyes with her apron*): Yes. She was so simple, or innocent, or somethin', that he deceived her. And—though she hopes otherwise—*I* think there's a misfortune coming o't.

JOHN DURBEYFIELD *starts up from chair.*

It do break my heart almost! Poor, deluded, unhappy girl! And we've always kept ourselves so respectable, too! And what makes it so unnatural is, that Tess don't love him one bit. Did ye ever hear such a thing? I believe that if she had cared for him much she might have got him to marry her, though he is a gentleman.

JOHN (*flings himself down tragically in chair*): My old ancient family come to this! To think that under the church at Kingsbere my ancestors lie—hundreds of 'em—in coats of mail and jewels, and great lead coffins weighing tons and tons. We've been here ever since the Conqueror's day, and all through Oliver Grumble's time we fought with the mightiest. There's not a man in the county o' Wessex that's got nobler skillentons in his family vault than I. And now this shame brought upon us!—it do make my knightly blood boil!

JOAN: Hang your old family blood! 'Tis what shall we do to keep our heads above water now this has happened to Tess.

JOHN: Do as you will. I've no more to say in it. Here was I, just thinking of sending round to all the old antiquarians in England to subscribe to a fund to maintain me. It would have been a most romantical, artistical, and proper thing to do. They spend lots of money in keeping up old ruins, and finding the bones o' rare animals, and such like; and *living* remains of such a family as mine must be more interesting. But now this mortification is come upon me, I shan't have the courage to do it, because my ancient pride is broken!

JOHN DURBEYFIELD *falls asleep in his chair.*

The boy, ABRAHAM, *enters with a note.*

JOAN (*calling*): Tess, here's a note for you.

The BOY *goes out.* TESS *comes forward and reads note.*

TESS: He's gone to London. He says I am to write to him there—if—if it is with me as you think. But I shan't.

JOAN: You won't?
TESS: I am not going to pray and beseech a man who has gone away!
JOAN: Well—something must be done.
TESS: Nothing can be done.

> BOY *re-enters: lays supper things on table under shed.*
> JOHN DURBEYFIELD *rises and goes out.*

JOAN: You'll soon leave off saying that. 'Tis a bad job, that's true; but, Lord, 'tis wonderful what things of that sort a body can get used to in time! It is a thousand pities it should have happened to you, of all others. But it is always so, and you must keep up your pecker. After all, 'tis a very dashing flirtation to have had wi' such a gentleman, and many's the girl that would envy 'ee if she knew.

TESS: Don't, mother, for God's sake! It is too thoughtless of you.

JOAN: That's right. Find fault with your mother for making the best of things.... You've had nothing to eat yet, you know; and nobody thinks of it if I don't. (*Turns to table under shed.*) Oh, that's right; the boy has brought the supper. (*Spreads supper.*) Do ye sit down. You must eat and drink whatever comes.... John!

> BOY *re-enters.*

BOY: Father says he don't want any supper, 'cause his family pride is shattered for ever.

> BOY *goes out.*

JOAN: Oh well—leave him alone. He's upset.—He'll have something inside with the children when they come in from the club dance....

> SHE *and* TESS *sit down to table. They eat and drink.*
> *Evening closes in as they talk.*

Trouble is trouble; but yours will be over some day; we must not forget that. You'll not be the first that have had a misfortune happen to 'ee in your time. Some of the highest in the land have had such a trouble, and have got over it and been thought little the worse, owing to their keeping it quiet.

TESS: And what shall I do when it is over?
JOAN: You must go away.

TESS (*hopefully*): Yes! Far away—where nobody knows me at all; and begin my life again. Oh will it be possible? and shall I ever be thought well of again, and the world be to me as it used to be?

JOAN: Yes, my dear. Only we must be careful, and you must live shut up private here till your trouble is over. Then you must go off—say to some dairy. You understand dairy-work well. I know a man who has a brother a dairyman on the other side of Wessex. You'd be safe there, if you only kept your own counsel.

TESS: I wonder! It seems almost too much to expect, after what I have done.... And perhaps I shall die.

JOAN: Nonsense. You won't die.

TESS: Well, something in me seems to bid me hope, and to say there is happiness in store yet. Yes; I'll go—out of the sound of all this—if I only get over my coming sorrow and have a chance of beginning my life again.

The CLUB GIRLS *come forward.*

GIRL: We are going to have one last dance in the twilight, and then go home. Won't you really join, dear Tess?

TESS *joins; but after a few turns shakes her head and steps out.*

TESS: No, no. I'm tired.

They dance in the gloom; JOHN DURBEYFIELD *enters.* TESS *and her parents look on;* TESS *occasionally wiping her eyes,* JOHN DURBEYFIELD *bowed sadly upon his stick,* JOAN *preserving her cheerfulness.*

END OF ACT II

ACT III

THE RALLY

SCENE: Talbothays Dairy

Two years have elapsed since the events of Act II.

The dairy barton, with the dairy-house adjoining, is viewed from the outside where a tree-trunk lies. Over the gate and rail fence are seen thatched cow-stalls, overhung by trees. Milkmaids and men, including MARIAN, IZZ, *and* JONATHAN, *are going to and fro with pails. Straw and mulch scattered about. Empty pails on stand. A large churn, yokes, a straw rick, troughs, etc.*

There enter in front, outside the gate, JOAN *and* JOHN DURBEYFIELD *and* TESS, *the former in visiting costume;* JOHN *supporting himself on stick; the latter in milking pinafore, and cotton bonnet. She is cheerful, bright, and rosy. While the two women converse standing,* JOHN DURBEYFIELD *sits down on a tree-trunk and dozes.*

JOAN: Well, I don't travel forty miles every day; and I thought that as I was in Casterbridge I would just run down and see you for half an hour, and brought Sir John, your father, to keep me company.

JOHN DURBEYFIELD *looks up, coughs, and dozes again.*

TESS: You'll stay and have some tea?
JOAN: No: I've got to catch the train back to Stourcastle, and then it's a long drive. And it's best that I shouldn't come in, considering. You needn't tell 'em who I be—'twould cause inconvenient questions perhaps? Of course they know nothing here about your misfortune?
TESS: Nothing.
JOAN (*to* JOHN DURBEYFIELD): Don't you go hearkening to what we are saying.
JOHN: No, no, my blood is above such as that. (*Nods.*)
JOAN: Well, now it's gone and past it will be forgot, I hope, even at Marlott. Thank God 'twas little known. It was a blessed thing for 'ee that the baby died—poor little thing.
TESS (*quickly*): Don't say that, mother. Don't talk about it! . . . Have you—kept his grave in shape?
JOAN: Well, I did at first. But, thinks I, he were such a terrible secret; and so terrible small, and such a come-by-chance little mortal and a little thing to be forgot as soon as possible, that— well, I haven't been that way, lately.

TESS (*moved*): You ought to, mother—you promised you would.

JOAN: Well, I'll see about it. But it was more than two years ago. (JOHN DURBEYFIELD *coughs*.) Now keep up your pecker. You be started afresh in the world, and can hold your own with anybody. Upon my word the milk and butter here agree with 'ee. Seeing how pink and blooming and girlish you look, my dear, nobody would think what you've gone through! They'll never guess such a thing is possible, if you don't tell 'em. . . . You've never seen him since, I suppose?

TESS: Who?

JOAN: Your gentleman—Alec D'Urberville. You knew who I meant well enough.

TESS: Oh, I want to forget him. He's like a horrid dream to me. No; I've never seen him since. And I hope I never shall. Please not to name Alec D'Urberville to me again.

JOHN (*looking up*): Who's that a-mentioning my family name?

JOAN: 'Tis nothing, Sir John. You rest there, deary.

JOAN (*after a pause, during which she looks over gate*): What sort of people be they here?

TESS: Very nice people indeed. Much nicer than Marlott folk. I have not been so happy for years: never, since that happened. I do almost as I like here. Their kindness is extreme.

JOAN: I could see you had fetched up wonderfully as soon as I set eyes on 'ee—couldn't you, Sir Jacky?

JOHN (*with a start*): Oh—ay! She's a finer girl now. 'Tis in such a proud race as ours to outgrow their humilities.

JOAN: Is it only their kindness that's so improved 'ee, Tess?

TESS: The air is good here, too.

JOAN: Ah yes. Good air. But so it was at Marlott. How many are you here altogether?

TESS: Besides the dairyman and his wife there are three indoor dairymaids and two outdoor ones. And two or three men milkers. And—the pupil.

JOAN: Who's he?

TESS (*with attempted nonchalance*): Oh—only Mr. Angel Clare.

JOAN: A pupil—a boy?

TESS (*with hesitation*): Oh dear no. A man of eight and twenty. He first thought of being a parson, or an author, or something of that sort. But now he's learning dairy-farming. He's really an educated gentleman.

JOAN: Oh? What's his father?

TESS: The vicar of Emminster. (*She looks around,* JOHN DURBEYFIELD *coughs.*) I don't see Mr. Clare just now; but he's in the barton somewhere.

JOAN: Ah. A gentleman. (*Looks narrowly and shakes her head at* TESS.) Now, Tess—I guess something! You sly girl—he's been paying 'ee attentions.

TESS: Well—as we are living in the same house, and keep running up against each other, and can't help meeting every hour, of course he's civil and all that.

JOAN (*pleased*): Ah—that's all very well. Now, he's your young man. Think o' that, Sir John!

TESS (*eagerly*): I haven't encouraged him once!

JOHN (*suddenly*): Well said, Tess!

JOAN: But I'll swear he is! I can tell by the looks of 'ee. But why didn't you write to me all about it? Of course I wish you well; and nothing would please me more than to know you were courted honourably by anybody, leave alone a gentleman.

TESS: Don't, mother, dear. There he is! Let us stand back. That's his brother Felix with him—the curate. I don't want to meet 'em just now.

JOAN (*to* JOHN DURBEYFIELD): Come along, Jacky.

He rises, coughing.

TESS, JOAN, *and* JOHN DURBEYFIELD *retreat in foreground. In the mid-distance enters* ANGEL CLARE, *dressed in drab cloth leggings and dark velveteen jacket, over the sleeves of which a milker's "keep cleans" are pulled; he is accompanied by his brother* FELIX, *dressed as a curate and in spectacles.*

FELIX: And you seem to have changed a good deal. I suppose it is farming or nothing for you now, my dear fellow. And therefore we must make the best of it. But I do entreat you to endeavour to keep as much as possible in touch with moral ideals. Farming, of course, means roughing it, literally; but high thinking may go with plain living, nevertheless.

ANGEL: Of course it may. Was it not proved nineteen hundred years ago—if I may trespass upon your domain a little? Why should you think, Felix, that I am likely to drop my high thinking and my moral ideals?

FELIX: Well, I fancied, from the tone of your letters, and our conversation—it may be fancy only—that you were somehow losing intellectual grasp. You seem to have become entirely absorbed in this life here, which, after all, is only a means to an end. These dairy nymphs and swains seem to have extinguished in you what you had of the scholar and thinker, and to have brought you to their sensuous, heathen level. I should guard against that if I were you, and keep up my dignity and culture. Remember you are only here to get information on dairy management.

ANGEL: Now, Felix: we are very good friends so far; and if we are to keep so, please don't lecture me on my mental state. You've the old conventional notion of Hodge as an animal merely. These people here are thinkers and feelers as much as you are—full of infinite differences. Some of them are bright, some stupid; some happy, and some unhappy; some refined, some boorish—just as people are in society so-called. They are not the dummy figures you fancy them, I can assure you. They and their lives have been an education for me—a finer education than I derived from Greek and Latin.... And how is father?

FELIX: He is as actively occupied as ever. He has just been to Trantridge, where he had a disagreeable experience. That upstart man you may have heard of, who calls himself D'Urberville—they were Stokeses originally—has come back to the Manor house there, after being away for a year or two; and father, knowing his character, thought it his duty to preach to him, taking for his text, "Thou fool, this night thy soul shall be required of thee." After service D'Urberville insulted father most grossly—told him to mind his own business, and came little short of striking him.

ANGEL: I wish father would not expose himself to such gratuitous pain from scoundrels.

FELIX: Oh, he took it calmly enough. The only pain to him was pain on the young man's account. We know he has had lots of such experiences, and his scorners have lived to thank him and praise God.

ANGEL: May this young man do the same. Though I'm afraid he won't from what I hear.

FELIX: How much longer do you mean to stay here?

ANGEL: Till I know all about the business; which will be about the end of the year, I suppose. Come and see the dairy. I have something more to tell you, too: a rather serious matter.

> THEY *retire through gate and remain in conversation at back.*

JOAN: Upon my body, Tess, you are lucky, if that's your new young man! What a one you are for gentlemen; 'tis they always that take notice of 'ee. Don't it make your buzzom plim!

JOHN: To be sure 'tis only gentlemen that think of her! Why ha'n't I got tons and tons o' titled bones, and lead coffins, and monnyments, down in Kingsbere Church? I ask that question! Tess knows what she's made of, thanks to me. (*Coughs.*)

JOAN: Hush a minute, Jacky. Now, Tess, don't you go making a mess of it this time, as you did last. Why don't you tell me straight out all about it?

TESS: Well, mother, because I didn't mean to speak of it. I thought I—I'd rather not, since it will not come to anything.

JOAN: Not come to anything? Why not?

> JOHN DURBEYFIELD *coughs.*

TESS: I couldn't let it go on to—to marriage.

JOAN: Couldn't let it? You don't mean to say that you would refuse him if he asked you to be his lawful wife?

TESS (*distressed*): My dear mother, I must, I must refuse him! Oh how can I do otherwise!

JOAN: Well; wait till he asks 'ee. 'Tisn't likely, after all. No such good luck for my children.

TESS: He has asked me.

JOAN: What?—really has asked?

JOHN DURBEYFIELD *coughs.*

TESS: And I have refused him. Yes, indeed I have. Oh, mother, and I do love him so, too! And I don't know what to do. He's so good, and noble, and educated, and altogether so pure and upright, that it would be a sin and a shame for me to—to let him marry me!

JOAN (*wringing her hands*): You've refused him, you've refused him; oh, you little, simple fool! That ever I should call 'ee so.

JOHN: That's right, Tess, stand out for your family.

JOAN: Shut up—you stupid,—with your family!

JOHN DURBEYFIELD *collapses.*

Oh, you be a fool, Tess, to throw away such a chance as that. Sir John—walk on: I'll overtake 'ee.

JOHN: Ah—I'll walk on. (*Walks, singing.*) I've got—a family vault—full—of—ancestors! Good-bye, Tess, my girl. You've the real blood in 'ee. And the world ought to know it.

TESS (*sadly*): Good-bye, father.

JOHN DURBEYFIELD *goes out.*

JOAN: He's had a drop o' drink at market to-day. That's all's the matter with en. . . . Tess, I say you be a born simpleton, to throw away this chance!

TESS: Yes, but I *must*. There's a double reason why..It would be a wrong to him—oh such a cruel wrong—and it would also be immoral in me. I am Alec D'Urberville's wife—made so by what has happened between us—worse luck for me, and though we parted those two or three years ago, and shall never see each other any more, I cannot be another man's wife while he lives, without deep sin. O mother, do see that it is so; do!

JOAN: But you don't love Alec. You dislike him; and he took advantage of 'ee by unfair means. And he's gone away to London or somewhere. You owe him nothing, Heaven knows. His wife, indeed! That's past and forgot.

TESS: Yes; but it is what I am, in relation to him, though I dislike him. How can I honestly be anybody else's as long as he lives? And even if I were persuaded that I could, I dare not marry Mr. Clare without telling him everything of my history.

JOAN: What! You'd tell him you've had a—

TESS: Yes. And then he would hate me, and wouldn't marry me—so respectable as he is—to bring disgrace on his family, religious church-people as they are.

> SHE *looks across hopelessly towards* ANGEL, FELIX CLARE *having his back turned.* ANGEL *catches sight of her and waves his hat;* SHE *bows and turns away in tears.*

No, I *mustn't*, I *mustn't* marry him. I must stay as I am, and die unmarried.

JOAN: Pooh! Accept him! Catch him while you can. You love him down to the ground.

TESS: Don't press me, mother. I *know* I love him—oh, *don't* I know it! . . . If I accepted him I must tell him, and then—'twould be all over, and I should go and drown myself!

JOAN: A pack of rubbish! I didn't tell your father everything I had done, and every man I'd spoke to, before I met him I can tell 'ee. No sensible young woman, that's had any face at all worth kissing, ever does such a stupid thing, or perhaps weddings would be fewer than they be, except over the broomstick. On no account must you say a word of your bygone trouble to him—especially as it was so long ago—and not your fault at all.

TESS: Yes, but on his account—

JOAN (*impatiently*): I shall answer the same if you ask me fifty times. . . . Now just for once show your sense, and if he ever asks 'ee again, marry him as soon as he'll take 'ee. Such an opportunity won't come many times in your life, I can tell 'ee. Here you've had two such chances, as never was. You might have married the first, if you'd played your cards well—if not before, after. Now the second comes along you refuse him. . . . Ah, well.

TESS (*impulsively*): Mother— let me make you known to him? Then you'd see how good he is. He's waiting over there to speak to me.

> SHE *turns, and* ANGEL *catches her eye, the attention of* FELIX *being again engaged the other way, they wave hands again.*

JOAN: No, no, no! Not for the world make such a rough woman as I beknown to such a gentleman as he. All the fat would be in the fire then, 'a b'lieve! If you married him I should never come near ye—you needn't fear. Don't you tell him who you've been talking to. Now my time is up, and I must go and overtake your father, if I mean to catch the train. You *must* encourage him to ask again—and say yes.—And you *must not* confess.

> JOAN *goes;* TESS *following to side of stage and watching her away waving her hand; then retreating to back shyly under* ANGEL'S *eye—where she joins* JONATHAN *and the other milkmaids.*
>
> ANGEL *and* FELIX *come forward, without encountering her, and walk up and down as they converse.*

ANGEL: I believe she is occupied with some one this afternoon, or I would introduce you.

FELIX: Oh, that can wait. It is such a new and startling thing altogether that you tell me that I don't know how to take it. Getting engaged before you've any place to take a wife to, or any income to depend upon. What will poor mother think of it? . . . But who is the lady?

ANGEL: She's not exactly what you would call a lady, though she's a lady in nature—the gentlest and sweetest specimen of virgin maidenhood—a lady born, not made. What is called a lady socially would be no good to me in the rural business I'm doomed to follow. As my father didn't think fit to send me to Cambridge, as he did you, but preferred to put me to farming, I must choose my mate accordingly and you at home must take the consequences. She's the most useful woman I could possibly have for a wife. She understands cows, butter-making and—

FELIX: Good Heavens—what is the woman? I hope you are not going to link your family on to—

ANGEL (*angrily*): Don't you fall down before you are hit, Felix. Never you be so anxious about our precious family—it doesn't quite become you as a minister of the Gospel. I tell you plainly—she is a milkmaid. She's here, in this very dairy. You were looking straight at her just now—when she was standing here with some one. Didn't you notice her?

FELIX: She—here? I recollect vaguely seeing some women—

ANGEL: It frightens you, doesn't it? Very well—you needn't meet her. What conceivable difference can it make to you whom I marry—since my plan is to go quite away from this part of the country—possibly abroad to a colony? If you *were* to condescend to talk to her you would find that what I say is borne out by facts. However, I would rather you didn't see her as she is here, in her work, and at a disadvantage. And she hasn't accepted me yet, either. In fact she has refused me so far.

FELIX: She's likely to refuse you!

ANGEL: Well, I hope she won't. I mean to try her again. But she's not a woman to be easily won, though you may think otherwise. As soon as I do get her consent—if I do—I shall go home, and tell father and mother the whole matter. I am sure they will see it as I do; and I am sure mother will love her. But I am my own master, and have made up my mind; though of course I don't wish to do anything against their wishes at home, if I can avoid it. . . .

TESS *advances from amongst the others at back.*

Ah—here she is coming. Will you wait and speak to her after all?

FELIX: No, no—not now—not now. She has not observed me, and I would rather not.

ANGEL (*sadly*): Very well. . . . Good-bye. . . . You'll hear from me soon about it, if I can only get her promise.

THEY *shake hands,* FELIX *goes.* TESS *advances further— but sheers off coyly.*

ANGEL: There you go, my Tessy. (*Goes to her.*) Do come this way a minute. We *must* have another talk. Yes, please. You've been too cruel!

He *takes her hand and* She *reluctantly comes through the gate to the front with him. When screened from the barton by the shed* He *kisses her.*

Tess (*distressed*): No, no!

Angel: But, dear one, surely I may! And now—that question I asked—you didn't mean no, really? My brother has been here—that was he you saw—and I hinted a little to him about ourselves. Now, come, say yes. You will be my wife?

Tess (*trying to escape*): I've got to go skimming—really I have.

During this conversation the other milkers go to and fro at back with pails.

Angel: There are plenty of others to skim. Now, to put it practically: I shall soon want to marry, and being a farmer I shall want a woman who knows all about the management of farms. Will you be that woman, Tessy?

Tess (*troubled*): Oh, Mr. Clare—I cannot be your wife—I cannot be.

Angel (*putting his arm round her*): But, Tess. Do you say no? Surely you love me?

Tess: Oh yes, yes! And I would rather be yours than anybody's in the world. But I *cannot* marry you.

Angel (*holding her at arm's length*): Tess, you are engaged to somebody else!

Tess: No, no!

Angel: Then why do you refuse me?

Tess: I don't want to marry. I have not thought of doing it. I only want to love you.

Angel: But why?

Tess (*hesitatingly*): Your father—is a parson; and your mother wouldn't like you to marry anybody but a lady.

Angel: You mistake my parents. They are quite unambitious, and unaffectedly religious. All they would really care for would be that my wife should be a sweet, innocent, chaste girl, such as you are, dear. . . . "Whatsoever things are true, whatsoever things are honest, whatsoever things are of good report"—to use their own

Scriptural phrase—are what they care for.

TESS (*faintly turning away*): I can't be your wife!

ANGEL: You utterly mistake my father, if you fear him! A more disinterested man never lived. Why, only the other day, he went away to preach at Trantridge, a place forty miles from here; and encountered there a rake-hell of a fellow—Mr. Alec something or other—and thought it his duty to expostulate with this young man for his goings on with women. It did no good, and he only insulted my father; though my father thinks that what he said to him may bear fruit in the young man's heart some day. However, I only mention this to show how you mistake my father if you think he is proud.... Now—my question, Tessy?

TESS: It *can't* be!

ANGEL (*capturing her to prevent her slipping away*): Now, you don't mean it, sweet? I am sure you do not! You have made me so restless by your evasions that I cannot read, or play, or do anything. I want to know—to hear from your own warm lips—that you will some day be mine. Any time you may choose, but some day? (TESS *shakes her head.*) Then I ought not to hold you in this way. (*With dudgeon.*) I have no right to. No right to seek you out, or walk with you. You love some other man!

TESS: How can you say it!

ANGEL: I almost know that you don't. But then, how can you say you won't accept me for a husband?

TESS: Ah—that's different. It is for your good—indeed! Oh believe me, it is only for your sake. I am *sure* I ought not to do it!

ANGEL: But you will make me so happy!

TESS: You think so. But you don't know. Don't ask me again. The struggle is too fearful—my own heart is so strongly on the side of yours! ... (*Aside.*) Two ardent hearts against one poor, miserable, little conscience! (*A pause.*)

ANGEL (*stooping and kissing the inside of her naked arm*): Do you know why I did that, Tess?

TESS (*awaking from her reverie*): Because you love me very much?

ANGEL: Yes. And as a preliminary to a new entreaty.

TESS: Not *again*!

ANGEL: Oh, Tess—I cannot think why you are so tantalizing. Why do you disappoint me so? You seem almost like a coquette—upon my soul you do!—a coquette of society. They blow hot and blow cold, just as you do; and it is the very last sort of thing to expect in *you*!

> TESS *turns away poutingly.*

And yet I know you to be the very reverse—the most unpractised creature with men that ever lived. So how can I suppose you a flirt? Why don't you like the idea of being my wife, if you love me as you seem to do?

TESS (*moved*): I have never said I don't like the idea, and I never could say it; b-b-because it wouldn't be true! (*She walks away.*)

ANGEL (*pursuing*): Tell me, for God's sake—do tell me that you won't belong to anybody else!

TESS: I *will* tell you. Heaven knows I will! I will tell you all that, and more—all about myself—all my experiences—all my history!

ANGEL: Yes, dear. Your experiences—any number. My Tess has, no doubt, about as many experiences as that wild convolvulus out there on the garden hedge, that opened itself this morning for the first time. Tell me anything; but don't use that wretched expression any more about not being worthy of me.

TESS (*weeping*): Will you go away—a few minutes—till I am myself again? and then I'll tell you. Please do!

ANGEL: Certainly.

> HE *retires through the gate, and stands leaning against the churn, his back to the spectator—*MARIAN *and* IZZ *come forward through gate.*

MARIAN: Oh—crying—crying! And Mr. Clare just left her.

IZZ: They've been quarrelling. (*To* TESS.) What—have you had a little tiff with him, dear? Never mind. Only a lovers' quarrel!

TESS (*with dignity*): Oh no—quite different. . . . But I have no objection to tell. He wants—I don't know if I ought to say—he wants to marry me!

MARIAN (*to* IZZ): I said so.

IZZ: Well—it was to be, I suppose. 'Twas no use our trying to get him away from her. He likes her best. (*To* TESS.) Is it to be soon? Why do you cry about it? I should jump for joy.

TESS (*bitterly*): No—you make a mistake! You wouldn't jump for joy. I ought not to have stood in your way, or anybody's, if you cared for him. But I couldn't help it, my dears. It is not—*ought* not—to be—ever!

MARIAN: Nonsense. Have him while you can. He don't want either of us, and never did.

TESS: I keep saying I can never be his wife—but—

IZZ: He's coming again. Come along, Marian—let 'em finish it. I shall go and tell the dairyman that you and Mr. Clare are going to be married soon!

TESS: No, no!

        IZZ *and* MARIAN *retire, passing* ANGEL.

IZZ (*slapping* ANGEL): Ha, ha! We know, sir.

        THEY *remain at back*. ANGEL *advances to* TESS.

ANGEL (*gaily*): Now, Miss Flirt—is it to be yes, at last?

TESS: You are back too quick. And you need not call me Flirt, Mr. Clare.

ANGEL: Call me Angel, then, and not Mr. Clare.

TESS: Angel.

ANGEL: "Angel dearest"—why not?

TESS: 'Twould mean that I agree, wouldn't it?

ANGEL: Well, you are going to agree, love!

TESS: Ah—but—there are other women worthier of you. Those, for instance. (*She indicates* MARIAN *and* IZZ.) Almost either of 'em would make—perhaps would make a more proper wife than I. And perhaps they love you as well as I—almost.

ANGEL: Oh, Tessy! No!

TESS (*with sigh of relief*): Don't you think so?

ANGEL: No. Now let us sit down here out of sight, and settle this little matter I've come back to have settled.

THEY *sit down on the tree-trunk*. IZZ, MARIAN, *and other milkers severally go away.*

Now we are all right. (*Takes her hand.*) Now permit me to put it in this way. You belong to me already you know; your heart, I mean—does it not?

TESS: You know as well as I. Oh yes, yes!

ANGEL: Then if your heart does, why not your hand?

TESS: My only reason was on account of you—on account of my position.—I have something to tell you—my history. I want you to know it—you must let me tell you—you will not like me so well.

ANGEL: Tell it then, if you wish to, dearest. This precious history; now. I was born at so-and-so, Anno Domini—

TESS: I was born at Marlott, and I grew up there. And I was in the Sixth Standard when I left school, and they said I had great aptness. But there was trouble in my family. My father was not very industrious and he drank a little.

ANGEL: Yes, yes. Poor child! Nothing new.

TESS (*her breath quickening*): And then—there is something very unusual about it—about me!

ANGEL: Yes, dearest! Never mind. (*Holds her hand.*)

TESS: I—I—am not a Durbeyfield, but a *D'Urberville*—a descendant of the old family of that name in this county in bygone times. And—we've all broken down and gone to nothing.

ANGEL: A D'Urberville! . . . Indeed! Why, it is the name that was taken by the family of that young rake I told you about—Alec D'Urberville, as he calls himself—though of course it is not his real name. My brother has been telling me of a most painful incident that occurred between him and my father. He insulted my father, merely for preaching a sermon that he thought would be for the young man's good. . . . Yes—the old family has gone to poverty, as you say. . . . And is that all the trouble, dear Tess?

TESS (*weakly*): Yes!

ANGEL (*joyfully*): Well—why should I love you less after knowing this?

TESS: I was told by the dairyman that you hated old families.

ANGEL (*laughing*): Well, I do, in one sense. I hate the principle of blood before brains, and I think the only pedigrees we ought to respect are those spiritual ones in which the wise and virtuous become successors to the virtuous and wise. But I am extremely interested in your news. I wonder that I did not see that your surname was a worn form of that old name. And *this* was the carking secret! Now you must spell your name properly from this moment. You've every right to it, and that stuck-up snob I told you of, who insulted my father—that Alec—has no right to it at all!

TESS (*agitated*): Angel—I think—I would rather not spell *my* name as he does—as you say—he does. It is unlucky—perhaps?

ANGEL: Now then, Mistress Teresa D'Urberville, I have you. Take my name, and so you will escape yours. The secret is out—why should you any longer refuse me?

TESS: Y-yes. The—secret is out.

ANGEL: Then say you will. I've told my brother that I mean to marry you, and I am going to tell my father and mother. They'll welcome you warmly—and though they are the most disinterested people in the world, they are human, and the fact of your being a real D'Urberville, and not a sham one like that scamp my father met with, will help you in winning their interest.

TESS: I—if it is *sure* to make you happy to have me as your wife, and you feel that you *do* wish to marry me—*just as I am—very very much—*

ANGEL: Yes—just as you are, of *course*!

TESS: To marry me, whatever my offences, it would make me feel that I ought to say—I will.

ANGEL: You will—you do say it, I know. You will be mine for ever and ever?

TESS: Yes.

> HE *embraces and kisses her. A pause.* TESS *suddenly bursts into a violent sobbing, loosens herself from his embrace, and turns herself away.*

ANGEL (*surprised*): Why do you cry so, dearest?

TESS: I can't tell—quite! I—I am so glad to think—of being yours, and making you happy.

ANGEL: But this does not seem very much like gladness, my Tessy!

TESS: I mean—I cry because I have broken down in my vow. I said I would die unmarried.

> JONATHAN KAIL, IZZ, MARIAN, *etc., enter at back, but they cannot see the pair.*

ANGEL: But, if you love me, you would like me to be your husband?

TESS: Yes ... yes! ... But oh—I sometimes wish I had never been born!

ANGEL: Now, my dear Tess, if I did not know that you are very much excited, and absolutely without experience of the male sex, I should say that remark was not very complimentary. How can you wish that, if you care for me? Do you care for me? If you do, I wish you would prove it in some way.

TESS: How can I prove it more than I have done? There!
> *Advances so as to enable him to kiss her.*

Now do you believe?

ANGEL: Yes. I never really doubted. Never—never!

> JONATHAN KAIL *comes forward; seeing the lovers embracing he turns quickly, as if he had not.* TESS *starts away from* ANGEL's *arms.* IZZ, MARIAN, *and other maids and men come forward.*

TESS: I knew how it would be. I said to myself, they are sure to come and catch us. But he wasn't really—

JONATHAN: Well, my maidy—if so be you hadn't told us you was catched a-cooing, I am sure we shouldn't ha' noticed you'd been a-doing of anything particular—now should we, Izz and Marian? Now that shows that folks should never fancy other folks be seeing things when they bain't. Oh no—I should never ha' noticed nothing, if she hadn't confessed to it!

ANGEL: We are going to be married soon, Jonathan.

JONATHAN: Ah—and be ye! Well I am truly glad to hear it, sir. I've thought for some time ye mid be drifting that way. She's a prize for any man.

ANGEL: She is! She is!

Holds TESS's *hand a moment, lets go, recedes and* JONATHAN *retreats.*

IZZ (*regarding* TESS): He's going to marry her. How her face do show it!

MARIAN: You *be* going to marry him?
They close up to TESS.

TESS: Yes.

ANGEL (*from the distance*): Don't tease her, girls!

IZZ: Going to marry *him*—a gentleman.

TESS: Are you sure you don't dislike me for it?

IZZ: I don't know. I want to hate 'ee for it; but I can't.

MARIAN: I feel the same. I can't hate her—somehow she hinders me.

TESS: He ought to marry one of you. You are both better than I.

IZZ & MARIAN: No, no—dear Tess.

TESS (*impetuously*): You are, you are! You would be better for him than—oh, I don't know what I am saying. Oh, oh!

ANGEL *advances with a pocket-book in his hand;* TESS *composes herself.*

ANGEL (*blithely*): There, I've just made a note of it. Yes—she has agreed at last. And only one more point remains to be settled—that is, the day! (*Embraces* TESS.)

END OF ACT III

ACT IV

THE WOMAN PAYS

SCENE: Wellbridge. Old manor-house.

The interior of a sitting-room in a farm-house, once an Elizabethan manor-house, as is shown by the mullioned and transomed window on left, moulded ceiling, and yawning stone-arched fireplace on right. Two paintings, built into wall, opposite the fireplace, represent two ill-featured dames of the last century. A heavy door beneath admits from without. At the back of the room a wide four-centred stone arch opens into a small inner chamber, where stands an Arabian bedstead with white dimity furniture; the curtains drawn back. The time is evening, the front room being lit by four candles, one at each corner of a small square dining-table, formally laid out for supper. High-backed chairs are ranged against walls, except two at the table. Fire burning. A settle beside it, facing spectator.

An aged FARM LABOURER *and his* WIFE, *both toothless, are moving about the room.*

LABOURER'S WIFE: Move the table a bit this way—that's better. They didn't zay what they'd want for supper, but I suppose they'll be hungered. How vur is it from Talbothays dairy to here?

LABOURER: Well—if you da goo round by the wold road it mid be a matter o' ten mile; but if so be you da come along straight, and don't mind hopping down zeventeen times to open zeventeen gates —well, you mid do it in nine mile.

LABOURER'S WIFE: What ever should make a new married couple come to such a' out-step place as this? If I was going to be married again—

LABOURER: Which you baint.

LABOURER'S WIFE: Don't you be too sure o' things. If I was going to be married again, which I'd scorn to do, considering, I should take care to go to a cheerfuller place than Wellbridge for my wedding jaunt. What did he zay wer his reason for coming here when 'a hired the chimmers?

LABOURER: I've told 'ee once, hain't I? 'A met maister just outside here, and 'a called en by name, and 'a said "That's a fine old building you live in, farmer; but his days be past and gone." "Yes," says maister, "but fine as 'a mid be, you mid live in en for I, and welcome, a damp, rotten wold place, thet ought to have been pulled down years ago." "I should be sorry to see that done," says my gentleman. And then 'a said that owing to the house having been once the family home of his wife that was to be, he'd like to bring her here, being a very romantical thing to do; and asked maister to let him have a couple of rooms for a few days. "Th' canst have the whole house if th'st want to," says maister, "if you can manage to do for yourself; I want to visit my daughter for a week." So then it was settled that we should come in from our house between whiles, and get their victuals for 'em and so forth, being such a' old aged couple, and not much good for anything else, you and I....

LABOURER's WIFE: Ugh!

LABOURER: Well, as all is ready, I reckon we mid as well go home-along.

LABOURER's WIFE: Somebody must bide till they come. I will, I think, being so much the youngest.

LABOURER: Ugh!

LABOURER's WIFE: Do 'ee go along, considering your afflictions, and lave the door on the latch till I come.

> LABOURER *finally arranges table, and goes.* LABOURER's WIFE *changes* LABOURER's *arrangement of table and stirs the fire.*
>
> *Presently* ANGEL CLARE *and* TESS *enter, in travelling clothes.* LABOURER's WIFE *half-curtsies and puts chairs.*

ANGEL: Good evening.—This is our room?

LABOURER's WIFE: 'Tis, sir.

ANGEL (*to* TESS): Welcome to one of your ancestral mansions, dearest. Your people owned this estate and house once, you know. Now it is a farm dwelling.

TESS: Did they? ... It is rather sad to think so.

ANGEL: Yes—it is, perhaps. I hope it won't depress you.

LABOURER's WIFE (*aside*): How be the mighty fallen!

ANGEL: Ah, I see now that I ought not to have brought you here!

TESS: Oh, don't say that, dear—I know you meant it kindly, even if it is a little depressing. (*She looks around; starts before the portraits.*)

ANGEL: What's the matter?

TESS: Those horrid women! How they frightened me.

ANGEL (*to* LABOURER's WIFE): Whose portraits are those?

LABOURER'S WIFE: I have been a-told, sir, by old aged folk that be now dead and rotten, that they were noble dames of the D'Urberville family. Owing to their being builded into the wall they can't be moved away without crumbling to pieces.

ANGEL: Ah—that must be so. Tess—they are your ancestral dames.

LABOURER'S WIFE: I think there's no more I can do for 'ee to-night, sir? I be living close by in my cottage, if you should want anything.

ANGEL: No—I think there is nothing more, is there, dear Tess? The man is coming directly with our things, and we shall be quite comfortable.

LABOURER'S WIFE: Good night, sir, and ma'am.

TESS & ANGEL: Good night.

LABOURER'S WIFE *goes out.*

ANGEL: Don't look at those horrid pictures any more, darling. Your nerves seem shaken by the least thing, to-day.

TESS: Yes! (*Looks round again at the paintings.*) The depressing thing about them is, that though they look so cruel and treacherous, they bear a terrible family likeness to me.

ANGEL: Well—of course, that's natural enough. Don't think of the house or the pictures any more. It was stupid of me, I see, to bring you here. I thought it would be romantic. . . . (*Looks at his watch.*) Jonathan ought to be here with our things soon. Now let us sit down and have some supper.

THEY *sit down to table.* TESS *begins meal.* ANGEL *regards her quietly.*

TESS: What are you thinking about me?

ANGEL: I'm thinking what a dear, dear Tess she is. I ask myself do I realize solemnly enough how utterly and irretrievably this little womanly thing is the creature of my good or bad faith? How dependent she is henceforth upon my fortune and friendship? What happens to me must in a way happen to her. What I become in the world she must become—such is the law. What I cannot be she cannot be. And shall I, then, ever neglect her, or hurt her, or even forget for a moment to consider her? God forbid such a crime!

TESS *sighs. Wind blows.*

TESS: What is that?

ANGEL: Only the wind. There is going to be a change in the weather. The cock crew late this afternoon.

TESS: That's an ill omen, isn't it?

ANGEL: No—it only means a change. (*Rain heard.*) Ah—I thought rain was coming. (*Pause.*)

TESS: Dearest, I wanted to tell you about something. I said—do you remember—that I would confess my faults—that I would write them down? Well, last night I did. And I crept upstairs afterwards with the note, to your room, and slipped it under the door. But—to-day when I looked to see if you had taken it, it was there just the same. It had gone under the edge of the carpet. So, as it was—too late—too late then for you to give me up, I destroyed it.

ANGEL (*heartily*): And quite right too. I am sure I wouldn't have wasted my time in reading your faults and confessions on my wedding morning—not I.

TESS (*with an uneasy laugh*): I wish you had. There seemed a fate in your not getting the note.

ANGEL (*again looking at his watch*): I wonder what can have happened to Jonathan? He is an hour late with our luggage.

TESS: I haven't so much as a brush or comb till he comes.

ANGEL: He'll come soon, I dare say. Tess, you are not a bit cheerful this evening—not at all as you used to be. Those harridans in their frames have unsettled you. I wonder if you really love me after all. . . . There, I did not mean it. You are worried at not having your things, I dare say.

A knocking.

Ah—there he is. (ANGEL *goes out and opens door.*)

JONATHAN (*entering*): I've brought the things for you and your mis'ess, sir; so to name what she lawful is.

HE *deposits box, portmanteau, etc., wipes his face.*

TESS: You are late, Jonathan.

JONATHAN: Well, yes, miss—ma'am, I would say, as your wedlock name. Yes, I've met with several hindrances. We've all a been gallied at the dairy, sir, since you left and your mis'ess—so to name her now. What's happened is that one of the girls hev tried to drown herself, and Marian has gone and got drunk. Some says it do mean one thing, and some another.

ANGEL: Ah.... Well, Jonathan—drink this cup of ale, and accept this from me for your trouble, and hasten back again as soon as you can, in case they should want you.

Gives ale and a gratuity.

JONATHAN: Thank 'ee, sir; thank 'ee—and your mis'ess to call her now by her lawful—

ANGEL: Yes, Jonathan. Thank you. Good night.

JONATHAN: Good night, sir, and ma'am—the same to you.

JONATHAN *goes out.*

TESS: I know why those girls acted so madly. They are breaking their hearts for you. It is very sad.

ANGEL: It is not worth their while. But no, no. I am so sorry he should have mentioned that. It's absurd.

TESS: They don't deserve to suffer; but I do ... and now I am going to tell you why.

ANGEL: Wait a while. All in good time. Now at last we have the place to ourselves. What a great empty place it is. It was very good of the farmer to give us so much room—more than we want. We'll make ourselves secure anyhow.

> TESS *leaves the table and sits down in settle by fire.* HE *goes out and is heard bolting and barring the outer door; returns; unpacks portmanteau. Takes out a piece of mistletoe,* TESS *watching him.*

TESS: What is that?

ANGEL: A twig of mistletoe—though it is rather squeezed.

He hangs it up under canopy of bed.

TESS (*turning away*): Oh—Angel. How romantic you are.

ANGEL: It's a romantic occasion, darling.

> HE *takes the portmanteau and box into bedchamber, unpacks night-dresses, etc. While he is away from her doing this* TESS *takes out a letter.*

TESS (*reading*): "What I said before, dear Tess, I say still, that on no account do you tell him of your past misfortune with Mr. Alec D'Urberville. No girl would be such a fool, especially as it is so long ago, and he is not at all likely to find it out. You be afraid that he will, I know, but he's too innocent to do that yet; and if he do at all, or anybody tells him, it will not be for some months, when you've been married long enough for him to get tired of 'ee, and not to care one straw whether anything happened in your past life or not. Then, dear Tess, keep up your spirits; and we mean to send you a hogshead of cider soon. So no more at present from your affectionate mother J. DURBEYFIELD." (*Puts away letter.*) O mother, mother.

> SHE *looks into fire.* ANGEL *comes up softly behind her, bends over her, takes her face between his hands, and kisses her. Then he sits down beside her. A knocking.*

ANGEL: What the deuce—somebody else? I wish they would leave us to ourselves. Who can it be?

> *Takes candle, goes and unbolts door, and peers out,* TESS *staring in same direction.*

MANSERVANT (*without*): Is this where Mr. and Mrs. Angel Clare are staying?

ANGEL: Yes. I am Mr. Clare.

MANSERVANT (*entering*): Oh yes, sir—I see you are now. I come from your old home, I was to give this into your own hands, and nobody else's. I reached Talbothays just too late to find you there—your wife and you had started a few minutes before; and so I have ridden on here, after you. It is from your father.

ANGEL: Oh yes. I see. Tess—here's something from father.

TESS: How good of him.

ANGEL: Will you rest a few minutes and have something?

MANSERVANT: Thanks, I've got the horse out here, and have a long way to go; so I won't stay. Good night, sir.

ANGEL: Good night. Tell my father and mother you found us well.

MANSERVANT: I will, sir.

> MANSERVANT *goes out.* ANGEL *re-bars door, and brings in packet about 9 by 6 by 4 inches—in brown paper—large red seals.*

ANGEL: Why, it is directed to you. Open it, Tess.

TESS (*handling it timidly*): I don't like to, dear. It looks so important.

> *Hands it back.* ANGEL *opens it. A jewel case is disclosed, with a note and key lying on it.*

ANGEL (*reads note*): "MY DEAR SON: Possibly you have forgotten that on the death of your godmother, she—vain, kind woman that she was—left to me a portion of the contents of her jewel case in trust for your wife, if you should ever have one, as a mark of her affection for you and whomsoever you should choose. This trust I have fulfilled; and though I feel it to be a somewhat incongruous act in the circumstances, I am, as you will see, bound to hand over the articles to the woman you have chosen. They become, I believe, heirlooms, according to the terms of your godmother's will. The precise words that refer to this matter are enclosed. Your affectionate father, JAMES CLARE." I do remember; but I had quite forgotten.

> *Unlocks case, and exposes necklace of brilliants with pendants, bracelets, etc.*

Take them out, darling.

TESS (*incredulously*): Are they mine?

ANGEL: They are certainly. (*He turns meditatively to the fire.*) Ah—my poor godmother. What expectations she had of me. (*While he stands with his back turned, thinking,* TESS *quickly puts on necklace and bracelets.*) I am afraid there is a little irony in this. But Tess is a D'Urberville after all: whom could they become better. Tess, put them on, put them on. (*Turns to help her.*) It ought to be a low one for a set of brilliants like that.

TESS: Ought it?

ANGEL: Yes—like this. Can't you tuck in the upper part—so—? Then it will be a little like an evening dress.

> HE *watches her while* SHE *tucks in the upper part of her dress, slightly assisting. When it is done he steps back.*

My God, how lovely you are! If you were only to appear in a ball-room.... But no, dearest; I love you best, I think, in the sun-bonnet and cotton neckerchief—better than in these—well as you support this display.

TESS: I will take them off. They seem to mock me.

ANGEL: No—let them stay a few minutes. Sit down here and let me see how they look in the firelight.

THEY *sit down.*

ANGEL: You must not think, because my father writes so stiffly, and all my relations declined to come to our wedding, that they are not going to forgive us. My mother, in particular, is not at all set against you so much as you suppose. She says to me in her letter, that though she may have wished me to marry otherwise, she knows you must be a good, and innocent maiden; and those are the chief things after all. I have it here. (*Pulls out letter and reads.*) She says: "I am sure she must be very pretty, Angel, or she wouldn't have won you. And that she is pure and virtuous goes without saying. Certainly, I could have wished for a more equal match; but there are worse wives than these simple, rosy-mouthed, chaste girls of the countryside. Living in such seclusion she naturally had scarce ever seen any young man of the social world till she saw you." Which is so. She goes on: "I have been reading to-night the chapter in Proverbs in praise of a virtuous wife. 'Who can find a virtuous woman? for her price is far above rubies.' I could not help thinking how very aptly some of the particulars applied to the one you have chosen. May Heaven shield her in all her ways." (*Puts letter away.*) Dear mother. I am sure she will soon get my father and brothers to see you in the same light. (*Turns to caress her; but* TESS *shrinks back.*)

TESS: No, no. I want to sit and talk here a little while.... I said I should like to tell you my history, didn't I? And now—

ANGEL (*securing her hand*): Ah yes; we said we would tell each other our faults, didn't we? Very well. Go it, little one. Much of a hidden past you must have—you little bird—about as much as a sparrow, or a half-opened rose-bud. But speaking seriously, *I* really have a grave confession to make—

TESS (*quickly*): Have you? You have to confess something?

ANGEL: And as this is a sort of proper occasion, I'll out with it now. I did not mention it, though I was going to tell you at the time you agreed to be mine, but I could not; I thought it might frighten you away from me, knowing nothing of what men are. But I *must*, now I see you sitting there so solemnly. I wonder if you will forgive me?

TESS: Oh yes—I am sure I shall.

ANGEL: Well, I hope so. But wait a minute. You don't know how bad it is. . . . You have thought too highly of me. Now listen. Put your head there, because I do want you to forgive me, and not to be indignant with me.

> HE *draws up to her and* SHE *puts her face against his shoulder.*

Of course men don't always tell these things; but I feel I shall seem more honest if I tell you. . . . I am a believer in good morals, Tess, as much as you perhaps. Though I am not religious myself, owing to my having grown up in a strictly religious family, I have always admired spotlessness, even though I could lay no claim to it. Well, a certain place is paved with good intentions, and having felt like that so strongly, you will see what a terrible remorse it bred in me when, in the midst of my fine aims, for virtue in others, I myself fell. (TESS *starts*.) You did not expect it.

It happened like this: I was tossed about by doubts and difficulties as to a profession, and other things. I went up to London, and there I was like a cork on the waves. . . . I met with a woman, and—well, I won't sully your ear with particulars—I plunged into a short, sensual dissipation with her. . . . (TESS *starts up*.) Happily I awoke almost immediately to a sense of my folly. I came home. I have never repeated the offence. But I felt I should like to treat you with perfect frankness and honour, and I could not do so without telling this. You forgive me?

TESS: Oh, Angel—yes, I *do* forgive you—because now *you* can forgive *me*. I have not made my confession yet.

ANGEL: Ah—to be sure.

> *Pulls her head again to his shoulder.*

TESS: Perhaps, although you smile, it is as serious as yours, or more so.

ANGEL: It can hardly be more serious, dearest.

TESS (*speaking low, and slowly*): It cannot—since it is the same sin. Yes, my husband; it is the same.

ANGEL (*mechanically*): The same?

TESS: Yes. I have committed the same sin. (HE *is about to start up;* SHE *puts her arms round his shoulders, and retains him in his seat.*) I—am not what you think me.... I grew up at Marlott, a lonely village. I was less than eighteen years when, as I told you, an antiquarian discovered that we were the lineal descendants of the ancient and powerful D'Urberville family and told it to my father. It turned the heads of my parents. I was told I must marry a gentleman... and was sent away—where there was a fast young man—and not understanding his meaning till it was too late—I—gave way to him.

ANGEL (*starting up*): You mean me to understand that the man seduced you?

TESS (*retaining her seat, and looking into the fire*): I do.

ANGEL: My God.

He walks away to the other end of the room, turns, and regards her.

And what—and what—

TESS (*still looking at the fire*): —and I had a child.

ANGEL: You had a child by him?

TESS: Yes.

ANGEL *regards her in silence; comes back; stirs the fire in a paralysed manner; puts down the poker, stands and faces her, she continuing to look down fixedly.*

ANGEL: Tess?

TESS: Yes?

ANGEL: Am I to believe this? From your manner I—I—it seems that I am to take it as true? Oh, you cannot be out of your mind? But you ought to be. My—wife—nothing in you warrants such a supposition as that.

TESS (*looking up at him*): I am not out of my mind.

ANGEL: And yet—(*Pauses—gazing vacantly; then almost shouts.*) God! why didn't you tell me before? Why didn't you? . . . (*Suddenly drops his voice to a murmur.*) Ah yes—yes—you wished to—in a way—I remember.

> HE *goes and leans over the back of a chair, covering his face.* TESS *rises slowly, follows him, and stands looking at him. Then she slips down upon her knees against his foot, and crouches in a heap.*

TESS (*huskily but emphatically*): Forgive me. In—the—name of our love—forgive me. (*Pause.*) I have forgiven you for the *same* sin. (*Pause.*) Oh forgive me, as you are forgiven. I forgive *you*, Angel.

ANGEL: Ah—you—yes. True—you do.

TESS: But you do not forgive me.

ANGEL (*writhing*): Oh, forgiveness does not apply to the case. You were one person: now you are another. My God—how can forgiveness meet such a—a grotesque—transformation as this. Ha-ha. Ha-ha. (*Laughs loudly and unnaturally.*)

TESS: Oh don't. Don't. It kills me quite—that. Oh have mercy upon me—have mercy. (*She springs up.*) Angel, Angel, what do you mean by that laugh? Do you know what this is to me? (HE *shakes his head with a wild reckless air.*) I have been hoping, longing, praying, to make you happy. I have thought what joy it would be to do it—to live to do that alone. That's what I have felt, Angel.

ANGEL: Have you?

TESS: I thought, Angel, that you loved me—*me*—my very self. If it is I that you do love, oh how can it be that you look and speak so? It frightens me. Having begun to love you, I must love you for ever—in all changes, in all disgraces, because you are yourself. Then how can you, O my own husband, stop loving me?

ANGEL: I repeat, the woman I have been loving is not you.

TESS: But who?

ANGEL: Another woman in your shape.

TESS: Oh—you look upon me—as having been a sort of impostor—a guilty woman—a cheat—a liar.

> SHE *turns, swerves, nearly falls*—HE *saves her and helps her to a chair.*

ANGEL: Sit down, sit down. You are ill; and it is natural.
> SHE *sits—gazing at him.*

TESS: I don't belong to you any more, then, do I, Angel? It is not me, but another woman that he loved, he says.
> *A pause;* SHE *bursts into tears.* HE *stands motionless, till her sobbing has exhausted itself, which it does all of a sudden, and she speaks naturally.*

Angel, am I too wicked for you and me to live together—as man and wife?

ANGEL: I have not been able to think what we can do.

TESS: I don't ask you to let me live with you. I suppose I have no right to. If you go away I shall not follow you, and if you never speak to me any more I shall not ask why. I shall obey you like a wretched slave, even if it be to lie down and die.

ANGEL: You are very good. But it strikes me that there is a want of harmony between your present mood of self-sacrifice and your past mood of self-preservation.
> TESS *winces as if struck; slips down on her knees from chair, and clasps her hands.*

TESS: I never meant to keep it secret!

ANGEL: But you did keep it secret.

TESS: I mean—I didn't—

ANGEL (*emphatically*): But you did!

TESS: Not to keep the secret longer than—

ANGEL (*yet louder*): But you did! (*Pause. He drops his voice.*) Tess, I cannot stay in this room—just now. I will walk out a little way.

TESS (*passionately*): Oh no, no, no. Stay with me,—stay. What have I done? What *have* I done? Nothing that I have said belies my love for you. You don't think I planned it, do you? It is in your own mind what you are angry at, Angel; it is not in me. Oh, I am not the deceitful woman you think me.

ANGEL (*flinging himself down in a chair*): H'm—well. Not deceitful. But not the same woman. *Not the same.*

TESS: I was a child—a child when it happened. I knew nothing of men. Then will you not forgive me?

Angel: I do forgive you as a human being. . . . But forgiveness is not all.

Tess: And love me?

> He *does not answer; walks out of the room;* She *sits down by table and remains with face in hands till he returns.*

Angel: Tess—(She *looks up with a start and buries her face again.*)—say it is not true. No—it is not true.

Tess (*in a low voice*): It is true.

Angel: Every word?

Tess: Every word—every word is true.

Angel: Is he living?

Tess: The baby died.

Angel: But the man?

Tess: He is alive.

Angel: Who is he?

Tess: Must I go further? and grieve you yet more? But I will tell you all. It was Alec D'Urberville—the same dissipated and reckless man who insulted your father in his ministry.—Oh, but hear me. It was owing to the antiquarian discovering who we were. My mother heard of the rich D'Urbervilles, and not knowing, poor simple woman, that they had only taken the name, and were not the real family, she sent me to their house to tell them we were kinsfolk. I was persuaded to stay there, and that's how it happened.

Angel: *That* man! God have mercy. Such a man.

Tess: Yes.

Angel: The deep deepens.

Tess: It was so unlikely that I should know. I had no other thought than that he was a sort of cousin of mine.

Angel: It was just like ten thousand cases. Every woman on the streets of London has precisely the same story to tell.

> Angel *takes two or three turns up and down the room.*

(*Abruptly.*) Our position is this. I thought—any man would have thought—that by giving up all ambition to win a wife with social standing I should secure rustic innocence as surely as I should secure pink cheeks; but—however, I am no man to reproach you; and I will not.

TESS (*looking up with some calmness*): It is unnecessary. I see *your* justification too well, too well.

ANGEL: Well—we must understand each other, anyhow. I cannot live with you—that I've decided—without despising myself, and what is worse perhaps, despising you.... Allow me to speak plainly, otherwise you will not perceive all our difficulties. How can we live together with that man hovering about you? Think of children being born to us, and this past matter getting known to them and others—for it must get known. Think of wretches of our own flesh and blood growing up under such a taunt. What an awakening for them—what a prospect! Therefore it is best to part now—before our marriage has been made real. Can you say "remain with me" after contemplating this?

TESS (*drooping*): I cannot. I cannot say Remain. I had not thought so far.... You must go away from me.

ANGEL: But what can you do?

TESS: I can go home.

ANGEL: Are you sure?

TESS: Quite sure. We ought to part, and we may as well get it past and over quickly. Otherwise I might win you to me against your better judgment; and that would be terrible.

ANGEL: Then it shall be so.

TESS *starts and steals an appalled glance at him.*

TESS: I will go to-morrow.

ANGEL: And I shall not stay here.... I think of people more kindly when I am away from them.... I want to think kindly of you again. I want to make your life as easy as I can. God knows; perhaps we shall shake down together some day in sheer weariness.... Thousands have done it. Anyhow let us not hate each other. There is no anger between us, though there is that which I cannot endure.... I will let you know where I go to as soon as I know myself.... And until I come to you it will be better that you should not try to come to me.

TESS: Until you come to me I must not try to come to you?

ANGEL: Just so.

TESS: May I write to you?

ANGEL: Yes. If you are ill, or want anything. But I'll make a provision for you, so that you will not till I write to you.... Now I will go and pack my things, and arrange matters.

TESS: I agree to the conditions, Angel; because you, my husband, know best what my punishment ought to be. Only—only—*don't* make it more than I can bear.

ANGEL: I will try that it may not be more than you can bear. But I cannot stay and condone this—I cannot—yet!

TESS (*sinking down*):Oh but it is, it is. My punishment is more than I can bear.

> SHE *sobs brokenly.* ANGEL *stands rigid, his gaze on the ground. He looks at her—then takes his hat, puts it on, looks back at her, goes out closing the door noiselessly.*
>
> TESS, *still sobbing, turns her head, stares round the room; and finding him gone rushes to the bedchamber, where she regards the mistletoe, the pillows, and the nightdresses. She flings herself on the bed, her previous quiet sobbing changing to uncontrollable hysteric grief.*

TESS: Oh—oh—oh. Oh—oh—oh!

END OF ACT IV

ACT V

THE CONSEQUENCE

SCENE I: Marlott Village. Interior of Joan Durbeyfield's cottage.

The time is daybreak in winter, and as the dawn advances the candles are extinguished. The furniture, which includes a clock, a dresser with plates, a warming-pan, etc., is undergoing removal. The boy ABRAHAM *and the girl* LIZA-LU, *in poor mourning, are carrying out articles.*

ABRAHAM (*sighing*): I wish the wagon would come, that we mid load the things. Have mother found a house for us yet, Liza-Lu?

LIZA-LU: Not yet. Folks don't want us in their houses, 'cause there's no man to pay the rent.

ABRAHAM (*aghast*): What—shan't we have no house at all to live in, now father is dead?

LIZA: I don't suppose we shall.

ABRAHAM: If father hadn't died should we have had to go away?

LIZA: No. We should have stayed. We had the house for his lifetime.

ABRAHAM: Then how could they say father was no good? How came he to die so soon, Liza-Lu?

LIZA: 'Cause he kept on coughing and coughing; and then he couldn't lie down at all. And then he went off like a candle-snuff when we was all asleep in the night.

ABRAHAM: 'Tis no good to belong to a' old ancient family, is it, Liza-Lu? You die just the same.

> JOAN *enters, in widow's mourning, with a candle, which she blows out.*

JOAN: Ah, my dears; that's good of ye to help.

> FARM BAILIFF *enters.*

BAILIFF: Come, ha'n't ye got no more of these things out yet? The other folk are to come in at twelve o'clock.

JOAN (*distractedly*): Got the things out! And only just daylight. And not a house over our heads, and no notion where to find one.

BAILIFF: Well, it's your own fault. You should have looked out before. Or you should have paid up your rent. I must obey orders.

> BAILIFF *goes out.*

LIZA: Oh, mother, it is so sad, all this. To see you so put to. What shall I carry out next? How sorry it will make poor Tess.

JOAN (*tartly*): O Lord—don't you talk about Tess. She, with her gentleman husband, indeed. A damn useful relation he is to a poor family in trouble. He marries her, and off he goes next morning and she's never seen him since, although 'tis a year agone and more. She don't care, or she'd have kept her secret for our sakes.

Liza: Mother, how can you speak against poor Tessy. You know she's gone to look for a place, and will write as soon as she has got it.

Joan: Well—'nation seize such husbands as she seems to get, say I.

Izz and Marian *enter, with bundles.*

Ah—Marian and Izz. I'm so glad to see you. Have you heard of anything?

Izz: Not a job in the whole country for outdoor workfolk, and not likely to be this side o' midsummer.

Marian: We be off on the tramp to look a little further, however; with hardly a sixpence in our pockets. But we thought we'd call up here, as we promised. Where's Tess?

Joan: God knows. She came home here once or twice and stayed a while, and now she's left again to get something to do, she says. Not a sound has she heard of her dear husband since she married him. He goes off to Brazil, and she comes home. She says he is going to send for her, but I don't believe it, nor she neither. When women marry, their husbands should keep 'em—that's what I say.

Liza: It is not Tess's fault, Izz and Marian. She gave us quite enough money to last more than a year; all that her husband gave her. Only the house wanted thatching, and we had to pay for that and a lot of bills came in when father died.

Joan: When I borrowed the money of Tess, that her husband had given her, I naturally thought he would send her some more. What was the use of her marrying a gentleman else? As I've been saying, much of a wife can she call herself. Never seeing him since the day she married him; and a full twelve months gone by.

Marian (*sighing*): Well I lost him, too, and I be obliged to comfort myself my own way. (*Drinks from a pocket bottle.*)

Joan: She ought to have married the first one she picked up with—Mr. Alec D'Urberville. He was the man for my money. But Tess is such a queer girl. Though he ruined her she never got fond of him; almost hated him.

MARIAN: But surely he never once thought of marrying her?
JOAN: Well, a good deal can be done by contrivance.
IZZ: He was a dashing fellow enough; but not a marryer.
JOAN: Have you seen anything of him lately?
MARIAN: Yes—rather lately. He came to her when she was working at Flintcomb with us a few weeks back. He had heard that she had been married and had had a split with her husband; and he came to see her on that account.
JOAN: Ah.... What did he say to her?
IZZ (*hesitatingly*): Well—between ourselves—he wanted her to go back to him. He said he'd keep her like a lady.
JOAN: Ah!
IZZ: He came several times, and coaxed her beyond everything. And he do know how to coax a woman, he do.
JOAN: What did she answer to it?
IZZ: She was in a rage at first. But she took it quieter afterwards. She seemed afeard of him; and of course, having given way to him once, it do make it hard for her to keep him off, poor girl. Well—I wonder—I wonder!
JOAN: What?
IZZ: If she will go back to him. I should feel it a strong temptation, if I were in her shoes.... "My sweet Tess," he said, "I've seen a lot of pretty women since I saw you last, but no such darling little witch as you! Why did I ever let you slip through my fingers, my Rose of Sharon," he says; and lots more o' the sort. Nobody ever says such beautiful language to I!
MARIAN: Nor to I. But there's comfort if you know where to go for it. (*Drinks.*)
JOAN: Then that letter I found was from him. Go on carrying out the things, children. (BOY *and* GIRL *take plates from dresser, etc.*) She left an old frock of hers behind, and in the pocket I found a letter with no name to it and torn in two halves. Now I see it must be from him. I've got the scraps here, and it need be no secret from you—for she scorned it plain enough. (*Goes to mantelpiece and takes letter from under candlestick.*) Here's what he says to her.
Fits the halves together and reads.

"Tess my Chick: Are you going to give me an answer or not? Why should such a sweet old girl as she go working in the fields again when she is shaped by nature to adorn any man's home in the world. Tess, remember the old time—the too short old time—when we were all to each other—at least, when you were all to me. Ever since I set eyes on you again, after our long separation, I have been on fire with love of you. You little wretch to leave me. Well, I did wrong you, that I know, but come to me again, and I'll make it all up to you. You goose!—what's the use of waiting for one who will never come back? He's not half so full of love for you as I, or he would not be able to remain away. You must come, Tess; yes, you must. I am dying to possess you again—to have you again for my own, as at that former time. Say you will—I insist, madam—you belong to me. I shall come to you in a day or two for your answer, which I won't allow to be anything but—'Yes.'"

Puts away letter.

Izz: Yes—it's from Alec D'Urberville. And did he come?

Joan: No—she went away before he could get here; and I suppose he heard she was gone.

Marian: Perhaps he has followed her? Poor thing. I hope he's not—got at her again.—Where is she gone to, did you say, Mrs. Durbeyfield?

Joan: She went first to Shottsford, and I sent Liza-Lu to her there to tell her we were turned out. Where she went next I can't say. She wouldn't leave word, and I thought it was because she didn't wish to be followed. When she found we were to be turned out of house she said she'd go and earn money, or die. She can't have done it yet, or she'd have sent us some.

Izz: He *may* have met with her at Shottsford.

Joan: I'll ask Liza-Lu. (*Calls.*) Liza-Lu. (Girl *enters.*) Did Tess say anything about Mr. D'Urberville when you went to her?

Liza: Yes—she did, mother.

Joan: What did she say?

Liza: She said he pestered her. But he was very kind.

Joan: How do you know?

Liza: He came while I was there and told her she could have

what money she wanted. But she wouldn't have any. And he said he'd pay up the rent of our house here, so that we needn't go away. And he sent her a watch; but she sent it back again.

JOAN: Why didn't you tell me this before?

LIZA: Tess—seemed to want me not to let you know.

JOAN: The Lord-a-Lord—if the rent were only paid! Well, Tess must please herself. I think I should ha' kept the watch, whether or not. But perhaps she was right.

A knock and a MANSERVANT *enters, with his arms full of packages.*

MANSERVANT: Is this where Mrs. Joan Durbeyfield lives?

JOAN: I be Mrs. Durbeyfield.

IZZ: Now, Mrs. Durbeyfield, we must get onward. I hope we mid meet wi' her somewhere, as we be going the same way. But the Lord only knows.

JOAN: Well,—good-bye to ye. I hope we mid meet again in happier times.

IZZ & MARIAN: I hope so. Good-bye all.

THEY *go to the door, but linger to hear the* MAN-SERVANT'*s business.*

MANSERVANT: I've orders to bring you all these articles, ma'am. This is a list of what's in the parcels, and I hope you'll find it correct. (*Reads.*) "Three pairs of blankets; five pairs of children's boots; ten pairs of stockings; one woman's cloak; one girl's jacket"; and so on. You'll examine for yourself. And this little packet—I've also to hand to you. (*Hands packet.*)

JOAN (*dazed*): Yes?

MANSERVANT: Take care of it. It contains something valuable. That's all my business, ma'am. I've travelled here o' purpose to give the things into your own hands. And now good morning.

MANSERVANT *goes out.*

JOAN (*turning to* MARIAN *and* IZZ *who come forward*): Did ye hear?

IZZ: It can't be from Tess, can it?

JOAN: No. Though I told her this was the day we should be out of house and home. What's in this I wonder? (*Opens packet.*) Dear, dear. 'Tis bank-notes!

MARIAN: It can't be from Tess.

IZZ: Perhaps it is from her husband!

JOAN: No—it must be from Mr. Alec. That's his man—I've seen him before.—That's who it is for certain. Well—he may have sent it out of kindness, on hearing of our misfortunes, considering what Tess was to him once. After all, he's the only husband she ever had, and was the father of her child; so this may be for the sake of the past. . . . Here, Liza-Lu—stop moving them things. We may not have to go after all, if another house can be got for the people who were coming here. I'll see the bailiff.

She begins replacing the bank-notes in the packet—starts.

[LIZA-LU *goes out.*]

Ah—here's a letter, too. Why—it is from—after all.

She reads the letter to herself, slowly. Retreats, looking down. Sits down, still looking on the floor.

IZZ & MARIAN: Not from Mr. D'Urberville?

JOAN (*after a pause*): No—it's from—Tess. . . .

MARIAN: Ah. And where is she, to be so well off?

JOAN: She don't say, but I think at—Sandbourne.

MARIAN: What a grand town. What's she doing there?

JOAN: I don't know—I must think of this. Good morning, Marian and Izz.

MARIAN & IZZ (*looking significantly at each other*): Good morning, Mrs. Durbeyfield.

They go out.

LIZA-LU *enters to* JOAN, *who still sits in a reverie.*

LIZA: Mother, a man called to see you just now, but he wouldn't come in while the others were here; and he went into the back garden to wait. He's coming in now.

JOAN: What sort of man? Not the bailiff again? I want to see him.

LIZA: Oh no—a sort of gentleman. He seems to have been ill. Ah, here he is.

JOAN: You'd better go away for a few minutes.

ANGEL CLARE *enters, pale, haggard, and travel-stained.*

LIZA-LU *goes out.*

ANGEL: Mrs. Durbeyfield? (JOAN *nods, still holding* TESS's *letter.*) I came just now—but I thought you were engaged and I've waited. ... We've never met before I think.

JOAN: I don't think we have.

ANGEL: I am Tess's husband—just come home from Brazil.—Where is my Tess? I want to see her at once.

JOAN: Do you, sir? (*Puts away letter.*)

ANGEL: Will you please inform me, Mrs. Durbeyfield?

JOAN: Lord! You ought to know better than I where she is. It is more your business than mine. She's your wife.

ANGEL: I admit that I ought to know. But I've been ill of fever for months in a foreign country, or I should have been back with her long ago. Where is she staying? I thought she was here, and am keenly disappointed.

JOAN (*placing her hand to her cheek in embarrassment*): I—don't know exactly where she is staying, at this minute. She was—but—

ANGEL: Where was she?

JOAN: Well, she is not there now. And the last time I heard from her the note was enclosed in a parcel, and she gave no address.

ANGEL (*anxiously*): But you must have some idea? Don't you think that Tess would wish me to try and find her—or has she forgotten me?

JOAN: I don't think she would. She may have—given you up, if not forgot you.

ANGEL: Are you sure she doesn't want to see me?

JOAN: I fancy she don't—*now*.

ANGEL: But I left her well provided for before I left home. I gave her all the money I had left.

JOAN: Well—I spent it. We've been unfortunate all round—till to-day; and her money went with the rest.

ANGEL (*turning back after moving to go*): I am sure she wishes to see me; and see her I will. I know her better than you do.

JOAN: That's very likely, sir; for I have never really known her. And I don't think even you have known her well, or you would have forgiven her wrong to 'ee.

ANGEL (*with sad and solemn emphasis*): Mrs. D'Urberville, I know it. I ought to have forgiven her; I have owned it. I have admitted my faults. They have been great and I don't wish to extenuate them. But a moment comes when a man who has always tried to be honest and straightforward according to his lights, feels that he must speak out. You say you have never really known me. I loved your daughter with all the devotion, truth, and sincerity that a man can wish to feel towards a woman of such charm, such beauty, and, as I thought, such innocence, as was hers. I had but one wish on earth—to make her happy. You know, or you ought to know, how I stuck to her against the wishes of my parents; how I resisted their arguments and how at last they gave way. They gave way because of my fervent representations to them, which arose from my belief in her purity, and her truth, and her worthiness to be their daughter. Old-fashioned clergyman as my father is, old-fashioned gentlewoman as is my mother, with all the stiffness of their class, they yet decided to welcome her as their own, on the strength of this one supposition, that she was an innocent unsophisticated maiden. Since she is a *virtuous* woman, said my poor mother, her price is far above rubies. . . . Well, I married her. Then the revelation came. I quite admit that she was the sinned against and not the sinner—poor darling.—But there was the fact. It could not be got over. It turned my light into darkness as black as hell. You have never been a man in such a terrible position: God forbid that my worst enemy should ever be in such a position as mine was when Tess confessed that damnable secret to me. It almost turned my brain—I hardly knew what I did after that blow had come upon me. Nothing so pure, so sweet, so virginal as Tess, had seemed possible.

He looks down and speaks to himself.
"But the little less, and what worlds away."

(*Pause.*) Well, Mrs. D'Urberville, in the sudden revulsion of feeling I acted hastily—without due deliberation; but I acted as I thought for the best. To gain time for reflection—to think of some mode of living the scandal down—I agreed to her suggestion that she should go home and live with you awhile in this quiet place. I made provision for her; and here I thought to find her.

JOAN: Ah, but as I said, her father died—I spent her money—I couldn't help it, and she was forced to go away—God knows where.

ANGEL: Well, it's bad luck, but find her I must. In my absence I have aged a dozen years. It is not the beauty of her life, but the pathos of her life, that attracts me now. I have learned to judge Tess by her aims and impulses, not by her achievements; and I think that her true history lies, not among things she has done, but among the things she has wished and striven to do. When she confessed to me the same sin that I had just confessed to her, I said it was not the same for the man as for the woman; the poor little thing (*He speaks emotionally.*) could not see the difference. She was right; there was no difference. The sin was the same. . . . I have come back with wider views. Let the world say what it will. I only hope she'll forgive me as I forgive her.

JOAN (*moved*): Sir, I think I mid have wronged 'ee. If I have, God knows I am sorry for it. People like us don't quite see at first how such a thing would strike people like you, with your nice notions on what women should be. . . . But oh, I wonder what has happened to her. I am afeard they have poisoned her mind against 'ee; and—and—

ANGEL: Tell me her address. Cannot you tell me, really?—in kindness to a lonely man who loves her with all his soul.

JOAN: I assure 'ee, sir, she didn't give her address. But I've reason to think she's at Sandbourne.

ANGEL: Whereabouts there? Sandbourne has become a large, fashionable place, they say.

JOAN: I don't know more particular than I have said. For my part I was never there, although it is such a short way off.

ANGEL: I'll go and search for her. (*Looks round the room.*) Are you in want of anything?

JOAN: No, sir. We've just been fairly well provided for. And I don't like to think the meaning o't.

ANGEL *pauses—then goes out.*

JOAN: Liza-Lu and Abraham. (THEY *enter.*) Don't go getting out any more of the furniture—I think we may have to put it all back again. We be better off now; and our bills can be paid. But . . . I don't know. (*Aside.*) If 'tis so, they'll say I drove her to it.

LIZA & ABRAHAM: Oh—bain't I glad—not going away?

JOAN: Well, we'll see. I am just going to the bailiff.

ABRAHAM: Mother, who was the yellow-looking gentleman that's gone? Is that the gentleman Tess is going to be married to next?

JOAN: No—she is married to him. . . . (*Aside.*) Good God, what will come of it all?

ABRAHAM: Is it Tess's husband who is going to pay our bills?

JOAN: No, no. Would to the Lord it were.

Enter BAILIFF.

BAILIFF: Well—about these things.

JOAN: If I pay you, can't the other people have the cottage farther on?

BAILIFF: *If* you do. But I should like to see you do it.

JOAN: Here's the money. Give me change. (*Hands a bank-note.*)

BAILIFF: Oh—ho. How's this? I saw you had a visitor.

JOAN (*loftily*): Yes. My daughter's husband. He's a born gentleman. And he's just come home from abroad. He's been ill, or he would have been here long ago.

BAILIFF: And he's paying up. Well done. It is well to have a gentleman son-in-law. I'll get change. You needn't hurry about moving out. I can say that on my own responsibility.

BAILIFF *goes out.*

ABRAHAM: But, mother, I thought you told us it wasn't Tess's husband who is paying everything, and giving us the things? And now you say it was?

JOAN: Oh, did I? . . . I don't know what I say sometimes!

The children begin replacing furniture. JOAN *sits down and remains musing, her hand to her face.*

END OF SCENE I

Scene II: Sandbourne

The interior of the first floor drawing-room of a well-furnished seaside lodging-house. At the back are folding doors, one of them communicating with a bedroom, one corner of the bed being visible. In the front room is a breakfast table laid for two. MAID-SERVANT *finishes the arrangements, places letters and a newspaper on the table.*

TESS *enters from the bedroom. She is in a dressing-gown and slippers, her hair being tied back so that it falls in a mass behind. She goes to the table, examines letters.*

TESS: Was the parcel of clothing sent off to Mrs. Durbeyfield? and the little packet?

SERVANT: Yes, m'm. 'Twas sent last night, so that she would get it early this morning.

TESS: Oh, that's right.

She takes up the newspaper. SERVANT *goes out.*

ALEC (*yawning and speaking from bedroom*): What time is it?

TESS: Nearly ten.

ALEC: By jove, is it?

TESS: Formerly it would have seemed to me that half the day was gone.

ALEC: But now you've gone up in the world, your day is not begun.

TESS: I don't think I have gone up. I've gone the other way—down—down.

ALEC: Pooh! that's like you, to be such a fool. Though you only sham it. You know better.

TESS (*bitterly*): I don't sham it. You know as well as I how I hate to be here. I'd much rather be pulling swedes at Flintcomb-Ash Farm.

ALEC: Well, all I can say is, you are infernally ungrateful. See what pretty things you wear. See what I've given you to send your people. A miserable, broken-down lot—why, if it hadn't been for me they'd have had to go to the workhouse to-day.

TESS: Don't say that—I won't have it. I hate my pretty things. As for the help to my poor mother and the children, that you brag of, if you had given help to them freely, that would have been generosity. But you didn't—your selfishness wouldn't let you. Everything you've given them I've had to buy of you, at a dear price enough.

She sits down at table and covers her face with her hands.

ALEC: What the devil are you doing? I won't stand these airs. Bring in the letters and paper. Do you hear?

TESS *returns to the bedroom with letters and paper, and the door is closed. A knocking is heard at the street door as she retreats. In a few moments there is a tap at the drawing-room door and the* LANDLADY *enters.*

LANDLADY: Mrs. D'Urberville? (*Seeing the room empty she goes and taps at the folding doors.*) Mrs. D'Urberville?

TESS *reappears, and closes the door behind her.*

TESS: Did you want me?
LANDLADY: Yes, ma'am. Somebody has called to see you.
TESS: Me? Who can have called at this time? Somebody on business?
LANDLADY: Well, I don't think so. 'Tis a gentleman. He wants particularly to see you, though I said you wasn't an early riser. He seems puzzled about your name, though I know 'tis you he means. He says I am to tell you his name is Angel.
TESS (*agitated*): Oh—I don't think—I can't—I did not expect—

ANGEL CLARE *enters.* TESS *waves her hand to the* LANDLADY, *and she leaves the room.* CLARE *rushes up to* TESS, *clasps her, and kisses her passionately.*

ANGEL: O my darling Tessie—at last—at last. Forgive me—forgive me—I've been wandering hither and thither to find you, and I never expected you would be in a town—I can't understand this. But I am come to you—I am come. (TESS *gently thrusts him back, shaking her head.*) What, don't you forgive me? I was very wrong I know. I was cruel in judging you so harshly. We'll never part again, never, if you'll forgive me. (TESS *withdraws herself further.*) How do you come to be in these strange circumstances? Your mother didn't explain. It was sheer misery that drove me away, Tess—believe me, dear, it was. But now we are both purified by affliction and—

TESS: Stop . . . stop . . . stop. There's something—a horrible something, between us—don't you see how it is—what it is? Doesn't it explain itself—all this? (*Points to the room, table, her dressing-gown, etc.*)

ANGEL: I don't understand. Can't you forgive me—can't you come to me? What are you doing here?

TESS: It is too late.

ANGEL: No. Though I did not think rightly of you—I did not see you as you were at first—I have learnt to since, Tessy mine.

TESS: Too late, too late. (*Waving her hand.*) Don't come close to me, Angel. No, you must not. Keep away.

ANGEL: But don't you love me, my dear wife? Is it because I have been so pulled down by illness? You are not so fickle? I am come on purpose for you. My mother and father will welcome you now.

TESS: Yes—Oh yes, yes. But I say, I say it is too late. Don't you know all—don't you know it? Yet how do you come here if you do not know?

ANGEL: I inquired here and there for Durbeyfield or D'Urberville and found the way, and—

TESS (*with sudden tender pathos*): I waited and waited for you. But you did not come. He kept on saying you would never come any more, and that I was a foolish woman to expect you. He has been very kind to me, and to mother, and to all of us, in our distress since father's death. He—

ANGEL: He? I don't understand.

TESS (*pointing to the folding doors and speaking in a low desperate voice*): He—Alec D'Urberville—he's got me back to him—to live with him. (*A pause in which* ANGEL *regards her with stupefied despair.*) He is in there. I *hate* him now because he has told me lies—that you were not coming again ever any more: and you have come. These clothes are what he has put upon me; I didn't care what he did with me. But hate him or not, here I am. But will you go away, Angel, please, and never come any more. Oh never think of me, or pray for me, or pity me. Only forget me.

ANGEL (*after a silence in which he turns aside*): Ah. . . . It is my fault—mine only—and his.

TESS (*in a whisper*): Will you—go?

ANGEL: There is nothing else left for me to do—nothing—nothing. While that man lives I am an outcast and accursed.—She has no kiss left for me.

> HE *goes out.*
>
> TESS, *her face buried in the sleeve of her dressing-gown, goes to folding door, opens it to enter, but returns, leaving it open, and falling on her knees over a chair sobs brokenly.*

TESS: He said, while that man lives she has no kiss for me. My own husband says it. While that man lives he is an outcast, he says. And I—Oh, oh, oh!—I love him true .

ALEC (*from bedroom*): What's the matter? . . . (*Pause.*) What are you doing? Who has been talking to you?

TESS: My husband.

ALEC: Who? What?

TESS (*sobbing upon chair*): How can I bear it? . . . My dear, dear husband has come home to me. . . . And I did not know it. . . . And you had used your cruel persuasion upon me . . . you did not stop using it—no—you did not stop. My little sisters and brothers, and my mother's troubles—they were the things you moved me by—and you said my husband would never come back, never; and you taunted me, and said what a simpleton I was to expect him. And at last I believed you, and gave way. . . . And then he came back. Now he is gone—gone a second time, and I have lost him now for ever . . . and he will not love me the littlest bit any more—only hate me. . . . Oh yes—I have lost him, lost him—again because of you.

ALEC: What are you whining about? *I* am your husband, young woman, for the present.

TESS: And he is dying—he looks as if he is dying. And my sin will kill him, and not kill me. Oh, you have torn my life all to pieces—made me a victim, a chained slave. My own true husband will never—

ALEC: Damn it, I tell you I am your husband, at any rate just now. Don't be so infernally virtuous. If you hadn't been willing to sell yourself, you wouldn't have been here, you little humbug.

TESS: O God—I can't bear this—I cannot.

ALEC: Then get along back to him. I don't want you any more, come to that. Or perhaps he came to make a quiet arrangement, for a consideration. A virtuous pair—you and he.

> TESS *springs up from the chair-seat over which she has been bending and rushes into the bedchamber, snatching a knife in passing the table. A rustling follows; then a silence. In a minute she comes back to front room, her countenance changed to a pallor; she carries in her arms her outdoor garments. She closes the door behind her, and quietly dresses herself before the chimney glass. When she has put on her hat and taken up her sunshade, she looks out of the window.*

TESS: I am coming, my love. You will love me now. He doesn't live and you are not an outcast any more.

> *She goes out by the landing door and the front door is heard to close. The room is empty for half a minute; then there is a knocking at the door.*

LANDLADY (*without*): Mrs. D'Urberville. (*Pause.*) Mrs. D'Urberville. There is a red stain in the ceiling below your bedroom; something soaking through.

> LANDLADY *enters. Finding the room empty she goes to the folding doors, knocks, opens one of them a few inches. Turns back in horror.* SERVANT *enters.*

LANDLADY: Oh, what has happened! Good God—the gentleman in bed is dying, or dead. He has been murdered—a lot of blood has run down on the floor. And the lady is not here.

She goes to the window and waves her hand. Some people enter, and cross to the bedroom. Confused conversation.

LANDLADY: The young lady has done it. I listened at the keyhole, and heard him call her names. She's not his wife, after all; and she has done it to get back to her husband, whom she loves very dearly. He called just now.

SERVANT: And I saw her go out and run along the road to overtake him. (*Rushes to window.*)

END OF SCENE II

AFTER-SCENE

TESS *is seen lying on a horizontal stone, from which* ANGEL *has just risen. His greatcoat, lined with red, beneath her. A small portmanteau near.*

The stage is in darkness; on its gradually lightening a view of Stonehenge is revealed. Daybreak.

ANGEL: Well what shall we do now, darling? We may find a better shelter further on.

TESS: I don't want to go any further. Can't we stay here?

ANGEL: I am afraid not. This spot is visible for miles by day, although it has not seemed so to us in the dark.

TESS: I should like to die here. One of my mother's people was a shepherd hereabouts, now I think of it. And you used to say that I was a heathen. So now I am at home. How lucky it was that I ran after you.

ANGEL: Yes. I had a presentiment that you were behind me. So I turned my head, and there I saw a distant figure waving her hand.

TESS: Oh, and I was in such a dread that you would go into the plantation before I could attract your notice, and tell you I was freed from him.

ANGEL: But I didn't. And we came together. And that made all the difference. And our spirits mixed and have been one ever since. (*Kissing her.*) I think you are lying on an altar.

TESS: Am I? I like very much to stay here. It is so lonely—after my great happiness in finding you and getting you to forgive me. It seems as if there were no folk in the world, but we two; and I wish there were not—except Liza-Lu. . . . Angel, when my end comes—and it will be soon—will you watch over Liza-Lu for my sake?

ANGEL: I will.

TESS: She has all the best of me without the bad of me. . . . How wicked and mad I was to do it. Yet formerly I could not bear to hurt or kill anything, not even a worm or a fly.

ANGEL: Don't talk of it. You had lost your reason for the time, Tess. I saw when you overtook me that you did not know what you were doing. Such aberrations are well known. The poor little overstrained brain gave way. (*Kisses her.*) However, we must get away.

TESS: Why should we put an end to all that's sweet? What must come, will come. All is trouble out in the noisy world: here it is all peace. . . . And I don't want to get away. I fear that what you think of me now may not last. I don't wish to outlive your present love for me. I would rather be dead and buried when the time comes that you will despise me, so that it may never be known to me that you despised me.

ANGEL: I cannot ever despise you.

TESS: That's what I hope. But considering what my life has been I cannot see how any man, sooner or later, can help despising me.

ANGEL: One cannot help loving—you—now and for ever. And I think we can escape, by getting out of this district and going straight north. Nobody will think of looking for us there. We shall be searched for at the Wessex ports if we are searched for at all.

TESS: I will go where you tell me, dear, of course. But my life can only be a question of a few weeks more or less.

ANGEL (*after looking around*): I fancy some one is about the neighbourhood, early as it is.

TESS: Let them be, so that you are near. Do you wish me to go on?

ANGEL (*peering into the distance*): I think we had better wait a few minutes. Somebody seems to be passing out there. And you are still sleepy. Lie down again.

TESS: Did they sacrifice to God here?

ANGEL: No.

TESS: Who to?

ANGEL: I believe to the sun. That high stone set away by itself is in the direction of the sun, which will presently rise behind it.

TESS: Tell me, Angel. Do you think we shall meet again after we are dead? I want to know. (HE *kisses her without replying*.) You and I, Angel, who love each other so well, are—sure—

SHE *falls asleep. Sun rises.*

ANGEL (*rising and looking round again; then turning to* TESS): Well, let her sleep. Who knows.... Ah! (*With a start*.) Here they are. Her story then is true. (*Stoops and gently wakes* TESS.)

TESS: What is it, Angel? Are they coming for me? (*Sitting up*.)

ANGEL: Yes, dearest. They are coming. I see them closing round us.

TESS (*standing up*): It is as it should be. I am almost glad—yes, glad. This happiness with you could not have lasted. It was too much. I have had enough and now I shall not live for you to despise me. (*She arranges her dress, they kiss each other, and await capture, looking off stage.*) Don't resist them, my dear husband. I am ready.

THE END

II. LORIMER STODDARD (1897)

TESS OF THE D'URBERVILLES

Dramatization in Four Acts

CHARACTERS

ANGEL CLARE
ALEC D'URBERVILLE
MR. CRICK
JONATHAN ⎫
JAMES   ⎬ *farm-hands*
TIM   ⎭
A SHERIFF
JOHN DURBEYFIELD, *otherwise* SIR JOHN
ABRAHAM, *his son, a boy of twelve*

JOAN DURBEYFIELD, *his wife*
TESS, *their daughter,* "TESS O' THE D'URBERVILLES"
LIZA LOO, *her sister, a little girl*
MARIAN ⎫
IZZ   ⎬ *milkmaids*
RETTY ⎭

ACT I

Scene: *The yard of Mr. Crick's house. To the left is a part of the house itself, which has a sort of enclosed portico under the low roof. To the right is a one-story building where Angel Clare sleeps. It has a door and a window with a wide sill. There are milking stools, a bench at left, a wheelbarrow, etc. At the back is the rolling country, a gateway, and a bit of hedge on each side of it. It is just after sunset. The long bright twilight of an English summer. Light enough to read. The whole scene is pastoral and beautiful.*

Joan, Sir John, *and* Abraham *enter through the gate from right.*

Abraham: Oh, mother, what a *grand* house! Is it there that Tess lives? I do not wonder she left Marlott.

Joan: Just 'ee wait—she'll have as grand a place all her own. If she be not a fool, Abraham.

Abraham: Oh, it's the biggest house I ever saw. Bigger than the Parson's.

Sir John: 'Tis big, but 'tis not old. The antiquireens would have none of it. 'Tis not a pinch to what our *mansion* was.

Abraham: *Ours*, father?

Sir John: The ancient home of the D'Urbervilles. 'Twas built in King John's time. King John! I be Sir John! Mayhap he was a cousin of the house. The antiquireens—

Joan (*impatiently*): Oh, peace to the antiquireens and the past. We have the present and Tess's future—our future to deal with, but I fear she be a fool.

Abraham: Our Tess a fool, mother?

Joan: Oh, run away.

Sir John: Joan, no D'Urberville can be a fool. We be the oldest family in the land.

Joan: Age be no prevention against foolishness. She be a fool, to write to me and ask if she could tell! And what's the use o' telling, I says? A shut mouth spills no ale.

Sɪʀ Jᴏʜɴ: Telling o' what? The history of our family?

Jᴏᴀɴ: No, no, her own.

Sɪʀ Jᴏʜɴ: 'Tis a thing to be proud of! There's not a family in all the county o' Wessex that's got nobler skeletons in his family vault than I.

Jᴏᴀɴ (*sitting on the bench*): *Her* story be a common one, alack.

Sɪʀ Jᴏʜɴ: And to think that if Parson Tringham, the antiquireen of Stagfoot Lane, had not a' told me, I'd still think I was plain John Durbeyfield, and never should a' known I'd be a baronet, and—

Jᴏᴀɴ: Drat the antiquireens! Has the drink muddled your head, John?

Sɪʀ Jᴏʜɴ: *Sir* John! *Sir* John!

Jᴏᴀɴ: Did I not tell 'ee Tess had written me that Mr. Angel Clare, son of the parson, wants to marry her? That's why we be here.

Sɪʀ Jᴏʜɴ: To *show* ourselves to him—that is *me*.

Jᴏᴀɴ: No! No! To keep her from telling.

Sɪʀ Jᴏʜɴ: Of what?

Jᴏᴀɴ: The other one. She writes and asks me if she ought not to tell him.

Sɪʀ Jᴏʜɴ: About our noble family?

Jᴏᴀɴ: Thou art beriddled! To tell him of the child—her child and Alec D'Urberville and all. She be a fool to dream of it. She'll not let this chance slip like the other one.

Sɪʀ Jᴏʜɴ: Aye. That would have been a grand match; though Alec D'Urberville be but of a young branch and far distant, still, he be a D'Urberville too and rich.

Jᴏᴀɴ: She might have been his wife to-day if she had not yielded to him. He'll never marry her now, nor the other, Mr. Clare, if he learns of it and the child. Thank the Lord it be dead, bless its soul.

Sɪʀ Jᴏʜɴ: 'Twas a double D'Urberville. It should lie in the family vault if it be left-handed.

Jᴏᴀɴ: And to think o' telling Mr. Clare, a gentleman, of things like that, and spoiling everything. *Gentlemen*, I tell 'ee, don't like such things in their wives.

Sɪʀ Jᴏʜɴ: I'll speak to him. *I* be the head of the family—

JOAN: Had I been on hand, she might a' married Alec D'Urberville, if she was but a dairymaid on his place. Mark 'ee, if she lose Mr. Clare, he will come forward. He's looking for her. He came to me to-day, but I put him off as to where she was working, as he would spoil this game. Oh, to tell of it! Think! Why we'd be rich too, if she'll hold her tongue.

SIR JOHN: Rich! 'Twould be but right. I was thinking o' selling the title to Mr. Alec for a thousand pounds, or—or fifty, not a penny less. I could live like a baronet, then.

JOAN: You could live like a baronet and I like a lady! O John, we could keep a cow!

SIR JOHN: She shall not speak. I will *command* her.

JOAN: No, let me. I was but a milkmaid yet I have a woman's wit.

ABRAHAM (*at the window at left*): Oh, mother! Look! Look! What be this?

JOAN: Why, it is a harp.

ABRAHAM: A harp. And see, mother, there be carpet—red carpet on the floor.

A burst of laughter from within the farm-house at left.

JOAN: They be at supper.

ABRAHAM: It makes me hungry.

SIR JOHN: I be thirsty.

ABRAHAM: I did not hear *Tess* laugh. I should think she'd laugh the loudest, mother, if she be going to be a lady.

SIR JOHN: Let's go in. I be thirsty. Being a baronet, they may offer us some ale.

JOAN: No, no. I must get at Tess first, alone. Let's go to the inn and get a drop o' gin. Abraham, wait round and let me know when they be through.

> JOAN *and* SIR JOHN *go through the gate.* ABRAHAM *wanders round Clare's house.* ANGEL CLARE *and* MR. CRICK *come from the farm-house at right. More laughter inside.*

CLARE: I'll figure this up and bring it to you, Mr. Crick. The noise in there disturbs me.

CRICK (*on the end of the portico*): I'm willing to go into it as far as I said, Mr. Clare, that is, if your calculation comes out as I think.

JOAN: 'Tis *he*, Tess's man.

CLARE: I'm sure it will be a good investment. My time of service —of learning farming from you, I mean, will be up in two weeks. I shall go to Brazil in a month—that is, if—

CRICK: I understand. You mean if Tess will go with you. She'll make a good wife, I've seen it all along.

CLARE: Yes, it's true. If she can't make up her mind, I shall go to Caracas earlier. I'll bring this to you as soon as I finish it.

CRICK: I expect a man to-night who wants your place here. It will be hard to replace you. You'll make a good farmer if you *are* a *gentleman*.

Goes into the farm-house.

SIR JOHN (*opening the gate*): It would be *best* for me to address him.

JOAN (*pulling him back*): No, no, the drink first.

SIR JOHN *hesitates, then they go off L.*

CLARE (*pausing at his door, which is opened*): A month of this calm life. And then, a new one in a new world. A new world with Tess and me alone in it, perhaps. Why does she put me off so? She says she loves me. Well, she's a woman! Brazil with her seems—paradise. Fifty sheep at twenty shilling a head will be—

Goes in and closes the door. RETTY, IZZ, *and* MARIAN *come from the farm-house laughing.*

MARIAN: Jonathan'll keep his promise, I tell 'ee.
RETTY: Fie! Shame on ye!
The light shines through Clare's window.
RETTY (*with a gasp*): Look! He has lighted his lamp!
The others stop laughing.
IZZ: Yes, he's reading or writing.
They all sigh.

RETTY: 'Tis a beacon light.

IZZ: Aye, for the shipwrecked.

MARIAN: No, 'tis a candle flame! And your wings be scorched by it, foolish moth!

RETTY: And so be *yours*, and *yours*, Izz.

MARIAN: Nonsense, Retty.

RETTY: I *know* you love him.

IZZ: Who would not? 'Tis not because he is so *good*.

RETTY: Nor so *very* handsome.

MARIAN: 'Tis because he's different from the men you see. A gentleman, the son of a parson learning how to farm, be no common thing. How foolish you be! The likes o' us! His thoughts be of other cheeks than thine.

IZZ: Retty *do* love him.

RETTY: *You* need not say anything, for I seed you kissing his shade.

MARIAN: *What* did you see her doing?

RETTY: He was standing by the whey tub, and the shade of his face fell upon the wall close to Izz. She set her mouth against the wall and kissed the shade o' his mouth. I seed it, though he didn't.

MARIAN: Oh, *Izz Hewett*!

IZZ: There was no harm in it, *you* need not talk.

RETTY: The other night I heard you cry in your sleep, "Angel Clare, oh, Angel Clare, I love thee," and then, Marian, you woke, and wept.

MARIAN: I—I— Oh, 'tis nonsense! He'll never come and ask the likes of us to marry him. He's going away to be a great landowner and farmer abroad. More likely to ask us to come with him as farm-hands, at so much a year. Oh, 'tis foolishness!

RETTY: 'Tis not foolishness since he loves Tess. She be one of us.

IZZ: Ah, but *she's* been to school. She can write like a lady, and read—books.

RETTY: So can you.

IZZ: I can—but I do not—nor do you, save the marriage service. I saw you.

RETTY: I wonder what he be doing.

MARIAN: You must not peep.
RETTY: I'm not peeping. I be but looking.
IZZ: Surely, 'tis no more harm to look in a window than to look out of it. If Mr. Clare chose to look at me—
MARIAN: He would not move to see you.
RETTY: Don't push! You be dying to look yourself.
MARIAN: Let's all of us.
They peep in the window.
RETTY: Is he not handsome?
MARIAN: Aye. Tess does not value him.
IZZ: I know she does. She loves him.
MARIAN: Why does she put him off?
RETTY: She be a woman.
MARIAN: Would *you*?
RETTY: I have no chance—nor any of us. We can weep together. She be the prettiest and the best. I do not blame him.
IZZ: Do ye remember how he carried the four of us over the stream that Sunday?
MARIAN & RETTY: Yes.
IZZ: He took the longest carrying Tess.
MARIAN: She be heavier.
RETTY: No, you be.
IZZ: I thought I'd faint.
RETTY: He told me I had a little foot.
MARIAN: Men do not marry for little feet.
RETTY: No, nor for big ones either.
IZZ: Look! look! He moves. I would he would play his harp.
RETTY: Last night I lay awake and listened.
MARIAN: And wept.
RETTY: I did.
IZZ: He's going away soon, and Tess will go with him.
RETTY: Draw close. We must feast our poor eyes every minute that we can.
MARIAN (*half to herself*): Going away?
IZZ: To Brazil.
RETTY: With Tess?

Izz: Don't 'ee *cry*.

Retty: Don't you! Don't you!

They stand with their arms around each other, looking in the window.

Enter from the farm-house, Jonathan *and* James.

Jonathan: Look!

James: They be daft, the whole women folk. Just because he be a gentleman.

Jonathan: And can play the harp.

James: Wait.

He steals up behind them and gives them all a hug.

Retty: How you startled me!

Marian: I thought it was the devil. To the devil with you!

Jonathan: I have something that will make you go there—gin!

They all sit. Marian *drinks from his bottle.*

Marian: 'Tis raw.

Retty: Marian, you should not drink so.

Marian: I never drink till work is done, and 'tis but a drop.

Izz: Such dropping will wear away the hardest stone.

Marian (*to* Jonathan): You need not squeeze so tight.

Retty (*sitting beside* James): I'll not kiss you.

James: Don't you like kissing?

Retty: Not with you.

Jonathan: 'Tis Mr. Clare she saves them for.

Retty: 'Tis not true.

Izz: Shame on you!

Jonathan: Ho, ho! (*Sings.*)

> I never loved but one fair maid,
> And she did prove untrue,
> Untrue to him, who to her paid,
> More love than was her due.
> Her wandering heart and faithless eyes,
> Made many a shepherd weep,
> Whilst all of them fought for the prize
> Which none of them could keep.
> Which none of them could keep.

The girls sigh. There is a silence, the men smoke. TESS, *unnoticed, walks along the portico of the farm-house.*

JONATHAN (*sings*):
>Merrily danced the barber's wife
>Sadly sat his sister,
>Nobody came so she blushed with shame,
>Nobody came and kissed her.

ALL (*joining in the chorus*):
>Nobody came, nobody came,
>Nobody came and kissed her.

JONATHAN (*sings*):
>The night grew dark,
>And her love arrived,
>He danced with the barber's sister,
>And all was well so you can tell
>That somebody came and kissed her.

RETTY (*rising*): Well kissing goes by choosing.

JONATHAN: Did I tell you what happened to Jack Dollup at Farmer Tott's?

RETTY: Jack Dollup be as rotten as touchwood.

JONATHAN: You know Jack Dollup has been courting the Widow Blake's daughter.

ALL: Yes, yes.

JONATHAN: Well it's all come out that he's deceived her as he deceived many before. But this time he had a different woman to deal with—her mother. Yesterday he saw her coming up to the door with a great brass-mouthed umbrella in her hands as would have felled an ox. "Do Jack Dollup live here?" she cried. "I want him. I have a bone to pick with he, I can assure 'n." And right behind her comes the girl, her handkerchief to her eyes, weeping like a watering pot. "O Lard a me! Here's a time!" cries Jack, looking out of the window. "Where shall I get? Where shall I get?" and with that he jumps into an empty churn.

MARIAN: Ha, ha.

JONATHAN: And shuts himself inside just as the widow burst in. "I'll claw his face for him! Only let me get at him!"

They all laugh.

Well, she hunted everywhere, ballyragging Jack by side and seam, and he laying a'most stifled in the churn, and the girl crying her eyes out at the door.

They all laugh.

It would have touched a marble stone, ha, ha.

ALL: Go on.

JONATHAN: How the woman had the wit to guess it, I can never tell, but she found he was inside. Without a word she took hold of the winch, and round she swung her, Jack a-flopping about inside. "Oh, let me out, I'll be churned to a pummy!" "Not till you make amends," she cries, and pumps the more. "Stop the churn, you witch," screams he. "Oh, you call me witch, do ye, when you ought to be calling me mother-in-law this long time." On went the churn. "I'll make amends," cries he. "I'll marry her," and she lets him out and he skips away and married another one to-day, a widow who has money.

MARIAN: O Lord, O Lord!

IZZ: Serves her right.

JAMES: Ha, ha, ha, ha.

JONATHAN: Let's walk down the lane. I expect Tim Smith. He's coming to see Crick about a place here.

MARIAN: 'Tis a good story.

JONATHAN: "I'll be churned to a pummy!"

They all stroll through the gate and go R., laughing and chatting. TESS *has buried her face on her arms against the post. She turns.*

TESS: Have they no hearts? How can they—how can they laugh at such a thing. If they knew, they'd laugh the same at me. They have no pity, they're like all the world. No—not all, he would not laugh. He'd weep, or thrust me from him. God give me the strength to tell him all. He must—be told. He loves me and may forgive me, as I would forgive him anything—everything.

Sits on the bench at left.

But if he—

ABRAHAM *creeps up to her.*

ABRAHAM: Tess.

Tess: Abraham!

Abraham: I am so glad to see 'ee, Tess.

Tess: Abraham! How came you here?

Abraham: I be a-visiting you. Mother and father too—they've gone to the inn for gin. Liza Loo's at home with Paul and little Johnny.

Tess: Mother and father!

Abraham: Aye, to see Mr. Clare here, the gentleman. So you're to be a grand lady.

Tess: Don't talk like that, dear.

Abraham: Mother says so. But she said that once before with Mr. Alec D'Urberville, and you be working still. Why didn't you marry him, Tess?

Tess: He did not ask me. Mother is wrong to put such ideas into your head.

Abraham: Oh, I have ideas of my own too. Be you not going to marry the parson's son?

Tess: Perhaps yes, and perhaps no.

Abraham: And be rich and wear silk and golden rings and chains? I be so glad! You'll give us many things, mother says; you'll give her a cow, and mend the roof, and give us a new horse. Oh we need one, poor Prince is so old. We came with him; he was so slow; he limped all the way.

Tess: Poor Prince, lame? What makes him so?

Abraham: I think it's having nothing in his stomach so often, and mother says you'll give us lots of everything good to eat.

Tess: That would be beautiful, Abraham.

Abraham: Wouldn't it?

Tess: Oh, if I only could! You should have everything you wanted. You, and Liza Loo, and all.

Abraham: And will 'ee live here?

Tess: I don't know—I don't know where I shall live. (*Aside.*) I don't know that I shall live at all.

Abraham: And will you give us another pretty baby to play with?

Tess (*starting up*): Oh don't! don't! Abraham, never speak of that. Promise me—promise never to mention baby—to any one.

It's dead, dear,—gone—gone. You will forget it, won't you? Won't you?

ABRAHAM: Yes, if you want me to! It was so pretty. I sometimes lay flowers on its grave.

> TESS *walks away, then comes back and puts her arms around him.*

TESS: I sometimes feel that you are all I shall have—you and Liza.
ABRAHAM: I tell 'ee we miss you at Marlott.
TESS: Do you, dear?
ABRAHAM: Yes. How soft your cheek is. Oh, see that shooting star! They're all coming out—one by one. Is it true they all be worlds?
TESS: Yes. They be worlds like this one, filled with sad, happy, suffering women, I suppose.
ABRAHAM: And no men?
TESS: If there were no men there, the women would not sorrow.

> CLARE *strikes a chord on his harp.*

Or be happy.
ABRAHAM: Listen, Tess. 'Tis like an angel.
TESS (*aside smiling*): 'Tis my angel.

> CLARE *plays, "Oh Believe Me If All Those Endearing Young Charms."* ABRAHAM *climbs up to the window; the music stops.*

ABRAHAM: Oh, he saw me.

> *The door opens and* CLARE *comes out. He has some paper, a pad, with a pencil attached, in his hand.*

CLARE: Hallo, my boy.
ABRAHAM: Hallo, sir.
CLARE: You like music?
ABRAHAM: I like yours, sir.
CLARE: Whence come you?
ABRAHAM: From Marlott. Be you the one, the parson's son, who is to make Tess a grand lady?
TESS: Abraham! What did I tell you? 'Tis my brother, Angel.
CLARE (*taking* ABRAHAM's *hand*): I hope to do more than make Tess a grand lady, I hope to make her a happy one.

ABRAHAM: But still a lady. Mother says—
TESS: Run away and fetch mother. Abraham!
Whispers.
Don't let father drink too much, please. Hurry now.
ABRAHAM: Good-bye, sir.
Runs through the gate and out R.
CLARE: Good-bye. A nice boy! Shall I take him to Brazil?
TESS: I wish you could, but we need him at home.
CLARE: We? Now, Tess—you told me you would let me know—
TESS (*changing the subject*): What is that, Angel, a poem?
CLARE: Far from it.
TESS: I would I could write poems. I would I could express myself as the trees do when the wind makes them whisper, as the river does over the stones. They all say something that they feel. I alone, cannot. You—you have your music, but I—I feel, in silence.
CLARE: Why, Tess!
TESS: And the trees have eyes. At least they seem to have, eyes that look deep into one's soul at night, and the river says, "Take care! Beware of me! Beware!"
CLARE: Why, Tess!
TESS: 'Tis only fancy. What is that?
CLARE: 'Tis a calculation for Crick. If it suits him, he's going to put some money in my scheme, in our farm in Brazil. Brazil! Do you know where Brazil is?
TESS: Yes, it's far—far off.
CLARE: Not so far. Only a few weeks, if you will say yes. You promised me an answer. Why do you put me off?
TESS: You know I love you. Oh, be content. Let me go on just loving you—loving you—I could do that though half the world should lie between.
CLARE: You strange child! Come now, your answer.
TESS: Your friends would scorn me. I am not a lady.
CLARE: God made you one the day you saw the light.
TESS: Your mother and your father.
CLARE: They have consented. You misjudge. My father is a thoroughly disinterested man, thoroughly kind. You can judge by

this. The other day, when he was away somewhere, he encountered there a wild young man of rank. A Mr. Alec something or other.

Tess (*aside*): Alec!

Clare: My father, feeling it was his duty, expostulated with him about his ways, and was bitterly insulted. Instead of being angry, my father forgave him and went to him again, and thinks he will be benefited by his words. You see he's very good, if a little narrow. The consent of your mother and father is all we need now. They've come here to give it, have they not?

Tess: What they say would not count against my heart and conscience. Angel, I will say something to you I never said to anyone before, something I never admitted to myself. Did you ever love anyone you could not respect?

Clare: Never. I could not.

Tess: Oh! I—I love my mother and my father, but try as I will, I cannot thoroughly respect them, though they may be good and do the best they can. That troubles me, makes me think perhaps—can you understand?

Clare: In that relationship, yes. I thought you meant differently.

Tess: Could you love a woman you did not respect?

Clare: No—I could not—because—I love you—I need think of no other. Ah, Tess, you are tantalizing. I sometimes think you are the greatest coquette in the world.

Tess: I, a coquette?

Clare: Or—that you love someone else.

Tess: You know it is not so! Does not every word I say, every look I give you, every tone in my voice cry, "Angel, I love you"?

Clare: Then why not answer, "Yes"? You are happy?

Tess: When I am with you.

Clare: Then be with me, always. Answer. . . .

Tess: You know nothing of me—I am not—

Clare: Nonsense—you worry about my family—because you were born in a different—

Tess: I be better born than you, sir, and I know you scorn old families. Yes, Angel, I am not plain Tess Durbeyfield, I am Tess of the D'Urbervilles, one of the noblest and oldest families in all

England. My father is a baronet by every right. Parson Tringham has traced us back—back to the deluge somewhere. I can't but be proud of it, though we be but peasants in our way of living. You would not marry such a pedigree as I?

Clare: Ha, ha. Why there's many a mushroom millionaire would pay his gold for such. That needn't trouble you. Your answer.

Tess: Wait—you know nothing of me, save what you see. I must—tell you—first of—my life.

Clare: That's what you always say. Well, go on, go on.

Tess: I—I—(*Aside.*) I—I—I can't tell him now. I—

Clare: Tell me about your home.

Tess: There is a hut at Marlott, smaller than that. There are three rooms in it, a kitchen with an earthen floor, my mother's bedroom, and a loft where all the children sleep. My mother was a milkmaid like myself. She can hardly read. Her Monday's work is done by Saturday, and sometimes 'tis not done. We have a horse, a cart, that's all. The horse is old and lame. He is the only one that works. He keeps the family. The money that he earns my father spends in drink. But they are fond of me. They sent me to a school where I learned—words—no more. I grew up like a weed with no one's hand to guide me—no knowledge of the world, no warning, no advice. They sent me out to service to a family of our name, a younger branch of the D'Urbervilles, where I—I—Oh, no, no, don't ask me to go on. Why did you choose me from all the rest?

Izz, Marian, *and* Retty *enter from round the farm-house.*

Look! There they stand, Izz, Marian, and Retty. Why didn't you love one of them? They be prettier, better, and more worthy than I. Why didn't you love one of them instead of me? They love you. Yes, as much as I—no, not as much as I, but they love you. I know it. Go to them—ask them. Any one of them will make you a good wife.

Clare: Nonsense. I love you and I'm going to marry you.

Tess: I must tell you something first. I can't now—I must think it over. I must find words.

CLARE: All right, dear. Tell me when I come back. I'll take these into Crick. Now don't be fanciful.

Tears sheet of the pad, leaves it on the bench, kisses her, and turns. The girls run out L.

CLARE (*laughing*): You see I've frightened them. Child, I only want you, and your answer. Tell me anything you wish.

Goes into the farm-house.

TESS: I must—I must. There's no more putting it off; when he comes back, I must tell him.

She walks up and down. JONATHAN *and* JAMES *come in from the gate at right, followed by* TIM *and another man.*

JONATHAN: Wait, Tim, Crick's pretty busy o' nights now, calculating. We'll see if he's busy now.

JONATHAN *and* JAMES *go to farm-house.*

TIM (*recognizing* TESS *as she turns*): Hullo, my lady! Remember me at Mr. Alec D'Urberville's?

TESS *shrinks from him.*

You left rather sudden—(*Laughs.*)

TESS: Don't.

TIM: Come—come—that's not the way to treat an old friend. We'll get on finely. I'm coming here to work. I say—a kiss now.

TESS *struggles with him.* CLARE *enters from the farmhouse.*

CLARE: Stop!

TIM (*with an insolent glance*): Oh, so you're the one now are you?

CLARE *knocks him down.* TESS *clings to* CLARE.

TESS: Go—go into the house. Angel—I beg of you.

She gets between him and the man. The man gets up sullenly.

CLARE: There is the gate.

The men go to it. TIM *turns.*

OTHER MAN: Made a mistake?

TIM: No, but I spare the gent's feelings.
   CLARE *starts towards him*—TESS *clings to* CLARE.
TESS: Angel! Angel! Don't follow them.
   He gently puts her aside and sternly follows the men out of the gate.
TESS (*wildly*): Oh what shall I do! If he should learn the truth from them—from them before I can tell him.

   IZZ, MARIAN, *and* RETTY *come from round farm-house at right. They rush at* TESS.

MARIAN (*like an accuser*): You be going to marry him?
TESS (*laughing wildly*): Ha, ha, ha, ha.
RETTY: I want to hate 'ee but I can't.
TESS (*turning on them savagely*): Don't! Don't! Don't! Go! Go! Oh, why couldn't one of you make him love you? Why didn't you try? I tried to make him go to you. 'Twould be far better for us all. You—you are good and true—while I— Oh what am I saying?
SIR JOHN (*who has entered from the gate, staggering*): Hush, not a word.
TESS: Go, please go.
   The girls retire to the house wonderingly.
SIR JOHN: I am come to congratulate you, I am—
   Tries to kiss her grandly. CLARE *enters from the gate. He springs forward and lays a hand on* SIR JOHN's *shoulder to drag him away. He meets* TESS's *eyes. The girls, grasping the situation, motion back* JONATHAN *and* JAMES *at the door.*

   All go in. CLARE, SIR JOHN, *and* TESS *stand there, looking at each other.*

I be the—
TESS: My father.
SIR JOHN: I be King Norman's—
   Staggers and almost falls. TESS *catches him.*
TESS (*across him to* CLARE): Go—I cannot bear it.
   CLARE *turns and goes into his house.*

TESS (*gently*): Father, how could you!
SIR JOHN: I want to greet you. I drank the noble—

ABRAHAM *and* JOAN *enter through the gate and come to them.*

TESS (*heartbrokenly*): Mother!
JOAN: Abraham! Take your father down the road. 'Tis cooler there.

ABRAHAM *leads* SIR JOHN *out of the gate to right.*

TESS: Mother, why did you let him?
JOAN (*who has been drinking*): Fiddle-dee-dee! Many's the time you've seen him that way and laughed. All gentlemen drink.
TESS: Mr. Clare saw him.
JOAN: Oh, well, 'tis natur! So you be going to marry him?
TESS: I don't know yet, mother, if I can.
JOAN: Don't know? Be you a fool? We've come all the way to give our blessings. Don't know! Don't he want to? You're not going to let the chance slip as you did the other one?
TESS: It is because of that other one that this may never be. Oh, mother, why did you send me there to claim relationship? Into the world without one word of warning. What could I know? What could I know of men? I was a child—as blind as innocent— Oh, mother, have pity on me—I am suffering so.
JOAN: But that's all gone—now 'tis different, Tess. How can that change this one?
TESS: He does not know of that.
JOAN: 'Ee won't tell? The Lord-a-Lord, that I should have such a fool for a child. 'Tis past and forgotten.
TESS: No, no.
JOAN (*violently*): Don't 'ee understand how we need money? Don't 'ee understand we don't have food enough? The roof drips on us. The horse is old, he can't last long, and Liza's sick.
TESS: I'll work my fingers to the bone for you, for them, but I will not deceive him.
JOAN (*imploringly*): No, no, Tess, you must not tell him.
TESS: I love him, therefore I cannot deceive him.
JOAN: But he'll not marry 'ee if he knows.

TESS: Then he'll not marry me. I'll not wed a man I love with a lie on my lips, a lie in my heart.

JOAN: But the child be dead.

TESS: Yes. But the past, mother, always lives—always. It is the one thing we cannot get away from.

JOAN: You must not tell—you must not.

TESS: I shall tell him to-night. If he forgives, mother, you shall have all you want. I should have told him long ago, at first. Oh, how can I go to him and—

She sinks on the bench—her eyes fall on the pad.

I'll write it to him—then I shan't see his face.

JOAN: No, 'ee shan't.

TESS: Yes, mother, give me that please. It would be easier than telling him.

JOAN: Oh, you be no child of mine.

TESS: Don't say that.

JOAN *goes up to the gate in a rage.*

No, I can't—I won't lie even for them.

She stands there, then goes to the window, taps, and opens it.

Angel, I will leave something on the sill here for you. Take it, and then, if you still love me, come to me without a word.

She closes the window and crosses. JOAN *unseen watches this.*

TESS (*writes*): "Angel! This—this is what I have to tell. When I went out to service, I—I was deceived—I did not know—the child died—"

ALEC D'URBERVILLE *has entered L.I.*

ALEC (*standing by her*): Well?

TESS (*starting to her feet*): Alec!

ALEC: Yes, Alec.

TESS: What have you come for?

ALEC: You.

TESS: Please go.

ALEC: Oh no, Tess, I can't live comfortably without you, I've tried and still returned to you. I've found you—I love you.

TESS *laughs bitterly.*
What are you doing, my pretty Tess?
  TESS: Writing my history of shame. Do you need to read it?
  ALEC: That is written above—with my name as author. Come now—your mother couldn't trick me—I followed her here to you. Come with me again, and you shall have everything. I'm richer than ever—and much handsomer. Look at me.
            Turns her around.
And they are poorer. Oh, I know. I've seen that they haven't enough to eat sometimes. I've been there often to find you. They wouldn't tell me where you were, but I found you just the same. You ought to feel flattered. You are the only one—the only woman I ever cared for, the only one who suited me. Think of the benefit to them, and yourself, and me. Will you come back?
  CLARE *strikes a chord with his harp.*
  TESS: No.
  ALEC: Think.
  TESS: I never wish to see you again. I loathe you.
  ALEC (*laughing*): All women say those things.
  TESS: Does it not strike you that what all women say, some may mean?
  ALEC: You'll come to me some day. You'll have to. It's Fate. I'll wait.

> *He strolls out L.* TESS *sinks down and covers her face with her hands, then madly finishes the note.*

TESS (*writing*): "The child died. Forgive me. I should have told you long ago. I dared not. But I love you, TESS."
> *She runs to the window, lays the note on the sill, takes a rose from her breast, kisses it, lays it beside the note, knocks on the window, and rushes across.* JOAN'*s arm is seen round the corner of the house.*

> *She quickly snatches the note. The window is raised.* CLARE'*s hand is seen; he takes the rose. The window is closed. There is a silence.* TESS *stands in agony not daring to look up. The door opens and* CLARE *comes out.*

The light streams from behind him on to TESS. *He opens his arms.*

CLARE: Tess.

TESS *turns, and with a wild cry of joy rushes into his arms.* JOAN *hastily goes out of the gate at right.*

CURTAIN

ACT II

SCENE: *A room in an old manor-house that once belonged to the D'Urbervilles. There is a window R.C., a door to the left of that. A door at left. A wide fireplace with burning logs at right. A couch near it, against the couch a table. A larger table, in the left upper corner, is laid for refreshments. The whole scene is solemn and impressive-looking. It is late in the afternoon.*

The door at back opens and RETTY *runs in.*

RETTY (*wildly*): I can't bear it! I can't bear it.
    She throws herself face down on the couch.
They must be married by now.
    Looks at the clock.
It be all—all over. Tess is his wife. He looked so happy and she looked so happy. Oh dear! And the parson said, "You take this woman for your wife." I hope they didn't notice that I run away. I had to. I be a fool! Come now, they be married, it's all over—and—and there's other men—lots—no there isn't—not for me.—But he'll be here. He mustn't see me cry. They'll all be here. Now laugh!

    She walks up and down, trying to laugh, and comes face to face with IZZ *who has entered at left.*

BOTH: You!
    They fall into each other's arms.
IZZ: I had to run away—I could not bear it—I cried so.

RETTY (*patting her on the back*): Poor Izz.
IZZ (*patting her on the back*): Poor Retty.
RETTY: We be fools.
IZZ: Yes. Now 'tis over. 'Tis over, and we have our lives to lead.
RETTY: Alas, yes.
IZZ: I shall marry as soon as I can.
RETTY: Marry! I don't ever want to marry.
IZZ: You must. They say one makes you forget another.
RETTY: I never can. Why Jonathan wants me and—
IZZ: Take him. He's not a gentleman—
RETTY: And can't play the harp.
IZZ: He's a good man.
RETTY: All the goodness in the world wouldn't make amends—
IZZ: Come now—they'll all be here soon. Let's watch for them.
Goes to the window.
How beautiful Tess did look.
RETTY: I can't hate her. He did right.
IZZ: And he'll be so happy in Brazil.
RETTY: It was strange that none of his family came to the wedding.
IZZ: Her family did, and 'tween you and me, 'twas stranger. If I had a drunken baronet for a father—well all his grand name and titles wouldn't let him in, I assure ye.
RETTY: I heard the door.

They run to the window. The door at back opens, and MARIAN *enters. She tosses her hat towards the couch, goes to the table wildly, and grasps decanter. Her hand trembles so it knocks against the glass. The girls turn.*

BOTH: Marian!
MARIAN: I don't care! I must have it.
Drinks.
You feel it as much as I do. You couldn't stay in the church any more than I could. Take some—it will be the only consolation we'll get.
RETTY: No, no.
IZZ: 'Tis false consolation.

MARIAN: What else can you do?
IZZ & RETTY: We be going to get married.
MARIAN: That be false consolation, too. To whom?
RETTY: Jonathan.
IZZ: Any one.
MARIAN: You'll be right. I'll join you. Let's drink to it, and then we'll go a man hunting.
RETTY: Didn't Tess look beautiful?
IZZ: Her gown must have cost two pounds.
MARIAN (*bitterly*): She did look beautiful. I trust she'll act so.
IZZ: What do 'ee mean?
MARIAN: If she ever fooled him, I'll be the first to let him know.
IZZ: Shame on you.
MARIAN: Yes, I will. He's too good to be fooled.
RETTY: Tess could not do that.
MARIAN: All women can. You could, both of you. I could. I only wish I had the chance.
RETTY: Don't take any more.
They try to stop her.
MARIAN: I will.

Voices outside. They put their hands to their hearts and listen. IZZ *and* RETTY *run to the window.* MARIAN, *with a defiant toss of her head, drains her glass and sets it down with a bang.* SIR JOHN, JOAN, ABRAHAM, *and* LIZA LOO, *in their best, enter at centre.*

JOAN (*with great satisfaction*): Well, 'tis done. And what's done can't be undone, I says.
MARIAN: Would 'ee have it so?
JOAN (*airily*): Oh, I be content.
MARIAN: Oh, you be mighty grand now! Your daughter is a lady, Joan Durbeyfield.
SIR JOHN: D'Urberville—'tis D'Urberville.
MARIAN (*with a curtsey*): I asks your pardon, Lady D'Urberville.
SIR JOHN: Tess was always a lady—a born one, of ancient family. I have a family vault at Kingsbere.
MARIAN (*with a curtsey*): Aye, Sir John.

The children examine the things on the table.

JOAN (*seating herself with great satisfaction on the couch*): 'Tis but due that Tess should marry a gentleman.

MARIAN (*with a curtsey*): Aye, my lady of the ancient family. My Lady D'Urberville's carriage blocks the way.

JOAN: You are envious.

MARIAN: Not I.

JOAN: I seed you run away from the church and cry, all of you.

MARIAN: Fiddle-dee-dee.

RETTY: 'Tis not true.

IZZ: We came to see that—that all was in readiness.

SIR JOHN: Wine! He understands what is due to such as I. In King Norman's time, my ancestors, them as lays in leaden coffins, weighing tons and tons, in coats of mail and jewels, we drank from goblets of gold.

MARIAN: Hee! Hee!

SIR JOHN: What did you say?

MARIAN (*with a curtsey*): Aye, Sir John.

SIR JOHN: This very house be part of one of the old manor palaces of the family, the most ancient family in Wessex.

MARIAN: Oh, 'tis grand.

SIR JOHN: 'Tis but a farm dwelling now.

IZZ, MARIAN, & RETTY (*curtseying*): Aye, Sir John, ha, ha, ha.

JOAN: Minxes! You be mad with jealousy. You wanted him for yourselves.

MARIAN: Oh fiddle-dee-dee!

RETTY: It is not true, for I am to marry.

IZZ: Yes, yes and I.

JOAN: Who?

RETTY: Jonathan.

JOAN: Has he asked you? And you, Miss Izz?

IZZ: I?

Inventing a name.

Edward de Courcey.

MARIAN: And I—I am to marry Granthor Blake—the most ancient man in all Wessex.

SIR JOHN (*drinking and looking around*): It went out of our hands in Oliver Cromwell's time. Parson Tringham—the antiquireen says we fought against him and lost all. I was thinking of sending round to all the antiquireens in England to subscribe a fund to maintain me. It would be the most remanticle, artistical, and proper thing to do. They spend lots of money in keeping up old ruins, and finding the bones o' rare animals and such like, and the living remains of such a family must be more interesting. But I need not now that Tess is rich.

LIZA LOO: And shall we wear fine clothes and ride in her coach?

IZZ, MIRIAN, & RETTY: He, he, he.

SIR JOHN: Hush—you know she be going to the Brazils, a grand place.

ABRAHAM: Father, where be the Brazils?

SIR JOHN: 'Tis an island, off the far coast of Americy. There be silver mines there and gold—and—and lions and tigers.

ABRAHAM: And bears?

SIR JOHN: And bears, and serpents, as long as—as this table—boy constructors. I drink to my ancestors, to Tess, and the island.

ABRAHAM (*examining the food*): And the bears.

LIZA: And serpents.

MARIAN: As you can't get your antiquireens to dig up your bones, you better eat, to cover 'em up, instead o' drinking.

JOAN: What do you mean?

MARIAN: Your family don't look over fat, my Lady Durbeyfield.

JOAN: Oh, we always have as much as we can swallow.

MARIAN: A mighty small swallow for so ancient a family. The boy looks starved.

ABRAHAM: I be. May I eat, mother?

JOAN: No, no, I tell 'ee. Wait till Tess—Mrs. Clare—comes. 'Tis company manners to wait.

ABRAHAM: Oh, it's always company manners to do what ye don't want.

SIR JOHN: To King Norman.

RETTY (*at window*): Here they be.

IZZ: Let's go and welcome them. Marian—Marian.

MARIAN: I'll not go.

> Izz, RETTY, *and the children run out back.* MARIAN *hesitates, and then rushes after them.*

JOAN: Sir John, drink to me, for 'tis I brought it all about. I'll join 'ee.

SIR JOHN: The likes o' them can't understand our ancient family feeling. Joan, my Joan, here's to you.

JOAN: You little know. I had two strings to my bow, sir. Mr. Alec D'Urberville's the other. Should this have failed—well he'd have come forward. I tell 'ee he wants her and he's rich.

SIR JOHN: To marry Tess?

JOAN: No, no 'tis too late for that.

SIR JOHN: I tell 'ee I won't have it, I—I—

JOAN: 'Tis best as it is. A right-handed marriage to a man as has some money be far better and more lasting than a left-handed one with a man as has more. And 'tis I, Joan—not ancient family, sir—that did it. And we'll have many fine things, I tell 'ee, and you can live like a gentleman. But leave the management o' things to me. A woman's wit is worth more than a man's family. I'll tell 'ee something, but you must keep it close.

SIR JOHN: Aye, aye.

JOAN: Mr. Clare knows nothing of the other and the child.

SIR JOHN: 'Tis well in such a family. She did not tell?

JOAN: She did far worse—she wrote it. Words on paper last the longest. I burned the note. It all went up in smoke, out of the chimney at Marlott.

SIR JOHN: Here's to ye.

> TESS *enters at centre with a child on each side of her. The three girls follow.*

TESS: Yes, yes and more too, Liza. Mother!
> *Goes to her.*

JOAN: Dearie, I be so proud. You look beautiful.

TESS: Mother, I feel beautiful.
> *The girls sigh.*

ABRAHAM: Tess, I be hungry.

LIZA: So be I.

TESS: Well eat then.
ABRAHAM: Mother made us wait.
TESS: Oh, mother.
JOAN: 'Twas but right. Folks should learn early to keep down their feelings, and the ways o' company. You may eat now.
TESS: Eat all there is.
ABRAHAM (*at the table*): We never can do that, Tess. There's plenty here for weeks and weeks. Tess, may I take home some cake to little Johnny?
LIZA: And I for Paul?
TESS: Fill all your pockets—full.

> *The children eat greedily.* SIR JOHN, *sitting at the right at table, still drinks.* JOAN *joins him and sits next him at the foot of the table.*

TESS: Izz, Marian, Retty won't you eat?
RETTY: I cannot eat.
IZZ: Nor I, dear Tess.
TESS: Then come and sit by me, all of you, close.

> *They sit on the couch.* MARIAN *stands apart.*

Marian, there's room for you, sit here.

> MARIAN *hesitates, then sits at her left.*

Give me your hand. Draw close. I want you near me, you three, who worked so often at my side. You won't forget me?
IZZ & RETTY: Never, dear Tess.
MARIAN (*in a hard voice*): I hope you will be happy.
TESS: I am happy.
MARIAN (*after a struggle with herself*): I mean—I wish you joy.
TESS: Thanks.
RETTY (*aside*): Poor Marian.
IZZ: How do you feel?
RETTY: Tell us.
TESS: I do not know. I never felt this way before. I can't find words to tell you. You will miss me?
ALL: Ah, we shall.
TESS: And you're not angry that I took him? I had to.
RETTY: We be glad.

Izz: Oh, 'tis far better so.

>CLARE *enters at centre. The girls start up and withdraw up R.* TESS *turns and faces* CLARE. *He comes and kisses her. The girls sigh.*

CLARE: My little wife.

TESS: Yes.

SIR JOHN: And it all went up in smoke, ha, ha.

JOAN (*pinching him*): Hold your tongue, I tell 'ee.

JOHN: Ha, ha.

CLARE: Your father is merry, Tess.

JOAN (*hastily rising*): Why should he not be? So be I, and you.

SIR JOHN: Ha, ha, all in smoke.

JOAN: He has drunk too often to his family, to the bride, and to you, sir.

To SIR JOHN.

Hold your tongue.

>SIR JOHN *half singing and banging the table.*

JOAN: Oh—oh—we must be going. We have a ways to go. It be late. Hush, John. Good-bye, my Tess, good luck to you.

TESS (*embracing her*): Mother!

JOAN (*patting her on the back*): There—there. Mr. Clare, take good care o' her.

CLARE: I will.

TESS: Good-bye, father.

SIR JOHN: I be more proud of my family than ever.

JOAN: Come, children.

>JOAN *leads* SIR JOHN *to the door, fearful lest he may say more. The children run to* TESS; *she kneels between them and kisses them.*

ABRAHAM: Good-bye, Tess. Oh, must 'ee go?

TESS (*embracing him*): Yes, dear.

LIZA (*feeling her gown*): Is that silk, real silk?

TESS (*nods*): And you shall have one like it.

JOAN: Come, children.

LIZA & ABRAHAM (*running to the door*): Good-bye, good-bye.

>ABRAHAM *runs back to* CLARE.

ABRAHAM: Don't let the bears eat Tess.

> *Runs out with his fists in his eyes.*

LIZA (*at the door*): Nor the serpents bite her.

> *They go out at back.* CLARE *takes* TESS *in his arms, the girls sigh audibly and hold on to each other.*

TESS (*whispers*): Angel. Go to them. Kiss them. Poor things. I have robbed them. Go kiss them.

CLARE: Well, girls, have you kissed the bride?

ALL: Yes, Mr. Clare.

CLARE: 'Tis but fair you should kiss me. Will you?

> *They do not answer.*

Come, Retty, you're first. Come, I won't bite you.

> RETTY *comes slowly forward and presents her cheek. He kisses it and turns to* TESS.

MARIAN (*aside*): Drat the drink! I did not dare to let him kiss my mouth.

> *They all stand there a second in slight embarrassment.*

RETTY: Well we—

MARIAN (*taking the lead*): Yes, we must go.

ALL: Good-bye, and good luck to you.

TESS & CLARE: Good-bye. Good-bye.

> *They follow them to the door; it closes. They stand and look at each other.*

CLARE: At last I can feast my eyes on you. Are you happy?

TESS: That's no word for it.

> CLARE *puts his arm around her and they come down to the couch.*

CLARE: And you're sure you're not frightened, dear, at the prospect of going so far into a new country?

TESS: How can I fear when I shall be with you?

CLARE: But all will be so different. We shall see no one that we know.

TESS: I shall see you. You won't be forced to leave me often, will you? I too can work in the fields, you know.

CLARE: It's very hot there.

TESS: Will you fetch your harp along, Angel? To play on in the cool of the evenings as you used?

CLARE: No, but we shall have a guitar and you shall learn to play on it.

TESS: I have no cleverness. I can only play upon the strings of my own heart.

CLARE: And mine.

TESS: Angel?

CLARE: Yes.

TESS (*smiling*): You won't let the bears eat me.

CLARE: No, nor hug you.

TESS: Nor the serpents bite me.

CLARE: They may be tempted, but you won't.

They are holding hands. There is a knock at the door at right.

CLARE: Come in.

JONATHAN enters C. hat in hand.

JONATHAN: Just come to wish you luck, Mr. Clare, and Miss— Ma'am, I should say—to call her by her lawful—

CLARE: Thank you, Jonathan.

TESS: Thank you.

JONATHAN: And your luggage is in the hall.

CLARE: Drink this cup of ale, and keep that for your trouble.

JONATHAN: Success in foreign parts—er—that's all.

TESS & CLARE: Good-bye, Jonathan.

He goes out back. They sit again.

CLARE: I hope you didn't mind my family not coming, dear. I did not ask them. I thought it best that—

TESS: I understand. How good you are. You wish to wait till I'm presentable. Oh yes—I shall be. I'll read and read—all those books you've told me of, and learn at your side, everything.

She lays her head against his shoulder. A knock at the door L.

CLARE: What the deuce! Can't they leave us alone! Come in!

MAN *enters with a package.*

MAN: A package, sir, for Mrs. Clare.
TESS: For me?
CLARE: Thank you. 'Tis father's writing.

MAN *goes out at left.*

CLARE: Thank Heaven!
TESS (*laughing*): Do you know, Angel, I never felt like saying "Thank Heaven" when any one left a room till now.
CLARE: Father's writing. It's a present for you.
TESS: Oh, open it. I never had a present before, save the Bible mother gave me.

CLARE *unties the package and drops the paper.* TESS *picks it up.*

TESS (*reading*): Mrs. Angel Clare. Angel! That's me, Mrs. Angel Clare.
CLARE: Don't you believe it?
TESS: I'll try.

Draws close to him.

What is it?
CLARE (*glancing over the letter*): I remember. My godmother left them in charge of my father. They're for you. Dear woman, she expected wonders of me. She left them to be given to my wife.

Opens the box.

TESS: Oh how beautiful! For me? Angel, I can never wear these. I shall just look and look at them.
ANGEL: Dear old lady!

Reads.

"MY DEAR ANGEL! I leave these to you or your wife. They have been in the family many years, and it is but right that you should have them. Give them to your wife on her wedding day. I know the woman that you choose will be good and pure and true. Your godmother, GERTRUDE."

Hands them to her.

On our wedding day. Now put them on. I'll help you.

TESS *stands there smiling. He puts a bracelet on her arm, a star in her hair, and tries the necklace over her gown.*

That's not right. Can't you make it look more like an evening gown? Tuck it away a bit at the neck. It should be lower. I'll help you. There.

TESS: I can't clasp it.

CLARE (*stepping back*): How beautiful you are! If you were to appear in a ball-room—and yet you're not a whit more so than when you wore a cotton gown with a rose at your breast. Look! I have it here.

He takes a rose from case in his pocket.

The only token you ever gave me. The one you left on the sill. Your explanation of yourself—a wildflower. You remember?

TESS *stands there, holding the necklace with both hands.*

TESS (*smiling tenderly*): The one I gave you with the letter.

The necklace falls at her feet with a crash. She looks straight ahead and her lips move. He stoops to pick up the necklace at her feet.

TESS: He does not know—he does not know.

CLARE *kneeling at her feet catches sight of her face.*

CLARE: Tess, what is it?

TESS: The letter.

CLARE: What letter?

TESS: On the sill. The night I told you—the night you came to me. Oh!

Wildly.

You must have got it. You must have got it. I laid it there, telling you all—all.

She sinks down on the couch and covers her face with her hands.

CLARE: Tess, my sweet, what troubles you? What was in that letter?

TESS: My life.

CLARE: How strange you are! I remember—you said you had something to tell, but you told me of your home. The wind must have blown it away—a trifle.

TESS: There was no wind.

CLARE: Never mind!
TESS: It—was—no—trifle.
CLARE: But do you remember what we said this morning—
TESS: I remember.
CLARE: About telling each other our faults—
TESS: I remember.
CLARE: We spoke lightly—but it was no light promise on my side. I—I have something to say. I know I am a peculiar man—I want to make a confession.
TESS (*with relief*): You have something to confess?
CLARE: Yes. I wonder if you will forgive me.
TESS: It is forgiven already.
CLARE: You don't know. You value me at far more than my worth. Draw close—because—I want you to forgive me. Of course men don't always tell things like this, but I shall feel more honest if I do. It is because you are what you are—so pure, that I must. I am not religious—I suppose because I grew up in a religious family, yet though I am not spotless myself, I admire that most in others, for I fell.

TESS *starts*.

I went to London, young, unsettled, full of life. I met a woman. I plunged into a short and sensual dissipation with her.

TESS *starts to her feet*.

And then I ended it—never to repeat it. I felt that to be honest I must tell you this. Do you forgive me?
TESS: I am so glad!
CLARE: Glad!
TESS: Yes—because then you can forgive me.
CLARE: Forgive you?
TESS: I told you all in that letter. I knew it was right that you should know. Give me your hand. I would you had read that note—it is so hard to tell. It was three years ago. We were told that we were noble D'Urbervilles—my father's head was turned. I was told that I could marry a gentleman. I must, they said, and I was sent away. I told you—to service, to the other D'Urbervilles. They thought I should be recognized. There was a son. They

thought that he would marry me. We often met, and he was very kind at first. He followed me, would not let me alone. I did not know—I was so young—I did not understand—until it was—too late.

CLARE (*starting up*): No—no.

TESS (*lost in her past*): Then I went home again. They met me at the door, my mother and my father. "And be you married yet?" they cried. I did not answer. I went upstairs into the loft where I had slept—I did not leave it till the child was born.

CLARE *walks to the mantel and leans his forehead against it.*

It was very frail. The vicar heard that it was ill—dying. He came to christen it. My father locked the door, he had to go away. The children sat with me. My child was dying. I took my Prayer Book from the shelf, I placed a candle at his head—I dipped my fingers in the bowl and made a cross upon its little head. I had to save its soul. I sprinkled water on it. I said: "I baptize thee in the name of the Father, and the Son. I name thee Sorrow!" That Sorrow died.

CLARE (*turning*): Tess, are you out of your mind?

TESS (*quietly*): I am not out of my mind.

CLARE (*crying out*): Oh! Why didn't you tell me! I remember.
She goes to him. He draws away in horror and does not look at her. She follows on her knees.

TESS: In the name of our love forgive me as I have forgiven you.

CLARE: Oh, Tess, Tess, forgiveness cannot apply to such a case. You were one person; now you are another. Such forgiveness cannot be. It would be grotesque.
He laughs horribly.

TESS: Don't! Don't! It kills me. Have mercy!
He still laughs.

What do you mean by that laugh?

CLARE: That it is impossible. Does that man live?

TESS: Yes.

CLARE: No—no—we might meet him.

TESS: We were going to Brazil.

CLARE: No—no! Go where we might he would ever come between us.

TESS: Can you not forgive me?

CLARE: I do forgive you, but forgiveness is not all.

TESS: I thought you loved me. Having begun to love you, I love you for ever, in all disgrace, because you are yourself. I ask no more. How can you, my husband, stop loving me?

CLARE: The woman I have been loving is not you. Another in your shape—a lie.

TESS sits down like a dead woman.

TESS (*after a pause*): I don't belong to you then, any more, do I? (*He never looks at her.*) Angel, am I too wicked for you to go on living with me?

CLARE: I can't think yet.

TESS: I shan't ask you to let me. If you go away, I'll try not to follow you. I won't unless you tell me to. I shall not speak to you if you bid me not. I shall not ask you why.

CLARE: And if I order you—

TESS (*proudly*): I shall obey.

CLARE: Listen, Tess, I shall go away to Brazil—at once.

TESS: Angel!

CLARE: Alone. You—you may write to me. Here is my address.

TESS: Angel, I—I can't let you go.

CLARE: You must. Oh!

Recovering himself.

You must not follow me.

TESS: I promise.

CLARE: It is the only way. We must be apart where we can think clearly. We will remember the best then—and value it. I shall write to my attorney to send you an allowance. Here is all the money that I have. Take it.

TESS: I cannot take it.

CLARE (*gently without looking at her*): I order you to, Tess.

She goes toward the table, then draws back.

TESS: No—I have no right.

CLARE: Take it.

Tess: Angel, it would be easier for me to take money from the father of my child—far, far easier from him than from you. I cannot. You are no more the man I loved than I am the woman you loved. I do not know you. You are a stranger.

Clare: Take it, Tess.

Tess: I will obey you in all but that.

Puts the note into his hands.

The only token you ever gave me.

Clare: How will you live?

Tess: By work, as I have always done. That's not a lady's hand. Do you want your ring, Angel?

Clare: No.

Tess: I have no right to it. I am not your wife.

She puts it on his little finger. He looks away from her. She takes the star from her hair, the bracelet from her arm, the necklace from the table and puts them into his hand.

They belong to your wife.

Clare (*after a second*): Good-bye, Tess.

She stands there immovable. The door closes behind him. She does not move, but gives a strange, low cry.

Tess: I must obey—I must obey.

CURTAIN

ACT III

Scene: *The kitchen in the cottage at Marlott. A low-ceilinged room. A door L. of C.; to the right of that rough steps lead up to the loft. A fireplace and oven at right, a small paned window at left. A table in the centre, two rough chairs, and some tubs. There is an old clock, a warming-pan, some brass candlesticks, and a few plates on shelf. It is early winter outside before snow.*

Abraham *is sitting on the floor before the fire.*

Abraham: Oh, I be so hungry it be pain.

Calls.

Mother! Mother! I wish Tess would get back. I don't feel so hungry when she's by. The only time I ever had enough to eat was when she married. I've been hungry ever since.

    LIZA Loo *enters at back. She has some straw and hay in her hand.*

LIZA Loo: I did not dare take more or Prince would have no supper. There's only a little left. Do you think we can get it down?

ABRAHAM: I must eat something. It keeps poor Prince alive.

    He chews some.

LIZA: Do you like it?

ABRAHAM: No.

LIZA: What does it taste like?

ABRAHAM: Little sticks. Try some.

LIZA (*chewing*): I be glad I am not a horse.

ABRAHAM: I be glad I'm not Prince. He be so old.

LIZA: Older than you?

ABRAHAM: No, but older as a horse. I feel as if I was a hundred.

LIZA: That's 'cause you're ill. I wish we had some o' that cake we had at Tess's wedding.

ABRAHAM: It do make me hungrier to think of it. Where be mother?

LIZA: Walking up and down the road watching for Tess. I hope she do get that place. 'Tis time she were back.

ABRAHAM: 'Tis a long way and Tess be ill. She would not take poor Prince but walked. If father were alive, all would be well.

LIZA: Oh, what did father do, but talk of the antiquireens and his ancient family. Be you going to drink when you grow up?

ABRAHAM: All gentlemen do. Mother says so. And I be one. I be a baronet. Sir Abraham now, Tess says so.

LIZA: When I get a husband, I tell 'ee, I won't let him go to the Brazils without me.

ABRAHAM: And mother said we would be rich and have a cow.

LIZA: And cake—

ABRAHAM: And everything, and Tess be working still.

LIZA: Or trying to. He's never written her. I hear her cry in the night. He never sent a word or money, and 'tis months and months since she came home. He must be a bad man.

ABRAHAM: No, he's not—Tess says so. He's not like Parson Alec who comes here so often.

LIZA: Then Tess must have done something wicked, or Mr. Clare wouldn't act so.

ABRAHAM: Tess! Shame on 'ee. Hold your tongue.

LIZA: I won't.

ABRAHAM: You shan't speak o' Tess so. Go away.

LIZA: Oh—oh—sick boy—sick boy.

JOAN *enters at back.*

JOAN: Hush yer noise.

ABRAHAM: Mother, has Tess come yet?

JOAN: No. What be that?

ABRAHAM: I be trying to eat it.

JOAN: Lord-a-Lord. Be you a fool? Poor boy, don't 'ee fret. 'Twill come out right when Tess gets back, for if she does not get that place, I have another plan, mark 'ee. Don't 'ee worry.

ABRAHAM: My stomach does.

LIZA: Is it another husband for Tess, mother?

JOAN: No, but just as good. Wait, I tell 'ee.

ABRAHAM: Mother, I be a baronet. Could I not sell the title? I would for a loaf of bread.

JOAN: Peace, I tell 'ee.

ABRAHAM: I cannot see what good a Sir before your name does. It did no good to father.

JOAN: Try to be as good as he was. He was a fine specimen, a gentleman, and a schollard, too, in his way. Have patience. 'Twill come out right in the washing. I'll make it so.

ABRAHAM (*aside*): Oh, I be so sick.

Enter TIM *and the* SHERIFF. *They stand in the doorway.*

SHERIFF: Well, Mrs. Durbeyfield, what am I to do?

JOAN: The sheriffs!

SHERIFF: Well!

JOAN: Oh wait, sir, wait.

SHERIFF: Sorry, Mrs. Durbeyfield, I have my orders. If you can't pay the rent, you must go out at once.

JOAN: O Lord-a-Lord, can't 'ee wait a second? I do expect my daughter back. If she gets the situation she's gone after, we can pay you. My daughter, Tess, it is.

TIM: Oh her, Tess of the D'Urbervilles, is it? I have a bone to pick with that lady. She lost me a good place last year at Farmer Crick's with her airs and fine gentlemen. Tess of the D'Urbervilles, I know her!

JOAN: You shall not speak so. My daughter be a decent married woman.

TIM: Well, she be lucky.

ABRAHAM: I be the head o' the house, and I'll not let you talk that way o' Tess.

TIM: Oh ho, my lad.

SHERIFF: Stop, Tim. We can wait about a bit if she can settle things. When do you expect her?

JOAN: At any moment, sir.

SHERIFF: We'll stroll about outside awhile. Come, Tim.

TIM looks at JOAN and laughs. They go out.

JOAN: Drat them! The rats! Tess o' the D'Urbervilles. It may be Tess o' Alec D'Urbervilles. And then, my men, you will toe the mark, I tell 'ee.

ABRAHAM: Is Mr. Alec coming here again to-day? I do not like him.

JOAN: Aye, and every day.

MARIAN enters at back.

Marian!

MARIAN sits and weeps.

JOAN: What ails 'ee?

MARIAN: I have lost my place.

JOAN: The Lord-a-Lord. And Tess be just getting one. How was it?

MARIAN: As it has been before. I—I took a drop too much and—

JOAN: Shame on 'ee not to know when to stop.

MARIAN: Do you? Did your late husband?
JOAN: I'll not hear one word against him, I tell you.
MARIAN: No—no—Mrs. Durbey—Mrs. D'Urberville. He was a fine man and gentleman. Where be Tess?
JOAN: She be gone to get another situation. She'll be here soon.
MARIAN: I have nowhere to go. May I spend the night with you?

    JOAN *laughs bitterly.*

Well, I'll go then.
JOAN: You do not understand. You can stay as long as we do. We may be put out at once, the sheriff's been here. It all depends on Tess. Lord, and she might be rich!
MARIAN: Has she no word from Mr. Clare?
JOAN: Not one. Devil take such husbands as she gets, I says. And she do write and write, and spend lots of money on postage. 'Tis o' the other I'm thinking, Parson D'Urberville.
MARIAN: A fine parson he! Tess be brave to have nothing to do with him. I don't like him.
JOAN: He be a fine figure of a man, but mighty mean. What's a few pounds to him? He knows we have not food enough to eat, or nothing since Sir John died, and not a penny will he give till he gets Tess. And Tess won't let me ask him. I tell 'ee, he loves her.
MARIAN: He'll never get her.
JOAN: Oh, he may.
MARIAN: Never. I wrote to Mr. Clare to warn him. Aye to Brazil—two months ago—when I seed Mr. Alec's hanging around. He means no good! Parson o' the devil! What made him take to preaching?
JOAN: To repent o' his sins, may be. Or because it was something new and different like.

    The door at back opens and TESS *enters wearily. She sinks back in a chair.*

JOAN: Well—what luck?

    TESS *shakes her head.*

Did 'ee not get it?
TESS: It was just taken.

JOAN: Oh, why didn't 'ee hurry? Why didn't 'ee take the horse?

TESS: Poor Prince is ill. He's all we have to depend on. He must be kept alive, mother.

JOAN: But if you'd got there in time.

TESS: It was twelve miles, mother. I fainted as I did before. I had to sit by the road a long time.

MARIAN: Tess, you can have my place, I've lost it.

TESS: Oh, Marian! Poor Marian!

MARIAN: Send the child there—you might as well have it.

TESS: Thank you, Marian. I've tried so hard. I've lost so many places; I'm so weak. If I don't get this place, I don't know what will happen—something terrible! I'm driven to desperation, Marian. I can't struggle much longer. I have no strength left, no will, no hope. Look at the children's faces and think o' the winter coming. Are you sure you've lost the place?

MARIAN: Yes.

TESS: Liza, take the horse and drive to Farmer Tott's at once, and ask him if I can have Marian's place. Tell him how much I need it and that I'm strong, very strong. I'll be better when I've rested. Hurry, but spare Prince all you can.

ABRAHAM: Can I go too?

TESS: No, dear, you are too ill, and it will be so much more for Prince to carry.

> JOAN *and* LIZA LOO *go to the door,* ABRAHAM *follows them out.*

MARIAN: Have you heard from him?

> TESS *shakes her head.*

MARIAN: Since when?

TESS: Not at all. Not since he left me.

MARIAN: Have you written?

TESS: Many, many times.

MARIAN: I did not think it o' him. He must be without heart. 'Tis cruel.

TESS: He is a very good man.

MARIAN: Then 'twas your fault. What did you do? Tess, you must have been a bad wife to him.

Tess holds up her hands.
Oh, if I'd but had the chance. I've written too—to warn him.

TESS: Warn him!

MARIAN: Of the other.

TESS: Why did you?

MARIAN: He's always here. I know. To save your soul, I suppose. He means no good, and I know women. You can't try them beyond their strength.

TESS: Not me, not me.

MARIAN: Forgive me, Tess. Tess, can I sleep here to-night? Your mother says I may if you are not put out. The sheriff's been here. I'll go up in the loft and lie down, I need it.
Comes back and puts her hand on Tess's shoulder.
I hope you'll get my place.
Goes up the stairs slowly and turns. Sighs.
If I had had her chance, how different things would be.

Tess sits there, looking straight ahead. Joan enters and lays her hand on Tess's shoulder.

JOAN: Be you tired, Tess?

TESS: Yes, mother, very tired.

JOAN: My poor Tess. Don't 'ee fret. Tess?

TESS: Mother?

JOAN: If you don't get that place, then—won't 'ee, Tess?

TESS: What, mother?

JOAN: You know.

TESS: Oh, not that again.

JOAN: He's been here and he's coming back. You'll have to, Tess. The sheriff's outside waiting. You'll have to.

TESS (*shaking her head*): No.

JOAN: Think! We be starving.

TESS: How can you ask me, mother, to be false to the man who honoured me and made me his wife? Mother?
Covers her face with her hands.

JOAN: What has he done for you? Has he not left you? Has he sent you word? Has he answered your letters? Has he sent you money? He has deserted you.

TESS: He has not deserted me. I can get money from his attorney any day if I choose.

JOAN: You could get money and you did not!

TESS: I will not take money from him as long as he is silent. I have written and told him how I shall believe. I'll believe he loves me still. I'll believe. I'll believe. I'll believe, and I'll not touch his money, mother.

JOAN: Oh!

TESS: I'll work my fingers to the bone first.

SHERIFF (*in the doorway*): Well, Mrs. Durbeyfield, what am I to do?

JOAN: Just wait a bit. She did not get that place, but she has another chance.

TIM (*in the doorway*): Oh, she be full of chances.

SHERIFF: Sorry, I can't wait. Tim, turn the table over.

They do so and begin to lay the chairs on it, JOAN *trying to prevent them.* TIM *takes hold of the chair in which* TESS *sits.*

TIM: Come, my lady, stand up.

TESS *rises but does not move.*

I'm even now.

TESS: For what?

TIM: The place you lost me.

TESS: I never harmed you; I did nothing.

TIM: No, but your man, your fine gentleman did.

TESS: He is my husband.

TIM: Ho ho, where is he now? A fine husband, and he knows he's got a fine wife.

JOAN: Tess—Tess—don't 'ee understand what they be doing? They be taking everything away, everything. Tess, wake up. They be taking the clock your father gave me, and the baby's chair. Ask them to wait—to wait.

TESS (*following the men around*): For the love of Heaven wait —just a little—can't you? Wait till the child gets back! She'll drive fast. If I get that place I can pay you soon. Don't put us out. It is so cold, and my brother is so ill. Look at him.

ABRAHAM *is lying on the floor by the fire in a heap.* And there are others upstairs—little ones, asleep. Have you no children?

SHERIFF: I'm sorry, ma'am, but—

TIM (*on the stairs*): We'd better get the beds down.

TESS: Oh have pity. Won't you wait? Don't wake them. Wait. That's all I ask.

TIM: No.

Goes on up.

MARIAN (*voice from above*): You'll not come up here I tell 'ee. Go back.

ALEC *enters C.*

ALEC: What's all this?

SHERIFF: Well, Parson—

ALEC: To the devil with Parson. What are you doing here?

JOAN: They're putting us out, they're putting us out.

SHERIFF: Only obeying orders, sir. They can't pay and must go.

JOAN: They won't wait.

SHERIFF: I waited all I could.

ALEC: Well, wait a little longer. Oh, I'll pay you for your time, and don't call me Parson unless you want to be kicked. Do you hear?

SHERIFF: Very well, sir, I'll wait five minutes.

ALEC: Understand, I'm no parson.

SHERIFF: You don't talk much like one.

ALEC (*laughing*): No, damn you! Now take your ugly faces elsewhere.

The men exit grinning.

ALEC (*to* JOAN): I'll settle with them. You shan't go.

JOAN: Oh thank you, thank you.

ALEC: Leave me with Tess.

JOAN *goes out R.* ALEC *approaches* TESS.

ABRAHAM (*aside sullenly, half rising*): I don't like that man. I hate him!

ALEC: Tess—Tess—don't you hear me?

TESS: I hear you.

ALEC: You have avoided me—kept away from me. Now you must listen.

TESS: Go on.

ALEC: Can't you thank me, Tess, for the little favour I just did?

TESS: I thank you.

She turns away.

ALEC: Is that all?

TESS: I thank you.

ALEC: Call me Alec.

She is silent.

You know why I am here.

TESS: I know why you are always here.

ALEC: Perhaps, Tess, you doubt the sincerity of my motive.

TESS: Are you here to save my soul?

ALEC (*laughing*): Go on, sneer at me. You never did believe in my sincerity.

TESS: How could I, knowing you so well? How could I believe in such a change—a reprobate become a leader of the church? What mortal thing could bring that change about?

ALEC: It was a man, a simple clergyman whose parting words sank into my soul, a man at whom I had scoffed and scorned. I was weary of the world and women after you left me. I thought over what he said. I took his advice. I tried it. It succeeded. He showed me a way to work, to be occupied, to do good to others, to be surrounded by the poor unthinking, to hold them in my hand and sway them. It was fine excitement, an exaltation, a dizziness of joy, while it lasted. To move and make the congregation weep and worship me. I seemed to have the spirit. I was sincere. I believed in my sincerity till I met you again.

TESS: Don't say that.

ALEC: It's true. You, a good woman, did me, a bad man, harm. The day you stood at the door of the barn listening to my sermon you stole my spirit from me. Did you not see how all my fire went out the instant that I saw your face?

TESS: No, no.

ALEC: Yes. I was a natural man again, and I was troubled, and I came to you. I came and begged you to pray for me. You only gave a bitter laugh.

TESS: I could not pray for you. I would not. I did not believe that the great power who made the world would alter his plans on my account.

ALEC: I came, still believing. I felt of all the persons in the world whom it was my duty and desire to save, you were that one, the woman I had wronged. You looked at me and said, "And have you saved yourself?"

TESS: And had you?

ALEC: I thought so till you came. But you were right. I had not. I found I did not want to. You made me feel that all my fervour was a physical excitement. When I touched your hand, I became a man again. And to you, my Tess, I owe my probable damnation.

TESS: No, no!

ALEC: And I'll be ready for it when it comes. But now I have my life to lead, the one I was fitted for. You fled from me, but still I follow you. You are the only woman in the world that ever suited, contented, satisfied me. I liked you first. I love you now; you have developed so. I did not despise you, as I did the rest, because you left me. And now that love has grown and grown till it fills all my life, and there is nothing in life for me but you—you. Nothing for me but you.

TESS: Oh, don't—don't. Go back to your church. Go back to it. Don't say I took you from it, or it from you. I have done harm enough already. Have I not kept from you? Did I not repulse you? Go back and try to have faith again.

JOAN *enters; stands at back of stage.*

ALEC: Never. I've chucked it all for you. I told them so when they came and begged me to rejoin them. You dear damned witch of Babylon, when I see that mouth, a thousand souls are nothing to me, and you are a temptress, say what you will! And my religion is you—you. Be mine, Tess, as you were.

TESS: You know what I have answered you before.

ALEC: You need me now, more and more. Give up this useless struggle against fate, against poverty and despair. You shall have everything a woman can ask for. Answer, "Yes."

JOAN (*who has been listening, comes forward*): Do, Tess, do. He loves you. There's a man for you as will stick by you.

TESS (*sternly*): Mother.

JOAN: Think o' me. Think o' me and the children. The boy there be so ill he cannot lift his head. Do it for them and for yourself.

TESS (*piteously*): I will work for you. Let me work for you.

JOAN: You need not. 'Tis not right. You are not strong now. No matter what place you get, you cannot keep it.

TESS: I shall try.

JOAN: He has a claim on you. He's more your husband than the other.

TESS (*in a low tone*): I love the other.

ALEC: You still think of that man, that whelp who deserted and despises you? What kind of a—

TESS: I swore to honour and obey him and I will. I will not doubt him. I will believe he loves me until he tells me not, and I'll wait. I'll wait. I'll wait.

JOAN: He'll never come back.

ALEC (*walking away, aside*): I'd wring his damned neck if he did.

JOAN: He does despise you. Are we to be put out into the cold because you won't take his money or this one's?

ALEC: They shall have all they need. Liza shall go to school and Abraham too.

ABRAHAM: I don't want to go to school. I want food, food. Mother, I'm starving.

TESS: I will wait.

ALEC: Tess, I—came to tell you something. Be prepared, he'll never come back, he's dead.

TESS (*after a pause*): He's not dead. He's not dead. Something would have told me.

ALEC: He is. I wrote. To-day I got my answer from Brazil. He died two months ago of yellow fever at Caracas.

TESS *puts her hand to her head.*
ALEC: Do you want to see the letter?
TESS (*in a strange voice*): I can't believe it—Angel dead—I—can people go out of our lives like that without our knowing it? Can they? Dead!
ALEC: Yes. Now, Tess, you will?
    ABRAHAM *gives a sharp cry of pain and starts to his feet and staggers forward and falls near* TESS, *face down.* TESS *looks at him, then seems to wake.*
SHERIFF (*at the door*): I can't wait all day.

    LIZA LOO *pushes herself past him and enters running.*

LIZA: Oh, Prince be dead, Prince be dead.
TESS (*wearily*): And the place, the place?
LIZA: It be just filled, he said.
SHERIFF: Tim, take the things.
    ALEC *stops them with a gesture.*
ALEC: Tess dear?
TESS (*in the same voice*): I don't care what happens. Take me.

    CURTAIN

ACT IV

SCENE I

A handsome sitting-room. A door L. of C., a toilet table with mirror, and a screen to the right of that. A wide window at left, through which the sun streams. A fireplace L., a door at right of breakfast table. R. of C. up stage a couch in front of the fireplace. The whole tone of the place is rich and comfortable.

    MARIAN, *dressed like a parlour-maid, enters C. with a tray. She sets it on the table softly, listens in the direction of the door at right, then goes to the mantel, takes a calendar, and sitting on the couch counts the weeks on it.*

MARIAN: Three months. That's four weeks over time, yet I won't believe he's dead. I won't. I think Tess would rather have him so, but if Mr. Clare had got my note and were alive, he'd have come back at any cost, even if he hates her, because he is her husband, and he would not have this. I made my letter plain and strong.

Recites from memory.

"Honoured Sir: Look to your wife. She is sore put to by an enemy in the shape of a friend. There is near her one who should be put aside. A woman should not be tried beyond her strength, and continual dropping will wear away a diamond—or a stone. A Well-Wisher." 'Tis plain enough. It reached there two months ago, and yet if—Oh, I am sure Mr. Clare is alive. I'd not have believed him dead till I saw him so.

> *There is noise at right.* Marian *starts, then goes towards the door at right hastily, as if to knock. It opens and* Tess *comes out. She wears a beautiful white wrapper.*

Marian (*stammering*): Breakfast, Tess, Mrs. D'Urberville, I should say.

Tess: Call me Tess, Marian. I never forget how long we worked side by side.

Marian: Aye, and suffered.

Tess (*sitting at the table*): It's the only name I have now.

Marian: I'm not so sure of that, Tess. I don't believe he's dead. Did you see that note from the Brazils? No. I won't believe in it. That man in there lies. Did you ever catch him at it?

Tess: Don't.

Marian: I have. I've heard him tell you lots.

Tess: Stop. Can't you see? Can't you see I want to think him dead? I can't believe, yet I must. I will. I'd rather far he was, than have him living on, unforgiving. And if he were, then this, all this would kill me.

Marian: What did you do that he could not forgive?

Tess: You know, now. It was the past.

Marian: Then why did you marry him? You had told him?

Tess: I thought so.

Marian: Thought so?

Tess: He did not get the note. I told him after—oh don't. Let me forget.

Marian: There's lies, and lies, somewhere.

TESS: If I were happy in my shame, there might be some excuse for your reproaches. Never speak of him again. Understand? I will not have it. I can't stand it. Every word is a stab. You have no right, for whatever I may be, I've been a friend to you, and because I am fallen myself, I have tried to save you from your demon—drink, and took you with me, from your poverty and misery. Now stop it—stop it I say. I have enough to bear without it. (*Hastily.*) Pour me some tea.

MARIAN: Will he want some?

TESS: No.

MARIAN: I—I love him still, that's why I spoke. Forgive me, Tess.

> ALEC *enters C. He is in evening dress and is a trifle drunk. He throws his hat and overcoat on the floor behind the screen.*

ALEC: Oh, you're up? Tea.
> *Sits at table.*

TESS (*pours it out*): There it is.

ALEC: Cream. Oh, its awful stuff!
> *Puts the cup down with a bang.* TESS *rises and wipes the spilled tea with her napkin.*

ALEC: Oh, let it alone, I pay for it.
> *To* MARIAN.

What are you standing staring at?

TESS: Go, Marian.

ALEC: No, wait. Where are the letters? Get them, Tess.
> *She does so and hands them to him.*

Don't look so damned resigned and patient.

TESS: I have to be.

ALEC: Oh, you're mighty sweet with your calm nerves. You've slept. I haven't. Talk! Can't you? What's the matter with her, Marian? Is she dumb? You've changed since you went up in the world.

TESS: I don't consider that I have gone up in the world.

ALEC: You have enough to eat, and you're growing fat on it, and that family of yours, too.

TESS: Leave us please, Marian.

MARIAN *goes out C.*

Whatever ugly thing you have to say, say it only to me.

ALEC: Ugly? To say you've gone up in the world?

TESS: I have gone down in the world, and you know it. I am infinitely more degraded now, than I was, when I first left you. Be careful, Alec. Be careful what you say or I shall strike you, as I did before. I'm not the patient woman that I was when I was hungry. I was patient then, because I had something to be patient for. I have not now. I have nothing but the day—each day—as it comes and goes, and I'll not stand much more.

ALEC: You're jealous, I suppose, because I didn't come home last night. I was very considerate. I only did it, because you say you don't like to see me drunk.

TESS: It makes little difference.

ALEC: Yes, so long as you get your pay.

TESS: That is all. All I expect. That was the only reason why I came to you. You know it. When a woman sells herself she deserves only her pay.

ALEC: But when a man buys a woman he expects a smile sometimes. You're disgustingly ungrateful. Look at the pretty things you have.

TESS: I hate them.

ALEC: And all I've done for those brother and sister brats of yours.

TESS: If you had given freely, it would have been a noble act of charity. As it is, it is part of the price. Say no more of it.

ALEC: Well, you get it, and that good old mother of yours, a fine specimen of virtue, helps quick to spend it.

TESS (*rising*): You may say what you please of me—but respect my mother at least, that quality you took from me. (*Sits again.*) Are you going to eat breakfast?

ALEC: No, I'm going to bed.

TESS: Then I'll ring to have it taken away.

Goes to left and rings.

ALEC (*throwing money at her feet*): There's all my leavings.

TESS (*quietly*): Thank you.

MRS. FISKE
Courtesy of Harvard Theatre Collection

He goes out and bangs the door.

TESS (*sitting on the couch*): How long can I stand this? (*Pointing to the money.*) For that.

> *She picks it up as if it sickened her and puts it in an envelope and directs it.*

Mrs. Joan Durbeyfield, Marlott, Wessex County. Mother, you may not have many more of these.

ALEC (*voice from the next room*): Come and close this window; it's beastly chilly here.

TESS: I am coming.

> *She goes out R. and closes the door after her.* ANGEL CLARE *enters C. He looks round in bewilderment. He has changed greatly and looks very thin and ill.* MARIAN *comes to the door behind him which he has left open. She starts.*

MARIAN (*aside in a hoarse whisper*): I knew he was not dead.

> TESS *comes in. She closes the door behind her.* MARIAN, *who has come a step forward, retreats.*

MARIAN: God! What's going to happen!

> *She goes out and closes the door.* TESS *turns and comes forward a step. She sees* CLARE, *and stands like one frozen. He holds out his arms. She does not move. They fall to his side. She stands in horror near the door. He goes to her. She seems to be trying to cover up all that is back of her.*

CLARE (*heartbrokenly*): Tess, can't you forgive me for going away? Can't you? Can't you come back to me? I forgave you long ago. I have been ill—very ill—for months.

TESS: It is too late.

CLARE: Oh, don't say that. I was wrong, I know. I was cruel to judge you so harshly. It was my great misery that drove me from you. I did not see you as you were, a good, pure woman. But I have learned—I understand now, and I am come to ask you to forgive me. I love you and we will never part.

TESS: Too late. Too late. Don't come near me, Angel! No, you must not. Keep away.

CLARE: Is your love dead? Have I killed it, or is it because I am such a wreck? You cannot be so fickle—my mother and my father will welcome you.

TESS (*almost shrieks*): But I say—I say it is too late. Don't you know all? Don't you know it? You must. How did you come here if you did not know it?

CLARE: I received a strange note. When I arrived, I searched for you everywhere. I went to your mother who told me at last you were at Sandbourne. I did not expect to find you in a town.

Looks round.

Like this. I inquired here and found you.

TESS: Oh, I waited and waited, but you did not come. I wrote and wrote, and you did not come. Still I believed. I trusted—I waited till he lied—he lied to me—he said he knew—he said that you were dead.

CLARE: He? I do not understand.

TESS: I am with him. Alec. He is there. He gave me these—all these, and helped us. I loved you all along. I hate him because he lied. He said that you were dead, and you are not. Now go—go.

CLARE (*in a half-whisper*): That man—again—between us.

TESS (*in a whisper*): Go—will you go?

> *He turns and goes blindly from the room.* TESS *sinks upon her knees, clasps her arms round her head, rocks back and forth, and moans.*

ALEC (*voice from the next room*): What's the matter? Who's with you?

TESS (*rising*): I hate him because I believed.

She opens the door a little.

Alec, he has returned.

ALEC (*from next room*): Who has?

TESS: The man you said was dead. My husband.

ALEC (*roaring with laughter*): Ha, ha, ha, ha. A little late, isn't he?

TESS clinches her fists.

Well, I'm your husband now; I foot the bills. Give him my love. Ha, ha! The cuckold!

Tess hastily closes the door and walks madly up and down as if looking for something. She walks into a table, tries to put it aside, sees the carving knife, and becomes as rigid as a statue.

Tess (*repeating* Clare's *words*): That man—again—between us.

The idea grows in her face. She takes the knife slowly, hides it in the folds of her dress, goes to the door softly, opens it, and goes in. There is a silence, then a strange cry, then more, but muffled as if with a pillow. Tess *comes out flying. She closes the door and stands there listening. She opens it and looks in. All is still. She goes madly about the room like a suffering animal trying to find something, then tries to think. She finds a stain on the lace of her gown, tears it off carefully, but doesn't know what to do with it. She finally drops it behind the toilet table. She fixes her hair in the glass, begins to take off her wrapper, puts it on again, pins up the train of the skirt, takes a long cloak with a cape from behind the screen, puts it on, also her hat. All with great deliberation.*

My gloves!

She goes out R., returns with them, holding up her skirt. She locks the door, crosses to the mantel, and hides the key in a vase, then turns to go out. Clare *stands in the doorway.*

Clare: I cannot leave you, Tess, no matter what has happened.
She signals him to be silent.

Tess: I have done it. I don't know how, but I owed it to you. I knew I should some day, when I struck him with my glove. I hated him. He called you a vile name. I have killed him—Alec. Don't you understand? I have killed him.

She takes his hand trustingly, and they go softly out.

Curtain

Scene II

The Heathen Temple at Stonehenge. Great pillars rise to the sky. To the right far below through them is seen a vast plain. It is not yet dawn.

TESS *and* CLARE *enter through the vines at left.*

TESS: I am so tired, Angel. Do you think they are following us?

CLARE: No, no, my darling, there's no one following us, don't think of that.

But he looks round.

TESS: Let us rest here.

CLARE: Let us move on. We shall find better shelter.

TESS: No, no, here we are with nature. Let us stay. The whole of the world outside is pain. Here it is rest.

CLARE: But this place can be seen for miles around when the sun rises.

TESS: It will be just as well, Angel. I care not now. I have been happy—very happy. Let us wait for them—I am ready. I am content. I have had my share of happiness these last, few days we have spent together, and yet I must be wicked, Angel, to be happy now. How can I? Yet I am. How did I do that? How could I—I—who never harmed a fly.

CLARE: Don't think of that. You've lost your reason, Tess. 'Tis often so. It will come back again. Forget it.

TESS: It's true what I told you. I cannot put it from me. It does not trouble me, yet I want to die. 'Tis only a few days, anyway. What must come, must. I want to die because I could not bear to live and know that you despise me.

CLARE: I never could do that.

TESS: But others will and you would see it. I don't wish to outlive by one second your present love for me. It cannot last.

CLARE: Always.

TESS: Ah!

CLARE: I cannot help but love you.

TESS: Promise to look after Abraham and the rest.

CLARE: I will.

TESS: See that Liza grows up—good.

CLARE: I shall.
TESS: Thanks, love, now let me sleep.
CLARE: Try—try to move on.
TESS: I am so tired—so tired. Let me sleep here. Was this an altar?
CLARE: Yes.
TESS: Did they, the ancients, sacrifice to God here?
CLARE: No, dear.
TESS: To whom?
CLARE: To the sun, I think.
TESS: Ah!

With a strange smile.

The sun will be up soon. I am so sleepy.

He fixes her cloak on the slab and makes a pillow. She lies down; he covers her with his coat and sits on the slab near her head.

Give me your hand. Kiss me once again, my love. I am so happy. Remember!

She drops asleep. He does not stir. The sky grows faintly pink. CLARE *looks up. There is a slight crackling of branches at right.*

CLARE: They are coming. What she said was true.

Five or six men enter at back silently. CLARE *holds up his hand.*

CLARE: Do not wake her.

They silently take off their hats and stand round. They have an air of absolute respect. Sky grows redder. TESS *moves.*

TESS: Angel dear.
CLARE: Yes.
TESS: The sun has come.

She moves, getting near him.

I love you.

She realizes that they are not alone. She does not look round, she shows no fear. She puts her arms around his neck and kisses him, then makes a move as if to rise to go.

CURTAIN

III. HARDY'S LONDON VERSION (1925)

TESS
OF THE D'URBERVILLES

A Tragedy
in Four Acts and an After-Scene

PERSONS REPRESENTED

ANGEL CLARE, *aged* 29
ALEC D'URBERVILLE, *aged* 28
JOHN DURBEYFIELD, *aged* 50
*a*MR. TRINGHAM, *an antiquary, aged* 65*b*
FELIX CLARE, *aged* 30
JONATHAN KAIL, *aged* 60
LABOURER, *aged* 75
*a*BOY, *aged* 12*b*

TESS, *aged* 18
JOAN DURBEYFIELD, *aged* 40
LIZA-LU, *aged* 12
SARAH, *a club girl, aged* 16
MARIAN, *a dairymaid, aged* 22
IZZ, *a dairymaid, aged* 20
LABOURER'S WIFE, *aged* 70
LANDLADY *of lodging-house, aged* 50
HER MAIDSERVANT, *aged* 20

*a*OTHER CLUB GIRLS; TWO FIDDLERS;*b* MILKMAIDS AND MEN; A MANSERVANT; RUSTICS; &C.

*a-b*Absent from Dorchester text.

---

*If desired the following modification may be adopted:

Several village girls in white, members of the Girls' Benefit Club, cross singing: "May Colvine & False Sir John."

  Lie there, lie there, thou false-hearted man,
   Lie there instead of me:
  For six pretty maidens thou hast a-drowned here,
   But the seventh hath drowned thee! . . .
  Then out the wily parrot spake
   Unto fair May Colvine,
  "What have ye done wi' False Sir John
   That you went with at e'en?" . . .
  "Oh hold your tongue, my pretty par-rot,
   Lay not the blame on me;
  And your cage shall be made of the glittering gold,
   With a door of the white ivor-ry."

Enter old MR. TRINGHAM, *an antiquarian. They curtsey to him and pass off. Enter* JOHN DURBEYFIELD *carrying a basket. He is met by* MR. TRINGHAM.

  SCENE I (*as opposite*)

FORESHOW[a]

Sliding Flats

A highway near Marlott Village. In the background stretches the beautiful Vale of Blackmoor.

TIME: *evening.* SEASON: *summer.*

*Enter JOHN DURBEYFIELD carrying a basket. He is met by old MR. TRINGHAM, an antiquarian.

SCENE I. JOHN DURBEYFIELD, MR. TRINGHAM

JOHN: Good night to ye.

MR. T.: Good night, Sir John.

JOHN (*turning*): Now, Mr. Tringham, begging your pardon as a great antiquarian, we met last market-day on this road, and I said good night, and you made reply, "Good night, Sir John," as now.

MR. T.: I did.

JOHN: And once before that—near a month ago.

MR. T.: I may have.

JOHN: Then what might your meaning be in calling me Sir John three different times, when I be only plain Jack Durbeyfield, the haggler?

MR. T.: It was my whim, on account of a discovery I made some little time ago, when I was hunting up pedigrees for the new county history. Don't you really know, Durbeyfield, that you are the lineal representative of the ancient and knightly family of D'Urberville, who derive their descent from Sir Pagan D'Urberville, that renowned knight who came from Normandy with William the Conqueror?

JOHN: Never heard it before, sir.

MR. T.: Well, it's true. Throw up your chin a moment, that I may catch the profile of your face better. Yes, that's the D'Urberville nose and chin—a little debased. Your ancestor was one of the

---

[a]Foreshow is absent from the Dorchester text.
*See variation on opposite page.

twelve knights who assisted the lord of Estremavilla in Normandy in his conquest of Glamorganshire. . . . You declined a little in Oliver Cromwell's time, but in Charles the Second's reign you were made Knights of the Royal Oak for your loyalty. Aye, there have been generations of Sir Johns among you, and if knighthood were hereditary, like a baronetcy, as it practically was in the old times, you would be Sir John now.

JOHN (*agape*): You don't say so!

MR. T.: In short, there's hardly another such family in England.

JOHN: Daze my old eyes, and here have I been knocking about year after year from pillar to post as if I were no more than the commonest feller in the parish! And how long has this news about me been known?

MR. T.: It had quite died out of knowledge till I rediscovered it.

JOHN: And where do we raise our smoke now? I mean, where do we D'Urbervilles live?

MR. T.: You don't live anywhere. You are extinct as a county family.

JOHN: That's bad.

MR. T.: Yes, what the mendacious family chronicles call extinct in the male line, which means, gone under.

JOHN: Then where do we lie?

MR. T.: At Kingsbere; rows and rows of you in your vaults under the church there, with your effigies under Purbeck-marble canopies.

JOHN: And shall we ever come into our own again?

MR. T.: That I can't tell.

JOHN: And what had I better do about it, sir?

MR. T.: Oh, nothing, nothing, except chasten yourself with the thought of how the mighty are fallen. Good night.

MR. TRINGHAM *goes*.

JOHN DURBEYFIELD *sits down on the bank, depositing his basket beside him. A* BOY *enters.*

SCENE II. JOHN DURBEYFIELD, BOY

JOHN: Boy, take up that basket. I want you to go on an errand for me.

Boy: Who be you, John Durbeyfield, to order me about, and call me "boy"? You know my name as well as I know yours.

John: Do you, do you! That's the secret. Well, I don't mind telling you that I'm found to be one of the noblest race in England. (*Stretches himself out.*) Sir John D'Urberville—that's what I am. Dost know of such a place, lad, as Kingsbere? Well, under the church of that city—

Boy: 'Tisn't a city—'tis a little one-eyed blinking place.

John: Never you mind the place, boy; that's not the question before us. Under Kingsbere church my ancestors lie—hundreds of 'em—in lead coffins weighing tons and tons. Now take up that basket, and go on to my house and tell my wife to put away that washing, because she needn't finish it. Here's for your labour, lad. (*Hands shilling.*)

Boy (*with alacrity*): Yes, Sir John. Anything else I can do for you, Sir John?

John: Nothing else now.

Boy *goes*.

Enter Joan Durbeyfield.

Scene III. John *and* Joan Durbeyfield

Joan: How's this, Jacky, that you haven't reached home? I've come to meet you.

John: Well, this is what's happened. We've been found to be the greatest gentlefolk in the whole county—reaching back to long before Oliver Grumble's time, to the days of the Pagan Turks, our real name being not Durbeyfield, but D'Urberville—

Joan: How wonderful!

John: 'Tis wonderful. But we've gone under entirely.

Joan: What's the good, then? But we can't all have gone under! Why, there's a rich family of the name out beyond Trantridge. Can't we claim kin with them?

John: I know nothing about a rich family.

Joan: You never know anything! And, when I think of it, 'tis an old lady and her son. We might send Tess, she being the brightest side of us. They'd be sure to take notice of her if we dress her up in her Sunday clothes. And who knows what may come of it?

JOHN: I can't say, I can't say. And I don't quite—like my child going away from home. As the head of the family the rest ought to come to me.

JOAN: But do let her go, Jacky! This young gent, her cousin, that we hear of, will perhaps marry her, and make a lady of her, and then she'll be what her forefathers were.

JOHN: Well, he certainly would improve his blood by linking on to the old line, if he belongs to a younger branch of us. And she can tell him that, being sunk quite from our former grandeur, I'll sell him the title—yes, sell it—and at no unreasonable figure.

JOAN: Not for less than a thousand pound!

JOHN: Yes, a thousand pound. Well, I'll take less when I come to think of it. He'll adorn it better than a poor rickety fellow like me. She can tell him he may have it for a hundred. But I won't stand upon trifles,—he shall have it for fifty pound. That's the lowest. Dammy, family honour is family honour, and I won't take a penny less!

JOAN: Well, anyhow, she shall go, and ought to make her way with her cousin, if she plays her trump card aright.

JOHN: Her trump card—her D'Urberville blood, you mean?

JOAN: No, stupid. Her face, as 'twas mine.

CURTAIN

END OF THE FORESHOW

*a*ACT I

Marlott Village

bOn the right is the exterior of the Durbeyfield's cottage, with the open shed attached, forming entrance to the dwellingc. Within

---

*a*The Dorchester text begins at this point.

*b*Dorchester text begins: SCENE. In the Dorchester text this word occurs before the descriptive stage direction for each act. For the rest, all numbered scene headings, with their lists of characters on the stage, are omitted in the Dorchester text. These omissions are not further noticed below.

*c*cottage

the shed are chairs, a table, etc. A green lawn in the centre towards the back. A highway on the left runs down to the front ᵈ *and is screened from the cottage and green by a tall hedge.*

SEASON: *autumn.*

JOAN DURBEYFIELD *and* SARAH *with several other village girls in white, members of the Girls' Benefit Club, are standing outside the cottage under the shed.* JOAN's *husband,* JOHN, *is sitting close by. Two fiddlers are near.*

SCENE I. JOAN, JOHN DURBEYFIELD, SARAH : *other club girls at back.*

SARAH: Had Tess's going away last June anything to do with your husband finding out that he was descended from the old ancient family of D'Urberville?

JOAN: Why, yes! As soon as Mr.ᵉ Tringham, the antiqueerian, told us that my husband is Sir John D'Urberville by rights, I thought of the rich lady and her son of that name, living at Trantridge; and I packed off Tess to claim kin—as of course he is a sort of cousin of hers. There she's been ever since—made much of, I believe.

SARAH: What has she been doing there all the time?

JOAN: Managing the chicken farm.

SARAH: That's not *much*, considering you are people of blood, and kin to the lady.

JOHN: That's what I da say. Surely they ought to honour us more, now I've discovered I'm a man of title.

JOAN: Nonsense.ᶠ 'Tis only to occupy her. Mr. Alec D'Urberville, the old lady's son, is a very handsome gentleman, and 'tis my belief our relations to 'em mid be closer some day. (*Nods knowingly.*) That he's fond of Tess I know.

JOHN: I don't like my daughter being there to work. We be the oldest branch of the family, and they ought to come to us, particularly if the young gent wants to marry her.

JOAN: True, Sir John. Well, now she's coming home for her holiday we shall hear all particulars. I tried her luck in the fortune-telling book, and it brought out *marriage*.

ᵈDorchester text adds: from the extreme back.
ᵉPa'son
ᶠPooh.

SARAH: Did it though!

JOAN: You should have seen how pretty Tess looked when she went away. Why, her skin is as sumple as a duchess's. She'd look well in the carriage beside Mr. Alec. And how she will take the shine out o' the folk here when she becomes his wife. . . . But what time is it? (*She puts her head inside window to look at the clock.*) She may be here before you've had another dance, if the carrier is up to his time.

> FIDDLES. *The* GIRLS *dance* g*at back*h *without male partners.*

> TESS *enters by the highway on*i *left front, in a pretty country frock and hat. She carries a bundle and sits down beside the hedge which screens her from the girls, resting with her head on her hand. The* DANCERS *recede and music softens.* JOHN *and* JOAN DURBEYFIELD *enter their dwelling.*

SCENE II. TESS *alone*

TESS (*looking around*): This is home! Oh how shall I tell 'em—how shall I?

> *She again rests her head on her hand.*

> ALEC D'URBERVILLE *enters by the same*a *highway, breathless and in riding costume.* TESS *looks up and starts. During the following duologue the* GIRLS *try dancing figures in dumb-show at back, without music.*

SCENE III. TESS, ALEC : GIRLS *at back*

ALEC: Why did you slip away by stealth like this? I only discovered by accident to-day that you were gone, and I have been riding like the very devil to overtake you. How unnecessary it has been for you to toil home like this! Do have a little sense, and come

---
g-hAbsent from Dorchester text.
ifrom
aAbsent from Dorchester text.

MRS. GERTRUDE BUGLER AS *TESS*
Photograph by W. H. Cumming, Dorchester

back!

TESS (*emphatically*): I shan't come back.

ALEC: I thought you wouldn't—I said so. It's like you. (*He lights cigar,* TESS *sighs.*) What are you so gloomy about?

TESS: I was thinking I was born here, and how different it was when I went away!

ALEC: Well, we must all be born somewhere.

TESS: I wish I had never been born—here or anywhere else!

ALEC: Pooh! Well, if you didn't wish to come to our house, why did you come?—not for love of me, I'll swear.

TESS[a]: 'Tis quite true. If I had gone for the love of you, if I had ever sincerely loved 'ee, if I loved you still, I should not so loathe and hate myself for my weakness as I do now. My eyes were dazzled by you for[b] a little while: that was all. (ALEC *shrugs shoulders.*) I didn't understand what you meant till it was too late.

ALEC: That's what every woman says.

TESS: How can you dare to use such words? My God, I could knock you down! . . . Did it never strike your mind that what every woman says some woman may feel?

ALEC (*laughing*): Fie, dear! That's temper! But I'm sorry to wound you. I did wrongly—I admit it. . . . Only you needn't be so everlastingly flinging it in my face. I am ready to pay to the uttermost farthing. You know you need not work in the fields or the dairies again. You know you may clothe yourself with the best, if you'll come back, instead of in the simple way you have lately affected, as if you couldn't get a ribbon more than you earn.

TESS (*her voice shaken*): I have said I will not take anything more from you, and I will not. I cannot! I *should* be your creature to go on doing that, and I won't!

ALEC: One would think you were a princess from your manner, in addition to a true and original D'Urberville, which I am not, ha-ha! Fancy your not knowing that one may assume any old name one pleases. (*He walks to and fro with his hands in his pockets.*) Well, Tess dear, I can say no more. I was born bad, and I have lived bad, and I shall die bad, in all probability. But upon

[a]Dorchester text adds: (*recovering emphasis*).
[b]Absent from Dorchester text.

my lost soul, I won't be bad towards you again, Tess. And if certain circumstances should arise, which may put you in difficulties, send me one line and you shall have what you require. I may not be at Trantridge—I am going to London for a time. But all letters will be forwarded.

 TESS *withdraws coldly, and takes up her bundle to depart.*
You are not going away like that, dear? Come! (*Throws cigar away and bends to her face.*)

 TESS (*indifferently*): If you wish. See how you've mastered me! (*Lifts her cheek and he kisses her.*)

 ALEC: Now the other side for old acquaintance' sake! (*Kissing her again.*) You don't give me your mouth*c* and kiss me back. You never willingly do that. You'll never love me now, I fear.

 TESS: Ah—true! I have never really loved you, and I think I never can. Perhaps of all things, a lie on that point would do me the most good now, for I may have the best of reasons for getting you to stick to me. But I have honour enough left not to tell that lie!

 ALEC (*after a pause*): Well, you are absurdly melancholy, Tess. As you know, I have no reason for flattering you *now*: but I can say plainly that you can hold your own for beauty against any woman of these parts, gentle or simple. If you are wise, you will go into the world and show it before it fades. . . . And yet, Tess, will you come back to me? Upon my sóul, I don't like to let you go like this!

 TESS: *d*Never!*e* I made up my mind as soon as I saw—what I ought to have seen sooner: and I won't come.

 ALEC: Then good-bye, my three months' cousin. Good-bye! Perhaps some day you'll be glad to come back to me.

   ALEC *retreats and disappears.*

 TESS *advances from the highway and comes round to the cottage door. The* CLUB GIRLS *at back see her and crowd around her.*

*c*lips
*d-e*Never, never!

SCENE IV. TESS, CLUB GIRLS

GIRLS: She's come! She's come!
TESS: Yes. I've come.
SARAH: What a conquest you've made, dear. We were just talking about it. I wish I had a rich cousin to fall in love with me! Is he fair?
ANOTHER GIRL: No. He's dark, I've heard.
TESS: Oh, he's not really my cousin—only of the same name. And I don't know that he's in love with me—please don't say it!
GIRLS (*severally*): She's shy!—she's shy! He's going to marry her, only she won't own it! ... (TESS *shakes her head sadly*.) Oh yes, he is—we know what we know. ... And he's been such a splendid heart-breaker—so we've heard. My—what a conquest!
    TESS, *distracted, turns away.*

ªEnter LIZA-LU.

LIZA-LU: Mother, mother, TESS has come home! (TESS *kisses her.*)
TESS: Dear Liza-Lu! Yes, I'm back.*ᵇ*
GIRLS: How pretty she is! And how that best hat and frock do set her off! I believe that they cost an immense deal and that they are a gift from him.

    JOAN *enters from the cottage.*

SCENE V. TESS, JOAN, GIRLS : *then* JOHN DURBEYFIELD

JOAN (*kissing* TESS): My dear Tess! Why didn't you come in? I didn't know you were here. So you've paid us a visit! How be ye? I'll call your father. John!

    Enter JOHN DURBEYFIELD *from cottage. Welcomes her.*

JOAN (*aside to* TESS): Have you come home to be married?
TESS: No, I've not come home for that, mother.
JOAN: Only for a holiday?
―――――
*ª-ᵇ*Absent from Dorchester text.

TESS: Only for a—holiday; a long holiday!

JOAN: What, isn't your handsome cousin going to do the handsome thing?

TESS: How could you think he was my cousin, mother? He's not my cousin—no relation at all. They are not real D'Urbervilles—they only took the same name when they had made their money.

JOAN: Oh! that's news to me. (*She turns to* JOHN.) Hear that, Sir John?

JOHN: Ah—these upstarts! Heaving out we old nobles o' the land!

JOAN: Well—is he going to marry 'ee?

TESS (*firmly*): No—he is not.

SARAH (*to* JOAN): She won't tell. She's as close as wax. I expect they mean to do it privately.

JOAN: I can't say. It depends upon her entirely, I reckon.

JOHN: You mean, she being of the old stock has more reason to be ashamed of such an alliance than he.

JOAN: Don't 'ee be so stupid, Sir John. Your brains don't reach the level of your blood, that I must say.

JOHN *turns to go indoors.*

GIRLS: But you'll come and have a dance with us, Tess?

TESS: No, thank you, dears. I'd rather not this evening.

JOAN: Nonsense, Tess. Just to keep up your return! If you won't, I will. Here, Sir John—come along. Fiddlers, "Haste to the Wedding." Some o' you chaps join in. What's a dance without men!

> *Tune "Haste to the Wedding."* SHE *drags out* JOHN DURBEYFIELD *and makes him dance as her partner in the figure of "Haste to the Wedding"—which he does unwillingly, using his stick to support himself as he dances.* RUSTICS, *including* SHEPHERD *with his crook, come forward and join in.*

JOAN (*as she dances*): I feel for all the world as if I was but just married to-day! (*Dance ceases.*) She seems tired. You must be, Tess. And you must want some supper. (*To* GIRLS.) You must excuse her.

GIRLS *retreat to back of stage and exeunt.* JOHN DURBEYFIELD *goes into the cottage.*

SCENE VI. JOAN, TESS

JOAN: But, Tess—bain't you really going to marry him?

TESS: It is as I say—there is no thought of marriage between us.

JOAN: But he's fond of 'ee. So it must be your own fault. . . . (*Pause—she regards* TESS *closely, up and down.*) Come—you've not told me all. What's the matter?

TESS *puts her face upon her mother's neck and whispers something.*

JOAN (*dumbfounded*): Tess, Tess,—can it be! . . . And yet th'st not got him to marry thee. Any woman would have done it, except you!

TESS: Perhaps any woman would, except me.

JOAN: It would have been something like a story to come back with if you had. After all the talk about you and him which have reached us here who would have expected it to end like this! (*Wipes eyes with apron.*) Why didn't 'ee think of doing some good for your family, instead of getting into a mess like this? See how I've got to teave and slave, and your poor father with his heart clogged like a dripping-pan. I *did* hope for something to come out o' this. To see what a pretty pair you and the young gentleman made*a*. See what things he's given us—all, as we thought, because we were his kin. But if he's not, it must have been done because of his love for you. And yet you've not got him to *b*wed you!*c*

TESS: Wed*d* me? He's never once said a word about making me his wife. He wants me to go back to him—that's all. If he had wished to marry me, I might have agreed, to save myself *e*from what may be coming*f*. But, mother, you don't understand my feelings towards this man. Perhaps it is unusual, unnatural; but there it is; and it is this that makes me detest myself. I have never cared deeply for *g*him. . . .*h* I was, I suppose, blinded by his *i* manners,

---
*a*Dorchester text adds: that day you drove away together, two months ago.
*b-c*marry!   *d*Marry
*e-f*Absent from Dorchester text.
*g-h*him and I don't now. I have dreaded him.   *i*Dorchester text adds: flash.

for he, in a way, dazzled me. But I soon despised him, and now I've run away from him. Go back to him as before I will not. I hardly wish even to marry him if I could, for my name's sake.

JOAN: Then you ought to have been more careful, if you didn't mean to get him to make you his wife.

TESS (*passionately*): O mother, my mother! How could I be expected to know? I was not much more than a child when I left this house three months ago. Why didn't you warn me there was danger in such men? I never had any chance of learning, and you did not help me.

JOAN: I thought if I cautioned you against his fond feelings and what they might lead to, you would keep him off, and so lose your chance of a more proper connection with him. . . .

Enter JOHN DURBEYFIELD.

Well, we must make the best of it, I suppose. 'Tis nater, after all, and what da please God.

SCENE VII. JOAN, TESS, JOHN

JOHN: What's that you must make the best of?
JOAN (*sighs*): Oh—something Tess has been telling.

TESS *retires*.

SCENE VIII. JOAN, JOHN

JOAN: Tess has been telling me a very unexpected thing.
JOHN (*sitting down*): Oh? Well?—
JOAN (*hesitating*): A dreadful thing has happened to her. I wish I had never let her go to that place. You ought to have looked into the matter more, before she went.
JOHN: I did. I said I didn't like my children going and making themselves beholden to strange kin. I'm the head of the noblest branch of the family, and we ought to live up to it.
JOAN: He's no kin to us—you ought to have known that!

JOHN: Well, what has happened? Have they been snubbing her?

JOAN: Worse than that. And how we hoped that it would be for her good to go there. . . . John, Tess has got into trouble with that young man.

JOHN: What?—You don't mean? . . . (*John starts up.*)

JOAN (*wiping her eyes with her apron*): Yes. . . . It do break my heart almost. Poor unhappy girl! And we've always kept ourselves so respectable too! And what makes it so onnatural is that Tess don't love him one bit. Did ye ever hear such a thing? I believe that if she cared for him much she might have got him to marry her, though he is such a gallant*a*-well-to-do!

JOHN (*flings himself down tragically in chair*): My old ancient family come to this. To think that under the church at Kingsbere my ancestors lie—hundreds of 'em—in coats of mail and jewels, and great lead coffins, weighing tons and tons. We've been here ever since the Conqueror's day, and all through Oliver Grumble's time we fought with the mightiest. There's not a man in the county of Wessex that's got nobler skelletons in his family vault than I. And now this shame brought upon us *b*by this upstart*c*.—It do make my knightly blood boil.

JOAN: Hang your old family blood! 'Tis what shall we do to keep our heads above water now this has happened to Tess?

JOHN: Do as you will. I've no more to say in it. Here I was just thinking of sending round to all the old antiquarians in England to subscribe to a fund to maintain me. It would have been a most romantical, artistical, and proper thing to do. They spend lots of money in keeping up old ruins, and finding the bones of rare animals, and such like; and living remains of such a family as mine must be more interesting. But now this mortification is come upon me, I shan't have the courage to do it, because my ancient pride is broken.*d*

*a*galliant
*b-c*Absent from Dorchester text.
*d*Dorchester text adds four speeches here which in the London text appear at the end of Act I; see pp. 147-8. They are preceded in Dorchester text by stage direction:

JOHN DURBEYFIELD *falls asleep in his chair.* LIZA-LU *enters with a note.*

JOAN: Well, something must be done.
TESS: Nothing can be done.

> LIZA-LU *re-enters: lays supper things on table under shed.*
> JOHN DURBEYFIELD *rises and goes out.*

SCENE IX. JOAN, TESS : LIZA-LU *at back*

JOAN: You'll soon leave off saying that. 'Tis a bad job, that's true; but, Lord, 'tis wonderful what things of that sort a body can get used to in time! It is a thousand pities it should have happened to you, of all others. But it is always so, and you must keep up your pecker. After all, 'tis a very dashing flirtation to have had wi' such a real dand, and many's the girl would envy you if she knew.

TESS: Don't, mother, for God's sake! It is too thoughtless of you!

JOAN: That's right. Find fault with your mother for making the best of things. . . . You've had nothing to eat yet, you know; and nobody thinks of it if I don't. (*[a]*JOAN *turns[b] to table under shed.*) Oh, that's better. Liza-Lu has brought the supper. . . . (*Spreads supper.*) Do ye sit down. You must eat and drink whatever happens. . . . John!

> LIZA-LU *goes out and re-enters.*

LIZA: Father says he don't want any supper, 'cause his family pride is shattered for ever.

> LIZA-LU *goes out.*

SCENE X. JOAN, TESS

JOAN: Oh well—leave him alone. He's upset.—He'll have something inside with the children when they come in from the old club dance. . . .

> SHE *and* TESS *sit down to table. They eat and drink.*
> *Evening closes in as they talk.*

*[a]-[b]*Turns

Trouble is trouble; but yours will be over some day; we must not forget that. You'll not be the first. Some of the highest in the land have had such a trouble, and have got over it and been thought little the worse, owing to their keeping it quiet.

TESS: And what shall I *a*do; I mean, afterwards?*b*

JOAN: You must go away.

TESS (*hopefullyc*): Yes. *d*When it's over, when it's over!*e* Far away—where nobody knows me at all; and begin my life over again: Oh, will it be possible? and shall I ever be thought well of again? And the world be to me as it used to be?

JOAN: Yes, my dear. Only we must be careful, and you must live shut up private here, 'till it is all past. . . . Then you must go off—say to some dairy. You understand dairy-work well. I know a man who has a brother, a dairyman on the other side of Wessex. You'd be safe there, if you only kept your own counsel.

TESS: I wonder! It seems almost too much to expect, after what I have done. . . . And perhaps I shall die.

JOAN: Nonsense. You won't die.

TESS (*brightly*): Well, something in me bids me hope, and to say to myself there is happiness in store yet. Yes; when it's over I'll go out of the sound of all this—if I only can, and have a chance of beginning my life again!*f*

The CLUB GIRLS *come forward again.*

*LIZA-LU *enters with a note.*

LIZA (*calling*): Tess, here's a note for you.

LIZA-LU *goes out.* TESS *comes forward and reads note.*

TESS: He's gone to London. He says I am to write him there—if—if—it is as you think. But I shan't.

JOAN: You won't?

*a-b*do afterwards?
*c*brightens up
*d-e*Absent from Dorchester text.
*f*This is the ending of Act I in the Dorchester text.
*The remaining material to the end of the act is transposed from its position in the Dorchester text, as noted on p. 145.

TESS: I am not going to pray and beseech a man who has gone away.

CURTAIN

END OF ACT I

ACT II

Talbothays Dairy

Two years have elapsed since the events of Act I.

The dairy barton with the dairy-house adjoining, as viewed from the outside, where a tree-trunk lies. Over the gate and rail fence are seen thatched cow-stalls overhung by trees. Milkmaids and men, including MARIAN, IZZ, *and* JONATHAN, *are going to and fro with pails. Straw and mulch scattered about. Empty pails on stand. A large churn. Yokes. A straw rick. Troughs, etc.*

There enter in front, outside gate, JOAN *and* JOHN DURBEYFIELD [a] *in visiting costume;* JOHN *supporting himself on stick;* TESS *in milking pinafore, and cotton bonnet. She is cheerful, bright, and rosy. While the two women converse standing,* JOHN DURBEYFIELD *sits down on tree-trunk and dozes.*

SCENE I. JOAN, JOHN (*in front*) : MILKMAIDS &c. *at back*

[b]TESS: Oh, mother, you've come. I am glad to see you.[c]

JOAN: Well, I don't travel forty miles every day, and I thought that as I was in Casterbridge I would just run down and see you for half an hour, and I've brought Sir John, your father, to keep me company. . . . What a time since we last saw you!

JOHN DURBEYFIELD *looks up, coughs, and dozes again.*

TESS: Yes. What a time. . . . [d]How are they all at home? Has Liza-Lu grown much?[e] You'll stay and have some tea?

JOAN: No. I've got to catch the van back to Stourcastle, and then it's a long drive. And it's best that I shouldn't come in, considering. You needn't tell 'em who I be—'twould cause inconvenient questions

[a]Dorchester text adds: *meeting* TESS; *the former.*
[b-c]Absent from Dorchester text.
[d-e]Absent from the Dorchester text.

perhaps. Of course they know nothing here about . . . that?

TESS: Nothing.

JOAN (*to* JOHN DURBEYFIELD): Don't you go hearkening to what we are saying.

JOHN: No, no, my blood is above such! (*Nods.*)

JOANs Well, now it's gone and past it will be forgot, I hope even at Marlott. Thank God 'twas not much known. It was a blessed thing for 'ee that it died—poor little thing.

TESS (*quickly*): Don't say that, mother. Don't talk about it. . . . Have you—kept his grave in shape?

JOAN: Well, I did at first. But, thinks I, he were such a terrible secret, to be forgot as soon as possible, that—well, I haven't been that way lately.

TESS (*moved*): You ought to, mother,—you promised you would!

JOAN: Well, I'll see about it. . . . But it was more than two years ago. (JOHN DURBEYFIELD *coughs.*) Now keep up your pecker. You be started afresh in the world, and can hold your own with anybody. Upon my word the milk and butter here agree with 'ee. Seeing how pink and blooming and girlish you look, my dear, nobody would guess what you have gone through! They'll never think such a thing was possible, if you don't tell 'em. . . . You've never seen him since, I suppose?

TESS: Who?

JOAN: Your gentleman—Alec D'Urberville. You knew who I meant well enough!

TESS: Oh, I want to forget him! He's like a horrid dream to me. No, I've never seen him since. And I hope I never shall. Please *f*do not*g* name Alec D'Urberville to me again.

JOHN (*looking up*): Who's that a-mentioning my family name?

JOAN: 'Tis nothing, Sir John. You rest there, dearie. (*After a pause, during which she looks over the gate.*) What sort of people be they here?

TESS (*cheerfully*): Very nice people indeed. Much nicer than Marlott folk. I have not been so happy for years; . . . . I do almost like it here. *h*They are as kind as they can be.*i*

*f-g*not to
*h-i*Their kindness is extreme.

JOAN: I could see you had fetched up wonderfully as soon as I set eyes on you*ʲ*, couldn't you, Sir Jacky?

JOHN (*with a start*): Oh—ay—! She's a finer girl now. 'Tis in such a proud race as ours to outgrow their little humilities.

JOAN: Is it only their kindness that's so improved 'ee, Tess?

TESS: The air is good here, too.

JOAN: Ah yes. Good air. But so it was at Marlott. How many are you here altogether?

TESS: Besides the dairyman and his wife there are three indoor dairymaids*ᵏ*, in addition to me,*ˡ* and several outdoor ones. And two or three men milkers. And—the pupil.

JOAN: Who's he?

TESS (*with attempted nonchalance*): Oh—only Mr. Angel Clare.

JOAN: A pupil—a boy?

TESS (*with hesitation*): Oh dear no. A man of eight-and-twenty. He first thought of being a parson, or an author, or something of that sort. But now he's learning dairy-farming. He's really an educated gentleman.

JOAN: Oh-h! What's his father?

TESS: The vicar of Emminster. (*She looks around;* JOHN DURBEYFIELD *coughs.*) I don't see Mr. Clare just now; but he's somewhere in the barton.

JOAN: Ah. A gentleman. (*Looks narrowly and shakes her head at* TESS.) Now, Tess—I guess something. You sly girl—he's been paying 'ee attentions.

TESS: Well, mother—as we're living in the same house, and keep running up against each other, and can't help meeting every hour, of course he's civil and all that.

JOAN (*pleased*): Ah—that's all very well. Now, he's your young man. Think o' that, Sir John!

TESS (*eagerly*): I haven't encouraged him once.

JOHN (*suddenly*): Well said, Tess!

JOAN: But I'll swear he is your young man. I can tell by the looks of 'ee. But why didn't you write to me all about it? Of course I wish you well; and nothing would please me more than to

*ʲ*ee
*ᵏ⁻ˡ*Absent from Dorchester text.

know you were courted honourably by anybody, leaving[m] alone a gentleman.

TESS: Don't mother, dear. There he is! Let us stand back. That's his brother Felix with him—the curate. I don't want to meet 'em, right[n] now.

JOAN: Nor I, I'm sure! (*To* JOHN DURBEYFIELD.) Come along, Jacky. (*He rises.*)

> TESS, JOAN, *and* JOHN DURBEYFIELD *retreat to side of stage R., in foreground. In the mid-distance enters* ANGEL CLARE, *dressed in drab cloth leggings, and dark velveteen jacket, over the sleeves of which a milker's "keep cleans" are pulled; he is accompanied by his brother,* FELIX, *dressed as a curate and in spectacles.*

SCENE II. FELIX, ANGEL : TESS, JOAN, JOHN *screened in L. foreground*

FELIX: And you seem to have changed a good deal. I suppose it is farming or nothing for you now, my dear fellow. And therefore we must make the best of it. But I do entreat you to endeavour to keep as much as possible in touch with moral ideals. Farming, of course, means roughing, literally; but high thinking may go with plain living, nevertheless.

ANGEL: Of course it may. Was it not proved nineteen hundred years ago—if I may trespass on your domain a little? Why should you think, Felix, that I am likely to drop my high thinking and my moral ideals?

FELIX: Well, I fancied from the tone of your letters, and our conversation—it may be fancy only—that you were somehow losing intellectual grasp. You seem to have become entirely absorbed in the life here, which, after all, is only a means to an end. These dairy nymphs and swains seem to have extinguished in you what you had of scholar and thinker, and to have brought you to their sensuous heathen level. I should guard against that if I were you, and keep up my dignity and culture. Remember you are only here to get information on dairy management.

[m]leave
[n]just

ANGEL: Now, Felix, we are very good friends so far; and if we are to keep so, please don't lecture me on my mental state. You've the old conventional notion of Hodge as an animal merely—the pitiable, caricatured, unvarying Hodge. These people here are thinkers and feelers as much as you are—beings of many minds—full of infinite differences. Some of them are bright, some stupid; some happy, and some unhappy; some refined, some boorish—just as people are in society, so-called. They are not the dummy uniform figures you fancy them, I can assure you. They and their lives have been an education for me—a finer education than I derived from Greek and Latin. . . . How is father?

FELIX: He is as actively occupied as ever. He has just been to Trantridge, where he had a disagreeable experience. That upstart man you may have heard of, who calls himself D'Urberville,—they were Stokeses originally—has come back to the Manor House there, after being away for a year or two, and father, knowing his character, thought it his duty to preach at him, taking for his text "Thou fool, this night thy soul shall be required of thee." After service D'Urberville insulted father most grossly—told him to mind his own business, and came little short of striking him.

ANGEL: I wish father would not expose himself to such gratuitous pain from scoundrels!

FELIX: Oh, he took it calmly enough. The only pain to him was pain on the young man's account. We know he has had lots of such experiences, and his scorners have lived to thank him and praise God.

ANGEL: May this young man do the same! Though I'm afraid he won't, from what I hear. (*Pause.*)

FELIX: How much longer do you mean to stay here?

ANGEL: Till I know all about the business, which will be about the end of the year, I suppose. Come and see the dairy. I have something to tell you, too; a rather serious matter.

They retire and remain in conversation at back.

JOAN: Upon my body, Tess, you are lucky, if that's your new young man! What a one you are for gentlemen; 'tis they always that take notice of 'ee. Don't it make your buzzum plim?

JOHN: To be sure 'tis only gentlemen that think of her! Why ha'n't I got tons and tons o' titled bones, and lead coffins, and monnyments, down in Kingsbere Church? I ask that question. Tess knows what she's made of, thanks to me!

JOAN: Hush a minute, Jacky! Now, Tess, don't go making a mess of it this time as you did last time. Why don't you tell me straight out all about it?

TESS: Well, mother, because I did not mean to speak of it. I thought I—I'd rather not, since it will not come to anything.

JOAN: Not come to anything? Why not?

JOHN DURBEYFIELD *walks around.*

TESS: I couldn't let it go on to—to—marriage.

JOAN: Couldn't let it? You don't mean to say that you would refuse him if he asked you to be his lawful wife?

TESS (*distressed*): My dear mother, I must, I must refuse him! How can I do otherwise?

JOAN: Well; good Lord!—But wait till he asks 'ee. 'Tisn't likely, after all. No such good luck for my children!

TESS: He has asked me!

JOAN: What?—really has asked—

JOHN DURBEYFIELD *coughs.*

TESS: And I have refused him. Yes, indeed I have! Oh, mother, and I do love him so, too! And I don't know what to do. He's so good and noble, and educated, and altogether so pure and upright, that it would be a sin and a shame for me to— *a* let him marry me!

JOAN (*wringing her hands*): You've refused him! You've refused him! Oh, you little simple fool. That ever I should call 'ee so.

JOHN: That's right, Tess, stand out for your family!

JOAN: Shut up, you stupid,—with your family! (JOHN DURBEYFIELD *collapses.*) Oh, you be a fool, Tess, to throw away such a chance as that! Sir John—walk on; I'll overtake 'ee.

JOHN: Aye—I'll walk on. (*Walks, singing.*) "I've got a family vault—full of ancestors!" Good-bye, Tess, my girl. You've the real blood in 'ee! And the world ought to know it.

TESS (*sadly*): Good-bye, father.

JOHN DURBEYFIELD *goes out.*

*a*Dorchester text adds: to.

SCENE III. JOAN, TESS : ANGEL *and* FELIX *in distance*

JOAN: He's had a drop o' drink at market to-day. That's all's the matter with him*a*. ... Tess, I say you be a born simpleton, to throw away this chance.

TESS: Yes, but I must! There's a double reason why. It would be wrong to him— *b* such a cruel wrong—and it would also be immoral in me. I am Alec D'Urberville's wife by the force of what's happened between us, worse luck for me, and though we parted these two or three years ago, and shall never see each other any more, I cannot be another man's wife while he lives, without deep sin. O mother, do see that it is so! do!

JOAN: But you don't love Alec! You dislike *c*him; he catched you by unfair means!*d* And he's gone away to London or somewhere. You owe him nothing, Heaven knows. His wife indeed! That's past and forgot.

TESS: Yes, but it is what I am, in relation to him, though I dislike him. How can I *e* be anybody else's wife as long as he lives? And even if I were persuaded that I could, I dare not marry Mr. Clare without telling him everything in my history.

JOAN: What! You'd tell him that you'd had a—

TESS: Yes. And then he would hate me, and wouldn't marry me—so respectable as he is—to bring disgrace on his family—religious church-people as they are.

> SHE *looks across hopelessly towards* ANGEL, FELIX CLARE *having his back turned.* ANGEL *catches sight of her, and waves his hat;* SHE *bows, and turns away in tears.*

No, I *mustn't*! I *mustn't* marry him! I must stay as I am, and die unmarried.

JOAN: Pooh! Accept him! Catch him while you can. You love him down to the ground.

TESS: Don't press me, mother. I *know* I love him—oh, *don't* I know it! ... If I accepted him I must tell him, and then—'twould be all over, and I should go drown myself.

a'en
*b*Dorchester text adds: oh.
*c-d*him!
*e*Dorchester text adds: honestly.

JOAN: A pack of rubbish! I didn't tell your father everything, and every man I'd spoke to, before I met him, I can tell 'ee. No sensible young woman, that's had any face at all worth kissing, ever does such a stupid thing, or perhaps weddings would be fewer than they be, except over the broomstick. On no account must you say a word—especially as it was so long ago, and not your fault at all.

TESS: Yes, but on his account—

JOAN (*interrupting impatiently*): I shall answer the same if you ask me fifty times.... Now, just for once, show your sense, and, if he ever asks 'ee again, marry him as soon as he'll take 'ee. Such an opportunity won't come many times in your life, I can tell 'ee. Here you've had two such chances as never was. You'd*f* have married the first if you'd played your cards well—if not before, after. Now, the second comes along and you refuse him.... Ah, well!

TESS (*impulsively*): Mother—let me make you known to him. Then you'd see how good he is. He's waiting over there to speak to me.

> SHE *turns and* ANGEL *catches her eye, the attention of* FELIX *being* *g* *engaged the other way; they wave hands again.*

JOAN: No, no, no! Not for worlds make such a rough woman as I beknown to such a gentleman as he. All the fat would be in the fire then, 'a b'lieve! If you married him I should never come near 'ee*h*, to disgrace 'ee*i*—you needn't fear.—Don't you tell him who you've been talking to. (*Going off.*) *j*You must encourage him to ask again—and say yes.... And you must not confess. Now my time is up, and I must overtake your father, if I mean to catch the carrier.*k*

> JOAN *goes out;* TESS *following to side of stage and watching her away, waving her hand; then retreating to back,*

*f*You might
*g*Dorchester text adds: *again.*
*h-i*Absent from Dorchester text.
*j-k*Rearranged from Dorchester text: Now my time is up, and I must go and overtake your father, if I mean to catch the train. You must encourage him to ask again—and say yes.—And you must not confess.

shyly, under Angel's *eyes[l]—where she joins* Jonathan *and the other milkmaids.*

Angel *and* Felix *come forward, without encountering her, and walk up and down arm in arm as they converse.*

Scene IV. Angel, Felix : Tess *in distance*

Angel: [a]She[b] is occupied with some one this afternoon, or I would introduce you.

Felix: Oh, that can wait. It is such a new and startling thing altogether that you tell me, that I don't know how to take it. Getting engaged before you've any place to take a wife to, or any income to depend upon. What will poor mother think of it?... [c]*But who is the lady?*[d]

Angel: She's not exactly what you would call a lady, though she is a lady in nature—the gentlest and sweetest specimen of maidenhood—a lady born, not made. What is called a lady socially would be no good to me in the rural business I'm doomed to follow. As my father didn't think fit to send me to Cambridge, as he did you, but preferred to put me to farming, I must choose my mate accordingly, and you at home must take the consequences. She's the must useful[e] woman I could possibly have for a wife. She understands cows, butter-making, and....

Felix: Good Heavens!—what is the woman? I hope you are not going to link your family [f] to—

Angel (*angrily*): Don't you fall before you're hit, Felix. Never you be so anxious about our precious family—it does not become you as a minister of the Gospel. I tell you plainly, she is a milkmaid. She's here, in this very dairy. You were looking straight at her just now—when she was standing here with some one. Didn't you notice her?

[l]eye
[a-b]I see she
[c-d]Absent from Dorchester text.
[e]helpful
[f]Dorchester text adds: on.

FELIX: She—here? (*Looking around.*) I recollect vaguely seeing some young[g] women—

ANGEL: It frightens you, does it? Very well—you needn't meet her. What conceivable difference can it make to you whom I marry since my plan is to go quite away from this part of the country—possibly abroad to a colony? If you were to condescend to talk to her you would find out that what I say is borne out by facts. However, I would rather you didn't see her as she is here, in her work just now, and at a disadvantage. And she hasn't accepted me, yet, either. In fact, she has refused me so far.

FELIX (*satirically*): She's likely to refuse *you*!

ANGEL: Well, I hope she won't. I mean to try her again. She's not a woman to be easily won, though you may think otherwise. As soon as I get her consent—if I do—I shall go home and tell father and mother the whole matter. I am sure they will see it as I do: and I am sure mother will love her. But I am my own master, and have made up my mind; though [h] I don't wish to do anything against their wishes at home, if I can avoid it. . . .

> [i]*Song heard off:*
> Arise, arise, arise!
> And pick your love a posy,
> All o' the sweetest flowers
> That in the garden grow.
> The turtle doves and sma' birds
> In every bough a-building,
> So early in the May-time
> At the break o' the day![j]

TESS *advances from amongst the others at back.*

Ah! here she is coming. Will you wait and speak to her after all?

FELIX: No! no!—Not now—not now! She has not observed me and I would rather not.

ANGEL (*sadly*): Very well. . . . Good-bye. . . . You'll hear from me soon about it, if I can only get her promise.

[g]Absent from Dorchester text.
[h]Dorchester text adds: of course.
[i-j]Absent from Dorchester text.

THEY *shake hands.* FELIX *ᵏcomes through the gates and goes out.ˡ* TESS *advances further—but sheers off coyly.*

SCENE V. TESS, ANGEL

ANGEL: There you go, my Tessy! (*Goes to her.*) Do come this way a minute. We must have another talk. Yes, please! You've been too cruel.

HE *takes her hand and* SHE *reluctantly comes to the front with him. When screened from the barton by the shed* HE *kisses her.*

TESS: No, no.

ANGEL: But, dear one, surely I may! And now—that question I asked—you didn't mean no, really? My brother has been here—that was he you saw—and I hinted a little to him about ourselves. Now, come, say yes. You will be mine?

TESS (*trying to escape*): I've got to go ᵃ skimming—really I have!

During the conversation other milkers go to and fro ᵇ with their pails.

ANGEL: There are plenty of others to skim. Now, to put it practically: as I said, I shall soon want to marry, and being a farmer I shall want a woman who knows all about the management of farms. Will you be that woman, Tessy?

TESS (*troubled*): Oh, Mr. Clare—I cannot be,—I cannot be.

ANGEL (*putting his arm round her*): But, Tess. Do you say no? Surely you love me?

TESS: Oh yes! yes! And I would rather be yours than anybody's in the world. But I *cannot* marry you!

ANGEL (*holding her at arm's length*): Tess, ᶜyou're not engaged to somebody else?ᵈ

TESS: No! no!

ᵏ⁻ˡgoes out R.
ᵃDorchester text adds: on.
ᵇDorchester text adds: at back.
ᶜ⁻ᵈyou are engaged to somebody else.

ANGEL: Then why do you refuse me?

TESS (*in low tones*): I don't want to marry. I have not thought of doing it. I only want to love you.

ANGEL: But, *why*?

TESS (*hesitatingly*): Your father—is a parson; and your mother wouldn't like you to marry anybody but a lady.

ANGEL: You mistake my parents. They are quite unambitious, and unaffectedly religious. All they would really care for would be that my wife should be a sweet, innocent maiden such as you are, my dear.... "Whatsoever things are true, whatsoever things are honest, whatsoever things are of good report"—to use their own Scriptural phrase—are what they care for.

TESS (*faintly—turning away*): I can't be your wife.

ANGEL: You utterly mistake my father, if you fear him! A more disinterested man never lived. Why, my brother has just been telling me that only the other day, he went away to preach at Trantridge, a place forty miles from here; and encountered there a rakehell of a fellow—Mr. Alec something or other—and thought it his duty to expostulate with the young man for his goings on. It did no good, and he only insulted my father; though my father took it quietly and meekly, and thinks and hopes what he said may bear fruit in the young man's heart some day. However, I only mention this to show how you mistake my father if you think that he is proud.... Now—my question, Tessy?

TESS: It can't be.

ANGEL (*capturing her to prevent her slipping away*): Now, you don't mean it, sweet? I am sure you do not. You have made me so restless by your evasions that I cannot read, or work, or do anything. I want to know—to hear from your own warm lips—that you will some day be mine. Any time you may choose, but some day? (TESS *shakes her head*.) Then I ought not to hold you in this way. (*With affected dudgeon*.) I have no right to, no right to seek you out, or walk with you. You love some other man.

TESS: How can you say it?

ANGEL: I almost know that you don't. But then, how can you say that you won't accept me for a husband?

TESS: Ah—that's different. It is for your good—indeed, oh believe me, it is only for your sake. I am *sure* I ought not to do it!

ANGEL: But you will make me happy!

TESS: You think so. But you don't know. Don't ask me again. The struggle is too fearful—my own heart is so strongly on the side of yours. . . . (*Aside*.) Two hearts against one poor little conscience! (*A pause*.)

ANGEL (*stooping and kissing the inside of her naked arm*): Do you know why I did that, Tess?

TESS (*awaking from her reverie*): Because you love me very much.

ANGEL: Yes. And as the beginning[e] of a new entreaty.

TESS: Not *again*.

ANGEL: Oh, Tess—*I cannot* think why you are so tantalizing! Why do you disappoint me so? You seem almost like a coquette—upon my soul you do!—a coquette of society! They blow hot and blow cold, just as you do; and it is the very last thing to expect in *you*.

TESS turns away poutingly.

And yet I know you to be the reverse—the most unpractised creature with men that ever lived. So how can I suppose you a flirt? Why don't you like the idea of being my wife, if you love me so[f] much as you seem to?

TESS (*moved*): I have never said I don't like the idea, and I never could say it; b-be-because it wouldn't be true! (*TESS walks away inclining to tears*.)

ANGEL (*pursuing*): Tell me—for God's sake—do tell me that you won't belong to anybody else!

TESS: I *will* tell you. Heaven knows I will! I will tell you all that and more—all about myself—all my experiences—all my history!

ANGEL: Yes, dear. Your experiences—any number! My Tess has, no doubt, about as many experiences as that wild convolvulus out there on the garden hedge, that opened itself this morning for

[e] preliminary
[f] as

the first time. Tell me anything; but don't use that wretched expression any more about not being worthy of me.

TESS (*tearfully*[g]): Will you go away—a few minutes—till I [h]can think? and[i] then I'll tell you. Please do!

ANGEL: Certainly.

> ANGEL[j] *retires through the gate, and stands leaning against the churn, or other object, his back to the spectator.* MARIAN *and* IZZ *come forward through the gate.*

SCENE VI. MARIAN, IZZ, TESS : ANGEL *in distance*

MARIAN: Oh—[a] crying! And Mr. Clare just left her!

IZZ: They have been quarrelling! (*To* TESS.) What—have you had a little tiff with him, dear? Never mind. Only a lovers' quarrel.

TESS (*drawing herself up with dignity, checking her feelings*): Oh no—quite different. . . . But I have no objection to tell. He wants—I don't know if I ought to say it—he wants to marry me.

MARIAN (*to* IZZ): I said so.

IZZ: Well—it was to be, I suppose. 'Twas no use our trying to get him away from her. He likes her best. (*To* TESS.) Is it to be soon? Why do you sigh about it? I should jump for joy.

TESS (*bitterly*): No—you make a mistake. You wouldn't jump for joy! I ought not to have stood in your way, or anybody's, if you cared for him. But I couldn't help it, my dears. It is not—ought not—to be—ever!

MARIAN: Nonsense. Have him while you can. He don't want either of us, and never did.

TESS: I keep saying I can never be his wife—but—

IZZ: He's coming again. Come along, Marian—let him[b] finish

[g]*distressed*
[h-i]am myself again? And
[j]He
[a]Dorchester text adds: almost.
[b]'em

it. I shall go and tell the dairyman that you and Mr. Clare are going to be married soon.

TESS: No, no!

    IZZ *and* MARIAN *retire, passing* ANGEL.

IZZ (*slapping* ANGEL): Ha!*c* We know, sir!

  THEY *remain at back*—ANGEL *advances to* TESS.

  SCENE VII. ANGEL, TESS : MARIAN *and* IZZ *at back*

ANGEL (*gaily*): Now, Miss Flirt—is it to be yes, at last?

TESS: You are back too quick! And you need not call me Flirt, Mr. Clare.

ANGEL: Call me Angel, then, and not Mr. Clare.

TESS: Angel.

ANGEL: "Angel dearest"—why not?

TESS: 'Twould mean that I agree, wouldn't it?

ANGEL: Well, you are going to agree, love!

TESS: Ah—but—there are other women worthier of you. Those for instance. (*She indicates* MARIAN *and* IZZ.) Almost either of 'em would make—perhaps make—a more proper wife than I. And perhaps they love you as well as I—almost!

ANGEL: Oh, Tessy! No!

TESS (*with a sigh of relief*): Don't you think so?

ANGEL: No. Let us sit down here out of sight, and settle this *a* matter I've come back to have settled.

  THEY *sit down on the tree-trunk.* IZZ, MARIAN, *and the other milkers severally go away.*

    SCENE VIII. ANGEL, TESS

ANGEL: *a*Now, we are all right.*b* (*Takes her hand.*) Now permit me to put it in this way.—You belong to me already, you know; your heart, I mean—does it not?

TESS: You know that as well as I do. Yes, yes!

*c*Ha!ha!
*a*Dorchester text adds: little.
*a-b*Absent from Dorchester text.

Angel: Then if your heart does, why not your hand?

Tess: My only reason was on account of you—on account of my position—I have something to tell you—my history. I want you to know it,—you must let me tell you—you will not like me so well!

Angel: Tell it then, if you wish to, dearest. This precious history; now. I was born at so and so, Anno Domini—

Tess: Yes. I was born at Marlott, and I grew up ^cthere, I^d was in the Sixth Standard when I left school, and they said I had great aptness. But there was trouble in my family. My father was not very industrious, and he drank a little.

Angel: Yes, yes! Poor child! Nothing new.

Tess (*her breath quickening*): And then—there is something very unusual about it—about me!

Angel: Yes, dearest. Never mind. (*Holds her hand.*)

Tess: I—I—am not a Durbeyfield, but a D'Urberville—a descendant of the old family of that name in this county in bygone times. And—we've all broken down and gone to nothing.

Angel: A D'Urberville! . . . Indeed! Why, it is the name that was taken by the family of that young rake I told you about—Alec D'Urberville, as he calls himself, though of course that is not his real name. Yes—the old family has gone to poverty as you say. . . . And is that *e* the trouble with dear Tess?

Tess (*weakly*): Yes!

Angel: Why should I love you less after knowing this?

Tess: I was told by the dairyman that you hated old families.

Angel (*laughing*): Well, I do, in one sense. I hate the principle of blood before brains, and I think the only pedigrees we ought to respect are those spiritual ones in which the wise and the virtuous become successors to the virtuous and the wise. But I am extremely interested in your news! I wonder that I did not see that your surname was a worn form of that old name. And *this* was the carking secret! Now you must spell your name properly from this very moment. You've every right to it and that stuck-up snob I told you of, who insulted my father—that Alec—has no right to it at all.

^{c-d}there. And I
^eDorchester text adds: all.

TESS (*agitated*): Angel—I think—I would rather not spell my name as you say he does. It is unlucky—perhaps?

ANGEL: Now then, Mistress Teresa D'Urberville, I have you! Take *my* name, and so you will escape yours. The secret is out—why should you any longer refuse me?

TESS: Y-yes, the secret is out! *f(Sighs deeply.)g*

ANGEL: Then say you will. I've told my brother that I mean to marry you, and I'm going to tell my father and mother. They'll welcome you warmly,—and though they are the most disinterested people in the world, they are human, and the fact of your being a real D'Urberville and not *h* one like that scamp my father met with, will help you in winning their interest.

TESS: I—if it is *sure* to make you happy to have me as your wife, and you feel that you do wish to marry me— *i*just as I am,—very—very—much—*i*

ANGEL: Yes—just as you are, of course!

TESS: To marry me, whatever my offences, it would make me feel that I ought to say—I will.

ANGEL: You will—you do say it, I know. You will be mine for ever and ever.

TESS: Yes.

> HE *embraces and kisses her. A pause.—An hysteric sigh escapes her; she loosens herself from his embrace and turns herself away.*

ANGEL (*surprised*): Why do you do that, dearest?

TESS: I can't tell—quite! I—I—am so glad to think of being yours, and making you happy.

ANGEL: But it does not seem very much like gladness, *k* Tessy.

TESS: I mean—it is because I have broken down in my vow. I said I would die unmarried.

> JONATHAN KAIL, IZZ, MARIAN, *enter at back, but they cannot see the pair.*

*f-g*Absent from Dorchester text.
*h*Dorchester text adds: a sham.
*i-j*These words are italicized in Dorchester text.
*k*Dorchester text adds: my.

ANGEL: But, if you love me, you would like me to be your husband?

TESS (*turning back to him*): Yes. . . . Yes. . . . But oh—I sometimes wish I had never been born!

ANGEL: Now, my dear Tess, if I did not know that you are very much excited, *l*and absolutely without experience of the male sex,*m* I should say that remark was not very complimentary. How can you say*n* that, if you care for me? If you do, I wish you would prove it in some way.

TESS: How can I prove it more than I have done? There!
Puts up her mouth so as to enable him to kiss her.
Now, do you believe?

ANGEL: Yes, I never really doubted it. Never—never! *o*(*Embraces her.*)*p*

> JONATHAN KAIL *comes forward; seeing the lovers embracing he turns quickly away, as if he had not.* TESS *starts away from* ANGEL's *arms*—IZZ, MARIAN, *and other maids and men come forward.*

SCENE IX. JONATHAN, TESS, IZZ, MARIAN, ANGEL

TESS (*confused*): I knew how it would be! I said to myself, they're sure to come and catch us! But he wasn't really—

JONATHAN (*interrupting*): Well, my maidy,—if so be you hadn't told us you was catched a-cooing, I'm sure we shouldn't ha' noticed you'd been a-doing of anything particular.—Now, should we, Izz and Marian? Now that shows that folks should never fancy other folks be seeing things when they bain't. Oh no—I should never ha' noticed nothing, if ye hadn't confessed to it.

ANGEL: We are going to be married soon, Jonathan.

JONATHAN: Ah—and be ye! Well, I'm truly glad to hear it, sir. I've thought for some time ye mid be drifting that way. She's a prize for any man.

ANGEL: She is! She is!

*l-m*Absent from Dorchester text.
*n*wish
*o-p*Absent from Dorchester text.

Holds Tess's *hand a moment, lets go; and he then recedes, and* Jonathan *retreats.*

Scene x. Tess, Izz, Marian : Jonathan *and* Angel *in distance*

Izz (*regarding* Tess): He's going to marry her. How her face do show it.
Marian: You be*a* going to marry him? (*They close up to* Tess.)
Tess: Yes.
Angel (*from distance*): Don't tease her, girls!
Izz: Going to marry him*b*—a gentleman!
Tess: Are you sure you don't dislike me for it?
Izz: I don't know. I want to hate 'ee for it, but I can't.
Marian: I feel the same. I can't hate her—somehow she hinders me.
Tess: He ought to marry one of you. You are both better than I.
Izz & Marian: No, no,—dear Tess!
Tess (*impetuously*): You are, you are. You would be better for him than—oh, I don't know what I am saying! (*Turns away from them.*)

Angel *advances cwith a pocket-book in his handd;* Tess *composes herself.*

Scene xi. Angel, Tess : Marian *and* Izz *behind*

Angel (*blithely*): *a*There, I've just made a note of it.*b* Yes—she has agreed at last. And only one more point remains to be settled —that is, the day.

Embraces Tess.

Curtain

End of Act II

*a*Word is italicized in Dorchester text.
*b*Word is italicized in Dorchester text.
*c-d*Absent from Dorchester text.
*a-b*Absent from Dorchester text.

ACT III

Wellbridge. Old manor-house.

The interior of a sitting-room in a farm-house, once an Elizabethan manor-house, as is shown by the mullioned and transomed windows on the left, moulded ceiling, and yawning stone-arched fireplace on right. Two paintings, built into the wall, opposite fireplace ^a*on right*^b, *represent two ill-featured dames of the eighteenth*^c *century. A heavy door beneath admits from without. At the back of the room a wide four-centred stone arch opens into a small inner chamber where stands an Arabian bedstead with white dimity furniture; the curtains drawn back. The time is evening, the front room being lit by four candles, one at each corner of a small square dining-table, formally laid out for supper. High-backed chairs are ranged against the walls, except two at the table. Fire burning. A settle beside it, facing spectator.*

An aged FARM LABOURER *and his* WIFE, *both toothless, are moving about the room.*

SCENE I. LABOURER, WIFE

WIFE: Move the things^d a bit this way—that's better. They didn't say what they'd want for supper, but I suppose they'll be a-hungered. How far^e is it from Talbothays dairy to here?

LABOURER: Well—^fif you go round by the old road it may be a matter o' ten mile; but if so be you come along straight, and don't mind hopping down zeventeen times to open zeventeen gates—well, you may do it in nine mile.^g

WIFE: Whatever should make a new-married couple come to such a' out-step place as this? If I was going to be married again....

^{a-b}Absent from Dorchester text.
^clast
^dtable
^efur
^{f-g}The Dorchester text uses more dialect: if you da goo round by the wold road it mid be a matter o' ten mile; but if so be you da come along straight, and don't mind hopping down zeventeen times to open zeventeen gates—well, you mid do it in nine mile.

LABOURER: Which you bain't.

WIFE: Don't you be too sure of things. If I was going to be married again, which I'd scorn to do, considering—I should take care to go to a cheerfuller place than Wellbridge for my wedding jaunt. What did he say[h] were his reasons for coming here when 'a hired the chimmers?

LABOURER: I've told 'ee once, hain't I? He met maister [i] outside here, and 'a called 'en by name, and 'a said, "That's a fine old building you live in, farmer; but its day[j] be past and gone." "Yes," says maister, "but as fine as 'a may[k] be, you may live in 'en for me[l], and welcome!—a damp rotten wold place, thet ought to have been pulled down years ago." "I should be sorry to see that done," says the[m] gentleman. And then 'a said that owing to the house having once been the family home of his wife that was to be, he'd like to bring her here, being a very romantical thing to do; and asked maister to let him have a couple of rooms for a few days. "Th' canst have the whole house if th'st wish[n] to," says maister, "if you can manage to do for yourselves—I want to visit my daughter for a week or so." So then it was settled that we would[o] come in from our house between whiles, and get their victuals for 'em and so forth, being such a old aged couple, not much good for anything else, you and I. . . .

WIFE: Ugh! Don't speak for two people, when you've hardly sense enough to speak for one.

LABOURER: H'm! Well, as all is ready, I reckon we mid as well go home-along?

WIFE: Somebody must bide till they come. I will, I think, being so much the younger.

LABOURER: Ugh!

WIFE: Do 'ee go along, considering your afflictions, and leave the door on the latch till I come.

> LABOURER *finally arranges table and goes.* LABOURER'S WIFE *changes* LABOURER'S *arrangement of the table and stirs the fire.*

[h]zay
[i]Dorchester text adds: just.
[j]days   [k]mid   [l]I
[m]my   [n]want   [o]should

Presently Angel Clare *and* Tess[p], *married that day,[q] enter in travelling clothes.* Labourer's Wife *half-curtsies and puts chairs.*

Scene ii. Angel, Tess, Labourer's Wife

Angel: Good evening.—This is our room?
Wife: 'Tis, sir.
Angel (*to* Tess): Welcome to one of your ancestral mansions, dearest little wife. Your people owned this estate and house once, you know. Now it is a farm dwelling.
Tess: Did they? . . . It is rather sad to think so!
Angel: Yes—it is perhaps. I hope it won't depress you.
Wife (*aside*): How be the mighty fallen!
Angel: Ah, I see that I ought not to have brought you here!
Tess: Oh, don't say that, dear—I know you meant it kindly, even if it is a little depressing. [a]It is so ungrateful of me to mind.[b] (*She looks round: starts before the portraits.*)
Angel: What's the matter?
Tess: Those horrid women. How they frighten me!
Angel (*to* Labourer's Wife): Whose portraits are those?
Wife: I have been a-told, sir, by old aged folk that be now dead and rotten, that they were noble dames of the D'Urberville family. Owing to their being builded into the wall they can't be moved without crumbling into pieces.
Angel: Yes—they must be so, Tess, they are your ancestral dames!
Wife: I think there's no more I can do for 'ee to-night, sir? I am[c] close by in my cottage, if you should want anything.
Angel: No—I think there is nothing more, is there, dear Tess? The man is coming directly with our things, and we shall be quite comfortable.
Wife: Good night, sir, and ma'am.
Tess & Angel: Good night.

Labourer's Wife *goes out.*

*p-q*Absent from Dorchester text.
*a-b*Absent from Dorchester text.
*c*be

Scene III. Angel, Tess

Angel: Don't look at those horrid pictures any more, darling. Your nerves seem shaken by the least thing to-day.

Tess: Yes! (*Looks round again at the paintings.*) The depressing thing about them is, that though they look so cruel and treacherous, they bear a *a* family likeness to me.

Angel: Well,—of course that's natural enough. Don't you think of the house or the pictures any more. It was stupid of me, I see, to bring you here. I thought it would be romantic.... (*Looks at his watch.*) Jonathan ought to be here with our things soon. Now let us sit down and have some supper.

They *sit down at table.* Tess *begins meal.* Angel *regards her quietly.*

Tess (*playfully*): What are you thinking *b*about?*c*

Angel: I'm thinking what a dear, dear Tess she is! I ask myself do I realize solemnly enough how utterly this little womanly thing is the creature of my good or bad faith? How dependent she is upon my fortunes and friendship? What happens to me must in a way happen to her. What I cannot be, she cannot be. And shall I then ever neglect her, or hurt her, or even forget for a moment to consider her? God forbid such a crime.

Tess *sighs. Wind blows.*

Tess: What is that?

Angel: Only the wind. There's going to be a change in the weather. The cock crew late this afternoon.

Tess: That's an ill omen, isn't it?

Angel: No—it only means a change. (*Rain heard.*) Ah, I thought rain was coming. (*Pause.*)

Tess: Dearest, I wanted to tell you about something. I said—do you remember—that I would confess my faults—that I would write them down? Well, last night I did. And I crept upstairs afterwards with a note to your room, and slipped it under your door! But to-day when I looked to see if you had taken it, it was there just the same. It had gone under the edge of the carpet. So, as it was too late—too late then for you to give me up, I destroyed it.

*a*Dorchester text adds: terrible.   *b-c*about me?

ANGEL (*heartily*): And quite right too. I am sure I wouldn't have wasted my time *d* reading your faults and confessions on my wedding morning. Not I!

TESS (*with an uneasy laugh*): I wish you had. There seemed a fate in your not getting the note.

ANGEL (*again looking at his watch*): I wonder what can have happened to Jonathan? He is an hour late with our luggage.

TESS: I haven't so much as a brush or comb till he comes.

ANGEL: Possibly he is gone to the mill-house by mistake—where I thought of going till I found these rooms more suitable. It is close by here—I'll cross the bridge and inquire. It will not take me five minutes.

*e*ANGEL *kissesf her and goes out.*

SCENE IV. TESS *alone*

aThereb is a knock at the front door.

TESS *c*(*to herself*)*d*: Perhaps that's Jonathan, and Angel has missed him.

Knock repeated.

Ah—there's no servant in the house—the old woman has gone home.

TESS *rises and goes to the door of the room and starts. Turns away.*

ALEC D'URBERVILLE *enters.*

SCENE V. TESS, ALEC

ALEC: Tess—it is I. Alec D'Urberville.

TESS: I see it is.

ALEC: Well—is that all?

TESS (*her voice trembling*): That's all.

ALEC: I could make nobody hear at the front door—so I came in.

---

*d*Dorchester text adds: in.
*e-f*Kisses
*a-b*Presently there
*c-d*Absent from Dorchester text.

I've just come from London. *After thinking a good deal about you lately, this*^b morning I got an anonymous note—"If you want to see your girl Tess again—you must be quick about it. There's another fellow in for her, and they'll be married shortly." Off I started and was on the road to Talbothays when a man said he had seen you driving to Wellbridge this afternoon. So I stopped here instead of going on to Talbothays, and passing this house I saw you through the window. You were talking to somebody, and I waited, and when I saw him go out, I came in. Why did you disappear into space in such a way, leaving me no clue to your address or anything? It was very shabby of you to serve me so. Have you come here to-day to keep Christmas with some relations? Was that your young man I saw? You don't care for him, I'll swear!

Tess^c: I wish you to go away! Why do you add to your old cruelty the cruelty of finding me ^d here?^e

Alec: I had a good reason. It is this—to inquire into your worldly circumstances^f. ^gHaving been what you were to me three years ago,^h I shouldn'tⁱ like to see you work hard. Now—not to mince matters, won't you be friends? (Tess *shakes her head*.) I wish you loved me, my dear.

Tess (*after a pause*): I love somebody else, Mr. D'Urberville.

Alec: The devil you do! I admire your spirit! . . . But has not a sense of what is right and proper any weight with you? (^j*Lower.*^k) You know you ^lare morally my little property, and^m can honestly be nobody else's in the world.

Tess: No! no! You are not to say it, sir!

Alec: You belong to me in honour.

^{a-b}This
^cDorchester text adds: (*agitated but peremptory*).
^dDorchester text adds: out.
^eDorchester text adds:
    Alec (*in a low voice*): You mean you are playing the maid again?
    Tess (*firmly*): I have begun another life, and I wish with all my heart you had not broke in upon it. You have refused my *last* request, not to come near me!
^fcondition   ^{g-h}Absent from Dorchester text.
ⁱdon't   ^{j-k}*Speaking lower.*
^{l-m}Absent from Dorchester text.

TESS: In dishonour.

ALEC: Well—in dishonour; and any love you may feel for another man is only a passing feeling—that'll come to nothing.

TESS: No, no! It is no passing feeling, and it *can't* come to nothing! Do you hear?

ALEC: Why can't it?

TESS: I have married him.

ALEC (*blankly, with a start*): Ah!

TESS: Go away! He is worthy and honourable, and his one wish is to make unworthy me, happy!

ALEC: Ah! . . . Well, does he know of our affair?

TESS: You and I are strangers: so will you *please* keep from questioning me, and leave this house?

ALEC: Strangers are we? Strangers! . . . Well, I swear I came here for your own good. I didn't know anything about ⁿa child° till a year and a half afterwards—and it was no use to offer you help in the matter then. . . . Who have you married? Where is he?

TESS (*looking up appealingly*): Don't ask what I don't wish to tell!

ALEC: When did you marry? Not to-day surely?

TESS: Yes.

ALEC: Good Lord. . . . Then I'd better be off. Ha-ha! Tess, don't look at me so like a startled fawn. I cannot stand your looks —they bewitch me! There never were such eyes before, surely! There—I won't lose my head.

TESS: Will you only go away? He will be here in a few minutes! Why do you trouble me so?

ALEC: Trouble you! How you keep on! I think you trouble me, dragging me here like this. Well—perhaps it is best that I should not look too often on you again—now you are married. I am older than I was.

TESS: I don't drag you, or can't help it, if I do!

ALEC: That's only my way of talking: you must not look so horribly concerned. Of course you have done no harm, except retain your pretty face, and your shapely figure. That nice frock

*n-o*what had occurred

sets it off, and that way of doing your hair suits you. You milkmaids should never dress so stylishly as you are dressed now if you wish to keep out of danger. And what a swell hat and handbag! We are getting on.

TESS: I don't want you[p] to look at my pretty things!

Takes up hat and handbag to put them away.

ALEC: Well, never mind that. Here am I, my love, as in the old time.

TESS (*recovering firmness*): No, *not* as of then—never as then—never! After what I have told you, that I am another man's wife—an upright, good man's—an educated man's—it is hard upon me to treat me to such talk! How *can* you if you care ever so little for me?

ALEC: He'll never stick to you—don't you believe it. The upright, educated man won't bring his name into disrepute by living long with *my* Tess, poor girl of you! But perhaps you have not told him?

TESS: Don't torture me in mercy's sake!—He will, he will! Oh, if you only knew the agony of....

ALEC: *You haven't told?* Good, I see it in your manner. Now believe me, he will spurn you if ever he knows. And therefore don't risk it! I see you are all nerves in my presence; so I'll be off! (*He retreats; then comes back.*) Tess, dear—you are mine! Come back to your own nest—come! ... Leave that stick you call husband, for ever. My trap is waiting round the corner. Darling mine —not his—you know the rest!

TESS *suddenly* [q] *hits him in the mouth with* [r]*muff, gloves, or*[s] *handbag she has retained in her hand.* ALEC *starts back and wipes lips with his handkerchief.*

ALEC: Damnation!

TESS (*with hopeless irony as she sinks down into chair*): Now punish me! You need not mind—I shall not cry out. Tell[t] my secret—anything! Once victim, always victim—that's the law!

---

[p]Italicized in Dorchester text.
[q]Dorchester text adds: *starts up and*.
[r-s]Absent from Dorchester text.
[t]TELL

ALEC (*recovering calm*): Oh no, no, Tess dear. I can make full allowance for this. You have been much tried; but you might have been civiler. (*His voice hardens.*) I was the owner of that pretty figure once, remember. (*He holds her by the shoulders.*) Do you hear, Miss Insolence? (*Lets her go.*) So much for our quarrel. You'll come to my arms again some day, my dear. They'll be open to receive you. I am the only husband you've really ᵘhad, whatever you may think of this contract.ᵛ Now I am going on. My blessing on your marriage, and take my advice; *Don't tell him.* Good-bye. Come—let us make it up and part friends. (*He holds out his hand but she does not respond.*) Come—do you hear, Miss Sulky? Shake hands! I am ashamed of you—nourishing enmity like this!

TESS: I don't nourish enmity. God knows I don't, against any living creature!

ALEC: Then give me your hand. (*A pause. She slowly and reluctantly gives her hand.*) That's a good girl. Now I am back again to London. Say we part friends.

TESS: Very well.

ALEC (*peremptorily*): Come—say we do!

TESS (*faintly, after a pause*): We do.

ALEC: That's right! Good-bye.

TESS: Good-bye! (*Faintly.*)

He goes out.

SCENE VI. TESS *alone : then* ANGEL

TESS *remains, looking on the ground as if stupefied.*
TESS: Oh, he's my master still!
Presently TESS *rises, puts away hat, bag, etc. and sits down.*

ANGEL *enters.*
ANGEL: Has he come yet?
TESS: Eh—Jonathan? No.
ANGEL: Oh, I thought I saw somebody leaving the gate. Well, he has not been to the mill either. We must wait. (ANGEL *again looks at his watch.*) I wonder what can have happened to Jona-

ᵘ⁻ᵛhad.

than. Surely he must be here soon. Tess, you are not a bit cheerful this evening—not at all as you used to be. Those harridans in their frames have unsettled you. I wonder if you really love me after all. . . . There . . . I did not mean it! You are worried at not having your things, I dare say!

A knocking.

Ah—there he is.

Angel *opens door.*

Scene VII. Jonathan, Angel, Tess

Jonathan (*entering*): I've brought the things for you and your mis'ess, sir; so to name what she lawful is.

Jonathan *deposits box, portmanteau, handbag, etc., wipes his face.*

Tess: You are late, Jonathan.

Jonathan: Well, yes, miss—ma'am, I would say, as your wedlock name. Yes, I've met wi' several hindrances. We've all been gallied at the dairy, sir, since you left and your mis'ess—so to name her now. What's happened is that one of the girls [a] tried to drown herself, and Marian has gone and got drunk. Some says it da mean one thing, and some another.

Angel: Ah—well, Jonathan—drink this cup of ale, and accept this from me for your trouble, and hasten back again as soon as you can, in case they want you.

Gives ale and a gratuity.

Jonathan: Thank 'ee, sir; thank 'ee and your mis'ess to call her by her lawful—

Angel: Yes, Jonathan. *Thank you.* Good night.

Jonathan: Good night, sir, and ma'am, the same to you.

Jonathan *goes out.*

Scene VIII. Tess, Angel

Tess: I know why those girls acted so madly. They are breaking their hearts for you. It is very sad.

[a] Dorchester text adds: hev

ANGEL: It is not worth their while; but no, no! I am so sorry that he should have mentioned that. It's absurd.

TESS: They don't deserve to suffer; but . . . I do . . . and now I'm going to tell you why.

ANGEL: Wait a while. All in good time. Now at last we have the place to ourselves. What a great empty place it is! . . . (*Looking round.*) It was very good of the farmer to give us so much room—more than we want. We'll make ourselves secure, anyhow.

> TESS *leaves the table and sits down on the settle by the fire.* HE *goes out, and is heard bolting and barring the outer door; returns; unpacks portmanteau; takes out a piece of mistletoe,* TESS *watching him.*

TESS: What is that?

ANGEL: A twig of mistletoe—though it is rather squeezed. (*He hangs it up under canopy of bed.*)

TESS (*turning away*): Oh, Angel. How romantic you are.

ANGEL: It's a romantic occasion, darling.

> HE *takes the portmanteau and box into the bedchamber; unpacks night-dresses, etc. While he is away from her, doing this,* TESS *takes out a letter.*

TESS (*reading*): "What I said before, dear Tess, I say still, that on no account do you tell him of your past with Mr. Alec D'Urberville. No girl would be such a fool, especially as it is so long ago, and he is not at all likely to find it out. You be afraid that he will, I know, but he's too innocent to do that yet: and if he do at all, or anybody tells him, it will not be for some months, when you've been married long enough for him to get tired of 'ee, and not care one straw whether anything happened in your past life or not. Then, dear Tess, keep up your spirits; and we mean to send you a hogshead of cider soon. So no more at present from your affectionate mother J. DURBEYFIELD."* (*Puts away letter.*) O mother, mother!

> SHE *looks into the fire.* ANGEL *comes up softly behind her, bends over her, takes her face between his hands,*

*London version marks the letter: Abridge this if necessary.

and kisses her. Then he sits down beside her. †*A knocking.*

ANGEL: What the deuce—somebody else? I wish they would leave us to ourselves. Who can it be?

Takes candle; goes and unbolts door, and peers out, TESS *staring in the same direction.*

MANSERVANT (*without*): Is this where Mr. and Mrs. Angel Clare are staying?

ANGEL: Yes, I am Mr. Clare.

SCENE IX. MANSERVANT, ANGEL, TESS

MANSERVANT (*entering*): Oh yes, sir—I see you are now; I was to give this into your own hands and nobody else's.—I reached Talbothays just too late to find you there—your wife and you had started a few minutes before; and so I have ridden on after you. It is from your father.

ANGEL: Oh yes, I see. Tess—here's something from father.

TESS: How good of him!

ANGEL: Will you rest a few minutes and have something?

MANSERVANT: Thanks. I've got the horse out here and I've a long way to go; so I won't stay. Good night, sir.

ANGEL: Good night. Tell my father and mother you found us well.

MANSERVANT: I will, sir.

MANSERVANT goes out. ANGEL *re-bars door, and brings in packet about 9 x 6 x 4 inches, in brown paper, large red seals.*

SCENE X. ANGEL, TESS

ANGEL: Why, it is directed to you. Open it, Tess.

TESS (*handling it timidly*): I don't like to, dear. It looks so

†London version marks material from here to dagger on page 179: Omit or not at option. (This material is absent from Dorchester text.)

important. (*Hands it back.* ANGEL *opens it. A jewel case is disclosed, with a note and key lying on it.*)

ANGEL (*reads*): "MY DEAR SON: Possibly you have forgotten that on the death of your godmother, she—vain, kind woman that she was—left me a portion of the contents of her jewel case in trust for your wife, if you should ever have one, as a mark of her affection for you, and whomsoever you should choose. This trust I have fulfilled and though I feel it to be a somewhat incongruous act in the circumstances, I am, as you will see, bound to hand over the articles to the woman you have chosen. They become, I believe, heirlooms, according to the terms of your godmother's will. The precise words that refer to this matter are enclosed.—Your affectionate father, JAMES CLARE." I do remember; but I had quite forgotten. (*Unlocks case, and exposes necklace of brilliants, with pendants; bracelets, etc.*)

TESS (*incredulously*): Are they mine?

ANGEL: They are certainly. (*He turns meditatively to the fire.*) Ah—my poor godmother! What expectations she had of me!
    While HE *stands with his back turned, thinking,* TESS
    quickly puts on necklace and bracelets.
I'm afraid there is a little irony in this! But Tess is a D'Urberville after all; whom could they become better? Tess, put them on, put them on. (*Turns to help her.*) Ah, you have done it.... But the gown is not right. It ought to be a low one for a set of brilliants like this.

TESS: Ought it?

ANGEL: Yes, like this. Can't you tuck in the upper part—so—? Then it will be a little like an evening dress.
    HE *watches her while* SHE *tucks in the upper edge of*
    her dress, slightly assisting. When it is done he steps back.

TESS: I will take them off. They seem to mock me.

ANGEL: No—let them stay a few minutes. Sit down here and let me see how they look in the firelight. (THEY *sit down.*)†

ANGEL: You must not think because *a*my father writes so stiffly and*b* all my relations declined to come to our wedding, that they

---

*a-b*Absent from Dorchester text.

are not going to forgive us. My mother, in particular, is not at all set against you so much as you suppose. She says to me in her letter, that though she may have wished me to marry otherwise, she knows you to be a good and innocent maiden: and those are the chief things, after all. I have it here. (*Pulls out letter and reads.*) She says: "I am sure she must be very pretty, Angel, or she wouldn't have won you. And that she is pure and virtuous goes without saying. Certainly, I could have wished for a more equal match; but there are worse wives than these simple, rosy-mouthed girls of the countryside. Living in such seclusion she naturally had scarce ever seen any young men of the social world till she saw you."—Which is so of course.—She goes on: "I have been reading to-night the chapter in Proverbs in praise of a virtuous wife. 'Who can find a virtuous woman? for her price is far above rubies.' I could not help thinking how very aptly some of the particulars applied to the one you have chosen. May Heaven shield her in all her ways!" (*Puts away letter.*) Dear mother! I am sure she will soon get my father and brothers to see you in the same light. (*Turns to caress her—but* TESS *draws back.*)

TESS: No, no! I want to sit here and talk a little while. . . . I said I would like to tell you my history, didn't I?

ANGEL (*securing her hand*): Ah, yes! we said that we would tell each other our faults, so we did. Very well. Go it, little one! Much of a hidden past you have—you innocent bird—about as much as a sparrow, or a half-opened rose-bud. But, speaking seriously, I really have a grave confession to make—

TESS (*quickly*): Have you? You have to confess something?

ANGEL: And as this is a sort of proper occasion I'll out with it now. I did not mention it, though I was going to tell you at the time you agreed to be mine, but I could not; I thought it might frighten you away from me, knowing nothing of what men are. But I *must*, now I see you sitting there [c] solemnly. I wonder if you'll forgive me?

TESS (*eagerly*): Oh yes—I am sure I shall!

ANGEL: Well, I hope so. But wait a minute. You don't know

---

[c]Dorchester text adds: so.

how bad it is.—You have thought too highly of me. Now listen. Put your head there, because I do want you to forgive me, and not to be indignant with me.

    HE *draws up to her and* SHE *puts her face against his shoulder.*

Of course, men don't always tell these things; but I feel I shall seem more honest if I tell you.... I am a believer in good morals, Tess, as much as you. Perhaps though I am not religious myself, owing to my having grown up in a strictly religious family, I have always admired spotlessness, even though I could lay no claim to it. Well, a certain place is paved with good intentions, and having felt like that so strongly, you will see what a terrible remorse it bred in me when in the midst of my fine aims for virtue in others I myself fell. (TESS *starts.*) You did not expect it!

It happened like this; I was tossed about by doubts and difficulties as to a profession, and other things. I went to London, and there I was like a cork on the waves.... I met [d] a woman, and—well, I won't sully your ears with particulars. (TESS *starts up.*) Happily I awoke almost immediately to a sense of my folly. I came home. I have never repeated the offence. But I felt I should like to treat you with perfect frankness [e]and honour[f], and I could not do so without telling this. You forgive me?

TESS: Oh, Angel—yes, I do forgive you—because now you can forgive me! I have not made my confession yet.

ANGEL: Ah—to be sure. (*Pulls her head again to his shoulder.*)

TESS: Perhaps, although you smile, it is as serious as yours or more so.

ANGEL: It can hardly be more serious, dearest.

TESS (*speaking low and slowly*): It cannot—since it is the same. Yes, my husband; it is the same.

ANGEL (*mechanically*): The same?

TESS: Yes.[g] (HE *is about to start up;* SHE *puts her arms round his shoulders, and retains him in his seat.*) I—am not what you think me.... I grew up at Marlott, a lonely village. I was less

    [d]with
    [e-f]Absent from the Dorchester text.
    [g]Yes: the same.

than eighteen when, as I told you, an antiquarian discovered that we were the lineal descendants of the ancient and powerful D'Urberville family and told it to my father. It turned the heads of my parents. I was told I must marry a gentleman . . . and was sent away—where there was a fast young man—and not understanding his meaning till it was too late—I—gave way to him.

ANGEL (*starting up*): You mean me to understand that the *h* man—!*i*

TESS (*retaining her seat and looking into the fire*): I do.

ANGEL: My God! (*He walks away to the other end of the room, and turns round, and regards her.*) And what—and what—!

TESS (*still looking into the fire*): And I had a—had—

ANGEL: You had *j* a child?*k*

TESS: Yes.

> ANGEL *regards her in silence; comes back; stirs the fire in a paralysed manner; stands and faces her;* SHE *continuing to look down fixedly.*

ANGEL (*slowly*): Tess!

TESS: Yes.

ANGEL: Am I to believe this? From your manner I—I—it seems that I am to take it as true? Oh, you cannot be out of your mind? But you ought to be. My—wife—nothing in you warrants such a supposition as that!

TESS (*looking at him*): I am not out of my mind.

ANGEL: And yet—(*Pauses—gazing vacantly; then calls out.*) Why didn't you tell me before? . . . Why didn't you! . . . (*Suddenly drops his voice to a murmur.*) Ah yes—yes—you wished to—in a way—I remember! I remember!

> ANGEL*l* *goes and leans over the back of a chair, covering his face.* TESS *rises slowly, follows him, and stands looking at him. Then she slips down upon her knees against his foot, and crouches in a heap.*

TESS (*huskily but emphatically*): Forgive me! In—the—name of our love—forgive me! (*Pause.*) I have forgiven you for the

*h-i*man gained you?
*j-k*a (*With bated breath.*) child?
*l*HE

same. (*Pause.*) Oh forgive me, as you are forgiven! *I* forgive *you*, Angel.

ANGEL: Ah—you—yes. True—you do.

TESS: But you do not forgive me! (*Still kneeling* SHE *clings to his knees as he stands, and weeps passionately a long time;* HE *stands*ᵐ *immovable.*) Oh forgive me—again I beg it—I have forgiven you for the same!

ANGEL (*writhing*): Oh, forgiveness does not apply to the case! You were one person; now you are another. My God—how can forgiveness meet such a—a grotesque—transformation as this! ... Ha-ha! ha-ha! (*Laughs unnaturally.*)

TESS: Oh don't! don't! It kills me quite—that! Oh have mercy upon me—have mercy! (*She springs up.*) Angel, Angel, what do you mean by that laugh? Do you know what this is to me? (HE *shakes his head with a wild reckless air.*) I have been hoping, longing, praying to make you happy. I have thought what joy it would be to do it—to live to do that alone. That's what I have felt, Angel!

ANGEL: Have you?

TESS: I thought, Angel, that you loved me—*me*—my very self! If it is I that you do love, oh how can it be that you look and speak so? It frightens me! Having begun to love you, I must love you for ever,—in all changes, in all disgraces, because you are yourself. Then how can you, O my husband, stop loving me?

ANGEL: I repeat: the woman I have been loving is not you.

TESS: But who?

ANGEL: Another woman in your shape.

TESS: Oh—you look upon me—as having been a sort of impostor—a guilty woman—a cheat—a liar! (SHE *turns, swerves, nearly falls—*HE *saves her, and helps her to a chair.*)

ANGEL: Sit down, sit down. You are ill; and it is natural.

TESS *sits and gazes at him.*

TESS: I don't belong to you any more, then, do I, Angel? It is not me, but another woman that he loved, he says.

A pause: SHE *bursts into tears.* HE *stands motionless, till*

ᵐ*standing*

her sobbing has exhausted itself, which it does all of a sudden, and she speaks naturally.

Angel, am I too wicked for you and me to live together as man and wife?

ANGEL: I have not been able to think what we can do.

TESS: I don't ask you to let me live with you. I suppose I have no right to.... If you go away I shall not follow you, and if you never speak to me any more I shall not ask why. I shall obey you like a wretched slave, even if it be to lie down and die!

ANGEL: You are very good. But it strikes me that there is a want of harmony *ⁿbetween yourᵒ* present mood of self-sacrifice and your past mood of self-preservation.

TESS winces as if struck; slips down on her knees from her chair and clasps her hands.

TESS: I never meant to keep it secret.

ANGEL: But you did keep it secret.

TESS: I meant I didn't—mean to longer than—

ANGEL (*emphatically*): But you did!

TESS: Not to keep the secret longer than—

ANGEL (*yet louderᵖ*): But you did! (*He drops his voice.*) Tess, I cannot stop in this room just now. I will walk out a little way.

TESS (*passionately*): Oh no, no, no! Stay with me! stay! What have I done? What *have* I done? Nothing that I have said belies my love for you. You don't think I planned it, do you? It is in your own mind what you are angry at, Angel; it is not in me. Oh, I am not the deceitful woman you think me!

ANGEL (*flinging himself down in a chair*): H'm—well. Not deceitful. But not the same woman. *Not the same.*

TESS: I was a mere girl when it happened. I knew nothing of men. Then you will not forgive me?

ANGEL: I do forgive you, as a human being.... But forgiveness is not all.

TESS: And love me?

HE does not answer; walks out of the room; SHE sits

ⁿ⁻ᵒbetween (*Pause.*) your
ᵖDorchester text adds: *and more emphatically.*

down by the table and remains with face in hands till he returns.

ANGEL: Tess—(SHE *looks up with a start and buries her face again.*) say it is not true! No—it is not true.
TESS (*in a low voice*): It is true.
ANGEL: Every word?
TESS: Every word—every word is true.
ANGEL: Is he living?
TESS: The baby died.
ANGEL: But the man?
TESS: He is alive.
ANGEL (*after a despairing sigh*): Is he in England?
TESS: Yes.
ANGEL: Who is he?
TESS*q*: Must I go further? and grieve you yet more? But I will tell you all. . . . It was Alec D'Urberville—the same man who insulted your father in his ministry. *r*Oh, but hear me! It was owing to the antiquarian discovering who we were. I was persuaded to stay at the rich D'Urbervilles' house.*s*
ANGEL: *That* man! God have mercy! *Such* a man!
TESS: Yes.
ANGEL: The deep deepens!
TESS: It was so unlikely that I should know. I had no other thought than that he was a sort of cousin of ours.
ANGEL: It was just like ten thousand cases. *t*(*Half aside.*) Every woman with a past of the kind has the same tale to tell.*u*

> ANGEL *takes two or three turns up and down the room:—*
> *v*abruptly, then:*w*

Our position is this. I thought—any man would have thought—that by giving up all ambition to win a wife with social standing I should secure rustic innocence as surely as I should secure pink cheeks; but—however, I am no man to reproach you; and I will not.

*q*Dorchester text adds: (*throws her head back*).
*r-s*Absent from Dorchester text.
*t-u*Absent from Dorchester text.
*v-w*abruptly:

TESS (*looking up with some calmness*): It is unnecessary. I see *your* justification too well, too well!

ANGEL: Well—we must understand each other, anyhow. I cannot live with you at present—that I've decided—without despising myself, and what is worse perhaps, despising you. . . . Allow me to speak plainly, otherwise you will not perceive all our difficulties. How can we live together, with that man hovering about you? Think of children being born to us, and this past matter getting known to them and others;—for it must get known. [x]Think of the wretches of our own flesh and blood growing up under such a taunt. What an awakening for them![y] What a prospect! Therefore it is best to part now, before our marriage has been made real. Can you say "stay[z] with me" after contemplating this?

TESS (*drooping*): I cannot. I cannot say "stay[a]". I had not thought so far! . . . You must go away from me.

ANGEL: But what can you do?

TESS: I can go home.

ANGEL: Are you sure?

TESS: Quite sure. We ought to part, and we may as well get it past and over quickly. Otherwise I might win you to me (*Bitterly.*) against your better judgment; and that would be terrible.

ANGEL: Then it shall be so.

    TESS *starts and steals an appalled glance at him.*

TESS: I will go to-morrow.

ANGEL: And I shall not stay here. . . . I think of people more kindly when I am away from them. . . . I want to think kindly of you again. I want to make your life as easy as I can. . . . God knows: perhaps we shall shake down together some day in sheer weariness and indifference. . . . Thousands have done it. . . . Anyhow, let us not hate each other. There is no anger between us, though there is that which I cannot endure. . . . I will let you know where I go to, as soon as I know myself. . . . And until I come to you, it will be better that you should not try to come to me.

  [x-y]Absent from Dorchester text.
  [z]remain
  [a]remain

TESS (*slowly*): Until you come to me, I must not try to come to you.

ANGEL: Just so.

TESS: May I write to you?

ANGEL: Yes. If you are ill or want anything. But I'll make a provision for you, so that you will not till I write to you. Now I will go back and pack my things, and arrange matters.

TESS*ᵇ*: I agree to the conditions, Angel; because you, my love and my husband, know best what my punishment ought to be. Only—only—*don't* make it more than I can bear!

ANGEL: I will try that it may not be more than you can bear. But I cannot stay—I cannot—yet.

TESS (*sinking down*): Oh but it is, it is! My punishment *is* more than I can bear!

> SHE *sobs brokenly.* ANGEL *stands rigid, his gaze on the ground.* HE *looks at her; then takes his hat, puts it on, looks back at her, goes out, closes the door, noiselessly.*

SCENE XI. TESS *alone*

> TESS *still sobbing turns her head, stares around*ᵃ *the room: and finding him gone, rushes to the bedroom, where she regards the mistletoe, the pillows, and the night-dresses.* ᵇ*She*ᶜ *flings herself on the* ᵈ*bed or floor*ᵉ*, her previous sobbing changing to uncontrollable* ᶠ*throes of*ᵍ *grief.*

TESS: Oh—oh—oh! . . . Oh—oh—oh! It *is* more than I can bear!*ʰ*

CURTAIN *ⁱ(to the chant-tune of* LANGDON *in F)ʲ*

END OF ACT III

*ᵇ*Dorchester text adds: (*with resigned dignity*).
*ᵃ*round
*ᵇ⁻ᶜ*Returning she
*ᵈ⁻ᵉ*table
*ᶠ⁻ᵍ*hysteric
*ʰ*Dorchester text adds: (*When* TESS *flings herself on Oak Seat then*—).
*ⁱ⁻ʲ*Absent from Dorchester text.

ACT IV

Sandbourne

More than a year has passed since the previous act.

The interior of the first floor drawing-room of well-furnished seaside lodgings. At the back are folding doors, one of which is open, communicating with a bedroom, a corner of the bed being visible. In the front room is a breakfast table laid for two. A MAIDSERVANT *finishes the arrangements, and places letters and a newspaper on the table. A ring at the front door is heard.* MAIDSERVANT *closes the bedroom door, and goes out of the front room by the other door.*

Re-enter MAIDSERVANT, *showing in* ANGEL CLARE, *pale and travel-stained, and* JOAN DURBEYFIELD *in widow's mourning.*

SCENE I. MAIDSERVANT, JOAN, ANGEL

MAIDSERVANT: I'll ask mistress if Mrs. D'Urberville can be seen yet. But I think it is too early.

JOAN: We can wait.

*Sits down—*MAIDSERVANT *goes out.*

SCENE II. ANGEL, JOAN

ANGEL: I thought she said "Mrs. D'Urberville"—not "Mrs. Clare"?

JOAN (*evasively*): Oh, Tess has never taken your name since you married her and went away from her, and that's more than a year ago, I'd remind you, sir. (*A pause.*) Since you would come here to Sandbourne, to hunt her up, you must put up with the consequences. But *I* don't know how she has been living since she left home!

ANGEL: How came she to leave you? I told her to go home when we parted, and to remain there. *ª And I stayed those months and months in Brazil with no other idea.ᵇ*

JOAN: Well, she did come for a time. But it was awkward, for

ª⁻ᵇAbsent from Dorchester text.

everybody got to know that you had deserted her, and guessed why. Then Sir John died, poor man, and as we held the house on his life only, we were turned out at the end of the quarter. A useful relation you've been, sir, to a poor family in trouble! Marrying her, and going off suddenly, and Tess never seeing you again all those long months. When women marry, their husbands should keep 'em—that's what I say!

ANGEL: I quite admit it. But I was ill of fever *c*such a weary time*d* in Brazil! and before I left England I gave her all the money I could.

JOAN: We were put to such straits that I had to spend it on the rest of the family. Tess had to work in the fields swede-hacking till her poor fingers were frozen, and she *e*had hardly enough to eat*f*.

ANGEL: How *g*terrible—and I not knowing!*h* I quite understood in addition to the money I left her, that my parents were seeing she wanted for nothing in my absence! I told her to apply to them in any difficulty.

JOAN: Tess had enough D'Urberville blood not to do it! She said she'd starve first*i*. Thinking they knew of your reason for leaving her, she was not going to people who would scorn her. . . . She *was* a little fool to confess to you as she did. If she had not squeaked, maybe*j* you would never have known, and all would have been well.

ANGEL: She was a good woman to tell me.—It was I who was the fool.

Re-enter MAIDSERVANT.

SCENE III.   MAIDSERVANT, ANGEL, JOAN

MAIDSERVANT: The lady is not ready yet, but she will be soon, if you can wait, or call again.

JOAN: We'll wait.

MAIDSERVANT *goes out.*

*c-d*for months
*e-f*was nearly starved
*g-h*terrible!
*i*Dorchester text adds: which she nearly did.
*j*Absent from Dorchester text.

Scene IV. Angel, Joan

Angel: *Yes, I ought to have forgiven her. I have owned it. I have admitted my faults. They have been great, and I don't wish to extenuate them. But*a* I loved your daughter with all the devotion and sincerity that one can wish to feel towards a woman of such charm, and, as I thought, such innocence, as was hers. *b*(Speaking rapidly.)* You know, or you ought to know, how I stuck to her against the wishes of my parents; and how at last they gave way because of my fervent representations to them of her worthiness to be their daughter. Old-fashioned clergyman as my father is, old-fashioned gentlewoman as is my mother, with all the stiffness of their class, yet they decided to welcome her as their own, on the strength of this one supposition, that she was an innocent maiden. . . .*c* Well, I married her. Then the revelation came. I quite admit that she was the sinned against, and not the sinner—poor darling! but there was the fact. It turned my light into darkness as black as hell. You have never been a man in such a terrible position; God forbid that my worst enemy should ever be*d*. It almost turned my brain—I hardly knew what I did after the blow came upon me. Nothing so pure, so virginal as Tess had seemed possible. *(He looks down and speaks to himself.)* "But the little less, and what worlds away!" *(Pause.)* Well, Mrs. D'Urberville, in the sudden revulsion of feeling I acted too*e* hastily; but I acted as I thought for the best. To gain time for reflection—to think of some mode *f*to live*g* the scandal down—I agreed that she should go home and live with you awhile. And there I thought to find her. . . . However, what's done can't be undone. I've come back. *(Looks round the room.)** Do you really mean to say that you don't really know what she's doing here, or how she's living? The girl called her "the lady."

*-*Marked in London version: May be omitted.
*a*Absent from Dorchester text.
*b-c*Absent from Dorchester text.
*d*Dorchester text adds: in such a position as mine when Tess confessed that damnable secret to me.
*e*Absent from Dorchester text.
*f-g*of living

JOAN (*evasively*): It is more your business as her husband to know, than it is mine! All I can say is that she has made enough money to pay our debts, and keep us in comfort ever since she . . . (*Pausing.*) took the position[h] here.

ANGEL (*puzzled*): But you must have some idea? (JOAN *shakes her head.*) Will she be glad that I've come back to her? Or do you think she has forgotten me?

JOAN: Not forgotten you. She may have given you up. (*Restlessly.*) You worry me, sir, with your questions!

ANGEL: Perhaps she doesn't wish to see me?

JOAN: I fancy she doesn't now! . . . Look here, Mr. Clare. You go out awhile, and I'll wait for her alone. I'll prepare her for your visit. It will be better than your bursting suddenly upon her.

ANGEL: Yes, you are right. I'll come back in ten minutes.

HE *goes out.*

SCENE V. JOAN *alone*

JOAN: Good God—what will come of it all? (*A pause.*)

> TESS *enters from the bedroom. She is in a dressing-gown and slippers, her hair being tied back, so that it falls in a mass behind. She starts at sight of her* [a]*mother, and her mother stands embarrassed at her appearance.*[b]

SCENE VI. JOAN, TESS

JOAN (*awkwardly*)[a]: You didn't think to see me, dear Tess, at this time of the day? But I've had to come—I'll tell you why directly. You barely gave me your address; you might have told me how you were living and where the money comes from that you've sent me[b]. Since you went away you've told us nothing about yourself.

TESS: *Told* you, mother! As if you couldn't guess! How do you suppose I could have kept you but for him?

---
[h]situation
[a-b]mother.
[a]Absent from Dorchester text.
[b]us

JOAN: Who?

TESS: Mr. D'Urberville, of course. You must have known that! I couldn't earn enough all at once to be so open-handed as I have been, except through him—it is affectation to pretend it.

JOAN: I'll take my oath I knew nothing for certain. I was not in a position to ask questions; though I did guess—that's true. Well, I've something to tell 'ee, and I don't know how to begin.

TESS: How did you get here so early?

JOAN: I got up at six o'clock. (*Hesitates*.)

TESS: Won't you stay here[c] till breakfast? I'll get you some downstairs—not here. I'll tell the landlady.

SCENE VII. JOAN

JOAN: No, no. . . . I don't like to see you. (*Turns away*.)

Exit TESS *to order the breakfast*.

I can't tell her, and I can't tell Mr. Clare. I wish I was well out o' this! I'll get away home again.[a] [*Re-enter* TESS.]

SCENE VIII. JOAN, TESS

JOAN: I can't stay, Tess. Don't order breakfast. I must go back. I merely came to say that somebody you know would call this morning—I'll come in again later.

SHE goes out agitated.

One of the folding doors to the bedroom is thrust open from inside.

SCENE IX. TESS, ALEC : *then* TESS *and voice of* ALEC

ALEC (*looking*[a] *from bedroom* [b]*in dressing-gown*[c]): Who was that talking to you?

[c]Absent from Dorchester text.
[a]Dorchester text adds: *Re-enter* TESS.
[a]*looks*
[b-c]Absent from Dorchester text.

Tess: Mother called. I had no idea she was coming.
Alec: Oh! What did she call for?
Tess: I don't know. She's going to call again later.
Alec: What time is it, then?
Tess: Nearly ten.
Alec: Well, she's got here early enough. (*Withdraws*^d *again to bedroom.*)
Tess: Early! Formerly it would have seemed to me that half the day was gone.
Alec ^e(*from bed*)^f: But now you've gone up in the world your day is hardly begun!
Tess: I don't think I have gone up. I've gone the other way—down—down!
Alec: Pooh! That's like you, to be such a prude! Though you only sham it! You know better.
Tess (*bitterly*): I don't sham it! You know as well as I how I hate to be here. I'd rather be pulling swedes at Flintcomb-Ash Farm!
Alec: Well, all I can say is that you're infernally ungrateful. See what pretty things you wear! See what I've given you to spend on your people! A miserable broken-down lot—why, if it hadn't been for me they'd have^g had to go to the workhouse.
Tess: Don't say that! *I won't have it!* (*With emphasis.*) I hate my pretty things. As for the help to my poor mother and the children that you brag of, if you had given help to them freely that would have been generosity. But you didn't—your selfishness wouldn't let you. Everything you've given them I've had to *buy* of you, at a dear price enough!

    She sits ^h *at table and covers her face with her hands.*

Alec: What the devil are you doing? I won't stand these airs. Bring in the letters and paper. Do you hear?

    Tess *returns to bedroom with letters and paper, and the door is closed. A knocking is heard at the street door as*

^d*Exits*
^{e-f}Absent from Dorchester text.
^gAbsent from Dorchester text.
^hDorchester text adds: *down.*

she retreats. In a few minutes[i] there is a tap at the drawing-room door and the LANDLADY *enters.*

SCENE X. LANDLADY

LANDLADY: Mrs. D'Urberville! (*Seeing the room empty she goes and taps at the folding doors.*) Mrs. D'Urberville!

TESS: Did you want me?

Comes from bedroom and closes the door behind her.

SCENE XI. LANDLADY, TESS

LANDLADY: Yes, ma'am. Somebody has called to see you. I believe, he's the same that called with an elderly woman ten minutes ago when I was at breakfast, before you were ready to be seen.

TESS: Who can it be at this time? Somebody on business?

LANDLADY: Well, I don't think so. 'Tis a gentleman. He wants particularly to see you, though I said you wasn't an early riser. He seems puzzled about your name, though I know 'tis you he means. He says I'm to tell you his name is ANGEL—

TESS (*agitatedly*[a]): Oh—I don't think—I can't—I did not expect—[b]I suppose I can't deny....

LANDLADY (*going to door*): The lady will see you, sir. Will you come up? (*Holds open the door;* ANGEL's *step is heard.*)[c]

ANGEL CLARE enters. TESS *waves her hand to the* LANDLADY, *and she leaves the room, closing the door.* CLARE *rushes up to* TESS, *clasps her, and kisses her passionately.*

SCENE XII. TESS, ANGEL

*ANGEL: O my darling Tessie—at last—at last! Forgive me—

[i]*moments*
[a]*agitated*   [b-c]Absent from Dorchester text.
*-*The London text says of this material: The following abridgment may be used at option:
ANGEL: Tess, can you forgive me for going away? Can't you come to me? How do you get to be like this?
  TESS *gently thrusts him back, shaking her head, and withdraws herself further, pointing to the room, her dressing-gown, etc.*
  TESS: It is too late.

forgive me—I've been wandering hither and thither to find you—
I am back*a*! (TESS *gently thrusts him back, shaking her head.*)
What, don't you forgive me? I was very wrong, I know. I was
cruel in judging you so harshly. We'll never part again, never, if
you'll forgive me. (TESS *withdraws herself further.*) How do you
come to be in these strange circumstances? Your mother didn't
explain. It was sheer misery that drove me away, Tess—believe me,
dear, it was! But now we are both purified by affliction, and—

TESS: Stop . . . stop . . . stop. . . . There's something—a horrible
something, between us—don't you see how it is? what it is? Doesn't
it explain itself, all this? (*Points to the room, table, her dressing-
gown, etc.*)

ANGEL: I don't understand. Can't you forgive your husband—
can't you come to me? What are you doing here?

TESS: It is too late!*

ANGEL: No! Though I did not think rightly of you—I did not
see you as you were at first—I have learnt to, since—Tessy mine!

TESS: Too late, too late! (*Waving her hand.*) Don't come close
to me, Angel! No, you must not. *b*Keep away.*c*

ANGEL: But don't you love me, my dear wife? Is it because I
have been so pulled down by illness? You are not so fickle! I am
come on purpose for you! My mother and father will welcome
you now!

TESS: Yes—oh yes, yes! But I say, it is too late. Don't you know
all—don't you know it? Yet how do you come here if you don't
know?

ANGEL: †I called at your mother's and got your address, and
then it occurred to me that it would be better for her to accompany
me. So we came together, much against her will. But I feared you
wouldn't forgive me unless I got her to plead for me.—She has
suddenly left me.—I don't know why.†

TESS (*with sudden and tender pathos*): I waited and waited for

*a*come
*b-c*Absent from Dorchester text.
†-†London text has a note: This speech may be abridged to the following:
I inquired here and there and found my way.

you.... But you did not ᵈcome, and I wrote to you and you didn't come.ᵉ He kept on saying that you would never come any more and that I was a foolish woman to expect you. He wasᶠ very kind to me, and to mother, and to all of us in our distress, afterᵍ father's death. He—

ANGEL: He? I don't understand.

TESS (*pointing to the folding doors and speaking in a low and desperate voice*): He—Alec D'Urberville—he's got me back to live with him.

A pause in which ANGEL *regards her with stupefied despair.*
He's in ʰ there. I *hate* him now because he told me lies—that you were not coming again any more; and you *have* come! These clothes are what he has put upon me; I didn't care what he did wi' me! But hate him or not, here I am! But you will go away, Angel, *please*, and never come any more! ‡Oh *never* think of me, or pray for me, or pity me. Only forgive me!‡

ANGEL (*after a stillness in which he turns aside*): Ah . . . it is my fault— ‡mine only—and his!‡

TESS (*in a whisper*): Will you—go?

ANGEL ‡(*continuing to look away from her*): There is nothing else for me to do—nothing—nothing! While that man lives I am an outcast and accursed.—She has no kiss left for me.‡

HE *goes out.*

TESS, *her face buried in the sleeve of her dressing-gown, goes to the folding door, opens it to enter—but returns, leaving it open, and falling*ⁱ *on her knees over a chair sobs*ʲ *brokenly.*

SCENE XIII. TESS *alone : then* TESS *and the voice of* ALEC

TESS: He said "While that man lives she has no kiss for me!" My own husband says it! While that man lives he is an outcast, he says—and I—Oh, oh, oh, I *love him true*!

ᵈ⁻ᵉcome.   ᶠhas been   ᵍsince
ʰDorchester text adds: bed in
ⁱflings herself
ʲsobbing
‡-‡London text marked: May be cut.

ALEC (*from bedroom*): What's the matter? ... (*Pause.*) What are you doing? Who has been talking to you?

TESS: My husband.

ALEC: Who? What?

TESS (*sobbing upon chair*): How can I bear it? ... My dear, dear husband has come home to me.... And I did not know it. ... And you had used your cruel persuasion upon me ... you did not stop! My little sister and brothers, and my mother's troubles—they were the things you moved me by—and you said my husband would *never* come back—*never*; and you taunted me, and said what a simpleton I was to expect him. And at last I believed you, and gave way! ... And then he came back! Now he is gone—gone a second time, and I have lost him *a* for ever ... and he will not love me the littlest bit any more—only hate me.... Oh yes—I have lost him,—lost him—again because of you!

ALEC: What are you whining about? *I* am your husband, young woman, for the present.

TESS: And he is dying—he looks as if he were dying! And my sin will kill him, and not kill me! Oh, you have torn my life all to pieces—made me *b*be what I prayed you in pity not to make me be again.*c* My own true husband will never—

ALEC: Damn it, I tell you I am your husband, at any rate just now. Don't you be so infernally virtuous! If you hadn't been willing to sell yourself, you wouldn't have been here, you little humbug!

TESS: O God—I can't bear this—I cannot!

ALEC: Then get back to him! Or perhaps he came to make a quiet arrangement, for a consideration? A virtuous pair— *d*you two.*e* *f*(TESS *sobs.*)

TESS: O God! O God!

ALEC: Oh, stop that infernal noise!

TESS: I can't bear it, I can't.*g*

> TESS *springs up from the chair-seat over which she has been bending and rushes into the bedchamber, snatching*

*a*Dorchester text adds: now
*b-c*a victim, a chained slave.
*d-e*you and he.
*f-g*Absent from Dorchester text.

up the carving[h] *knife in passing the table. A* [i]*cry within*[j] *follows, then a silence. In a minute she comes back to front room, her countenance changed to* [k] *pallor. She carries in her arms her outdoor garments. She closes the door behind her, and quietly dresses herself before the chimney glass. When she has put on her hat and taken up her sunshade, she looks out of the window at the sky.*

SCENE XIV. TESS *alone*

TESS (*exclaiming to herself*): I am coming, my love![a]

She crosses and goes out as in a dream; her footsteps are heard descending the stairs, and the front door is heard to close. The room is empty for half a minute; the LANDLADY *is heard running up the stairs; then there is a knocking at the door.*[b]

LANDLADY (*without*): Mrs. D'Urberville. (*Pause.*) (*She half opens the door.*) Mrs. D'Urberville! There's a red stain in the

[h]Absent from Dorchester text.
[i-j]*rustling*
[k]Dorchester text adds: *a.*
[a-b]You will love me now! He doesn't live, and you are not an outcast any more! (*Pause.*) Ah, I hear a step!

Re-enter ANGEL.

ANGEL: I felt I must see you *once* more! Then I'll go for ever.
TESS (*calmly*): Angel, things have changed. I have dressed to go with you. May I?
ANGEL (*bewildered*): You really wish to?
TESS: My tie with him is broken. It can never be renewed. (*Pause.*) He's dead.
ANGEL: Dead?
TESS: May I go with you? We can hide in the New Forest. I'll tell you as I go. I am free.
ANGEL: I don't understand. But, anyhow, come with me.

They go out by the landing door and the front door is heard to close. The room is empty for half a minute; then there is knocking at the door.

ceiling below your bedroom; something soaking through. Drip, drip, drip, as the red of blood!*c*

CURTAIN

END OF ACT IV

AFTER-SCENE

Stonehenge

The stage is in darkness; on its gradually lightening a view of the ruin is revealed.

Daybreak

TESS *is seen lying on a horizontal stone, from which* ANGEL *has just risen. Her hair is down and his greatcoat, lined with red, is beneath her. A small portmanteau near.*

SCENE. ANGEL, TESS

ANGEL: Well, what shall we do now, darling? We may find a better shelter further on.

TESS (*drowsily*)*a*: I don't want to go any further. Can't we stay here?

ANGEL: I am afraid not. This spot is visible for miles by day, although it has not seemed so to us in the dark.

TESS: I should like to die here. One of my mother's people was a shepherd hereabouts, now I think of it. And you used to say I was a heathen. So now I am at home. How lucky it was that I *b*followed after you that day last week I escaped!*c*

ANGEL: Yes. I had a presentiment that you wanted to see me

*c*Dorchester text adds:
  LANDLADY *enters. Finding the room empty she goes to the folding doors, knocks; opens one of them a few inches. Turns back in horror.* SERVANT *enters.*

LANDLADY: Oh, what has happened! Good God—the gentleman is dying or dead. He has been murdered. The young lady has done it.
*a*Absent from Dorchester text.
*b-c*came with you!

again. So I looked back, and there you were ^drunning! running after me!^e

TESS: Oh, and I was in such dread that you would have gone forever before I could let you know that I was free from him. . . . *f*

*g*TESS: I don't know how I did it—I felt I owed it to you and to myself. . . . I feared long ago when I struck him on the mouth that I might do it some day, after his wrong to you through me. He came between us and ruined us, and now he can never do it any more. I never loved him at all, my own dear, as I love you. You know it, don't you? You believe it?

ANGEL: I do.

TESS: You didn't come back to me, and I was obliged to go back to him—that was the sum of it! But I don't blame you: only, have you forgiven me my sin against you now that I've killed him? It came to me as a shining light that I should get you back that way. You don't know how unable I was to bear your not loving me. Say you have, dear, dear husband, say you have, now I have killed him; and I will go back to whatever fate awaits me.

She flings her arms around him.

ANGEL: I do love you still, Tess, and have forgiven you. It has all come back. (*Enclosing her in his arms.*) But by saying so often you have killed him do you mean you have killed your love for him?

TESS: No. I mean that I have.

ANGEL: What bodily? Is he dead?*

TESS: Yes. It was as I have told you. He called you by a foul name. And then I did it.

ANGEL: It is very—very— . . . if true. Perhaps you tried to? . . . Anyway I will not desert you now.^h Our spirits have mixed and have become one ever since. (*Kissing her.*) I think you are lying on an altar.

*d-e*looking out of the window, ready!
*f*Dorchester text adds:
ANGEL: But your spirit whispered it to me, and made me turn. And that made all the difference.
*g-h*Absent from Dorchester text.
*Compare the Dorchester explanation of Alec's murder at the end of Act IV, p. 198, n. *a-b*.

Tess: Am I? I like very much to stay *here—so*ʲ lonely—after my great happiness in finding you and getting you to forgive me. All those days we have had together in the Newᵏ Forest it seemed as if there were no folk in the world, but we two! and I wish there were not—except Liza-Lu. Angel, when my end comes,—and it will soon—will you watch over Liza-Lu for my sake?

Angel: I will. But your end is not—

Tess: She has all the best of me without the bad of me. . . . How wicked and mad I was to do it! Yet formerly I could not bear to hurt or kill anything, not even a worm or a fly.

Angel: Don't talk of it. You had lost your reason for the time, Tess. I saw when you said you were coming with me that you did not know what you had been doing. Such aberrations are well known. The poor little over-strained brain gave way. ˡ(*Supports her.*)ᵐ However, we must get away.

Tess: Why should we put an end to all that's sweet? What must come, will come. All is trouble in a noisy world; here it is all peace. . . . And I don't want to get away. I fear that what you think of me will not last. I would rather be dead and buried if aⁿ time ever comes that you may despise me, so that it may never be known to me that you despised me.

Angel: I cannot ever despise you.

Tess: That's what I hope. But considering what my life has been, I cannot see how any man, sooner or later, can help despising me.

Angel: One man cannot help loving you—now and for ever! And I ᵒthink, dearest, weᵖ can escape, by getting out of this district and going straight north. Nobody will think of looking for us there. We shall be searched for at the Wessex ports if we are searched for at all.

Tess: I will go where you tell me, dear, of course. But my life can only be a question of a few weeks more or less.

ⁱ⁻ʲhere. It is so
ᵏAbsent from Dorchester text.
ˡ⁻ᵐ(*Kisses her.*)
ⁿthe
ᵒ⁻ᵖthink we

ANGEL (*after looking round*): I fancy some one is about the neighbourhood early as it is.

TESS (*calmly*): Let them be, so that you are near. Do you wish me to go on?

ANGEL (*peering into the distance*): I think we had better wait a few minutes. Somebody seems to be passing out there. ⁹Are you still sleepy?ʳ Lie down again.

TESS *lies down.*

TESS: Did they sacrifice to God here?

ANGEL: No.

TESS: Who to?

ANGEL: I believe to the sun. That high stone set away by itself is in the direction of the sun, which will presently rise behind it.

TESS: Tell me, Angel. Do you think we shall meet again, after we are dead? I want to know. (HE *kneels and kisses her without replying.*) ˢOh, Angel, I fear that means no. And I wanted so much to see you again.... So much—so much!ᵗ You and I, Angel, who love each other so well, are—sure—sure—

SHE *falls asleep. Sun rises.*

ᵘCONSTABLE'S *shadow appears.* ANGEL *starts as if for defence.*

CONSTABLE (*speaking from off*): It's no use, sir. There are sixteen of us on the plain, and the whole country is reared.

ANGEL (*in broken voice*): Let her finish her sleep! (THEY *wait.*)ᵛ

TESS (*waking*): What is it, Angel? ʷHave they comeˣ for me? (*Sitting up.*)

ANGEL: Yes, dearest. They ʸhave come.ᶻ

TESS (*standing up*): It is as it should be. I am almost glad—yes —glad! This happiness with you could not have lasted. It was too much! I have had enough, and now I shall not live for you to

ᵠ⁻ʳAnd you are still sleepy.
ˢ⁻ᵗAbsent from Dorchester text.
ᵘ⁻ᵛANGEL (*rising and looking round again: then turning to* TESS): Well, let her sleep. Who knows! ... Ah! (*With a start.*) Here they are. Her story, then, is true! (*Stoops and gently wakes* TESS.)
ʷ⁻ˣAre they coming
ʸ⁻ᶻare coming. I see them closing round us.

despise me. (*She arranges her dress, they kiss each other, and await capture, looking off stage.*) *ᵃ* I am ready.

CURTAIN

THE END

ᵃDorchester text adds: Don't resist them, my dear husband!

APPENDIX

TESS IN THE FILMS

THE screen version of *Tess of the D'Urbervilles* made by Goldwyn Pictures Corporation in 1924[1] was a travesty from beginning to end. Some of the shots were made in England (for instance, in the enclosure of an abbey), as suggested by Hardy when the director and photographer called on him for his opinions; the costumes were supposed to be as near as possible to Herkomer's drawings; the director of the Goldwyn Corporation said that every effort would be made to treat *Tess* "worthily and reverently"; Harper and Brothers thought Goldwyn would make "a true and accurate picture": nevertheless, the result was bathos and license. J. T. Grein called it "that monstrosity that amounted to a sacrilege which was presented to us as a film."[2]

Imagine Conrad Nagel playing Angel Clare as a modern young officer with a wrist-watch and Blanche Sweet playing Tess in the manner of *Rebecca of Sunnybrook Farm,* or imagine Hardy's Wessex before 1891 with up-to-date motor-cars, telephones, and night clubs! A protest to the editor of the London *Observer* written by Clive Holland, October 19, 1924, says: "Even the use of a Colt revolver (as in a recent film play) by a highwayman in the time of George III, is not a greater anachronism. One can, indeed, laugh at the lapse in this last named effort; but, indeed, almost weep over Tess of the night club, and the wilful destruction of the whole atmosphere of the tragic and wonderful story of the Wessex peasant girl."

There were other loud and bitter protests against the Paris gowns, taxis, and night clubs. One letter ended by the writer's expressing his deep regret that Tess was subjected to "ruthless and unforgivable treatment at the hands of a philistine producer. Every Hardy lover will hope that in the future Mr. Hardy's works may be preserved from the merciless onslaughts of the screen-producing vandals."[3]

[1] There had been an earlier version in 1919 which Mrs. Hardy said was not convincing.
[2] *Theatre*, December, 1925.
[3] Reprinted in the *Stage*, December 21, 1924.

Cinematographic technique should have the advantage over the stage in giving atmosphere and background. Marshall Neilan, the director of the Goldwyn film, evidently failed to take this advantage. With too much Hollywood, too little Wessex, it must have told a commonplace story.

But it is interesting to observe its fidelity to the book in one particular episode—the letter's going astray. In the film Tess slips her full confession under the door and inadvertently under the carpet as well, so that Angel does not receive it. The moving picture could and did show Tess quietly climbing the stairs to Angel's room as she does in the novel. The fidelity to the novel in this respect, however, did not save the picture.

It is the lack of any native and 'ninety-ish hall-marks—and all that goes with them—that deprives this film version of *Tess* of everything approaching the book's grim distinction. The characters retain their names and roles; but it is as if they had strayed into the wrong wardrobe of the film factory and ingeniously disguised themselves in the nearest and dearest trappings that offered. It should, of course, have been a costume piece. As it is, Tess begins her tragic career in a little muslin frock and hat that would be considered chic on a musical comedy queen; and she enacts its more lurid episodes in an ultra-fashionable confection that would turn even a Los Angeles vamp green with envy. But, considering the pep that is put into her downfall, and the *savoir faire* with which she enters the various smart motors, night clubs and palatial bedrooms of her seducer, one cannot pretend that she is unsuitably dressed. So, too, with Angel Clare—preposterous fellow! He changes from plus fours to the latest thing in faultless evening dress with the ease and assurance of a leading man in revue; and his tiresome character is not helped thereby.

The Hardy atmosphere cannot stand this kind of thing. It turns the main features of a Victorian masterpiece—which are all that survive in the film—into crude melodrama, and affects one much as the conversion of Westminster Hall into a cabaret might affect a serious minded archaeologist. Call the result anything but *Tess of the D'Urbervilles*, and one could accept it as an efficient if not very remarkable example of modern American photo-play. But, doubly labelled as it is, one can only regret that an outstanding literary landmark has been abused, and that the name of Thomas Hardy has been taken in vain.[1]

[1] Unidentified clipping, bearing the title "Thomas Hardy Screened," October 12, 1924, signed H. H. (Harvard Theatre Collection).

APPENDIX

Most admirers of Hardy's novel who saw the film would probably agree with Clive Holland who said:

> ... I had doubts that *Tess* would film well. But I confess I did not anticipate the length to which the producers have gone altering a classic.
>
> To have crudely brought up to date, as has been done, this masterpiece of tragic fiction is an outrage upon literature. One wonders—if he has seen it—what Mr. Hardy thinks of the version that has been produced for the screen.[1] The great charm of *Tess of the D'Urbervilles* is, of course, the wonderful character drawing, the beautiful descriptions of scenery, and that elusive quality described as "atmosphere." Practically all this must of necessity be lost in "screening." But dairymaid Tess in Paris gowns—not even of her period—a rusher about in taxis, and a frequenter of night clubs! Bathos and license in screen production could not go further. ...
>
> *Tess of the D'Urbervilles* as conceived by the producers of the screen version is poor melodrama at best. It will give no one who has not read the story any idea of the greatness of the book. It will surely disgust all who have an acquaintance with Mr. Hardy's masterpiece.
>
> Knowing Wessex well ..., the same scenes of the story, and something of the country folk in Tess's land, I can only express my profound regret that the tragic story should have been so mishandled and distorted by a clumsy producer evidently out after "effects" at all costs.[2]

[1] I do not know whether Hardy accepted the invitation but I found a letter inviting him to attend the press and trade review of the film *Tess* on October 21, at 11 o'clock at Messrs. Pykes' Cinematograph Theatre, 105 Charing Cross Road (Cambridge Circus) W.C.

[2] Clive Holland, letter to the *Observer*, October 19, 1924.

PIRACIES AND FARCES OF *TESS*[1]

PERHAPS there is no better indication of the dramatic appeal of *Tess of the D'Urbervilles* than that given by the large number of unauthorized versions. From 1894, *Tess* has been melodrama, farce, and burlesque. Mrs. Hardy refers to the first of these versions. "At the end of a week he [Mr. Hardy] fetched his wife from Hastings, and after more dinners and luncheons he went to a melodrama at the Adelphi, which was said to be based without acknowledgement on *Tess of the D'Urbervilles*."[2] Later Mr. Harry Mountford arranged a dramatic version of *Tess,* in which Maud Walsh enacted the title role, at the Grand Theatre, Blackpool, January 5, 1900. In America there were also a number. Mrs. Fiske and Harper, however, suppressed some through legal means.

Among the American actresses, authorized or not, who played Tess were Rebecca Warren, Carline Rohr, Mary Lawton, Isabelle Fletcher, and Evelyn Vaughan.

Rebecca Warren played Lorimer Stoddard's version of *Tess*, presented by Melville B. Raymond, at the Columbia Theatre in Boston on February 8, 1894. The *Boston Evening Transcript* says of her:

> She was especially convincing when, in the second act, after her marriage to Angel, she played the part of the happy bride, and the rapid change from joy to sorrow when she learned that her new husband had not found and read the letter she wrote as her confession was poignant with the pain she expressed in face and figure. Her despair when Angel left her affected her hearers, who paid her the tribute of appreciative silence. As well done was the passage in Alec's lodgings, where she, the faithless wife, is compelled to bear the insults of her master, anguish and torture, the stinging rebukes of the man who has tired of her—the former expressed without the aid of words, the latter repelled with tragic scorn; these fitted the exacting scene so well

---

[1] A somewhat abbreviated account of these piracies and farces appeared under the title of "Farces and Piracies of Mrs. Fiske's *Tess*" in the *Colby Library Quarterly* for June, 1945.

[2] F. E. Hardy, *Life of Thomas Hardy*, II, 32.

that, whatever may be Miss Warren's defects in the part, she is still amply to be praised for her endeavour and its success.[1]

When Mary Lawton played Tess in the same arrangement with a stock company at the Castle Square Theatre, Boston, on September 1, 1905, a critic commented that she had a difficult task following Mrs. Fiske. "Miss Lawton is too often mechanical, and although she shows training, it is not the training of the school of experience. Throughout the earlier acts she was disappointing, and it was only during a few moments in her scene with Alec when he returns intoxicated, and in her utterance of 'Marian' when she learns that her friend has lied to her, that she rose to the demands of the part."[2]

In California, *Tess* was played at least three times between 1909 and 1936. I do not know whether the last was a piracy or not, but Mrs. Fiske must have still had the American rights through 1910. On January 18, 1909, Isabelle Fletcher played *Tess* in Ye Liberty Playhouse, Oakland, Calif., with the Bishop's Players. Under the direction of Fred J. Butler, Evelyn Vaughan played *Tess* February 28, 1910, in San Francisco, with the Alcazar stock company of which Belasco and Mayer were proprietors. The last record of a production that I was able to find was of one in California on May 19, 1936. From the arrangement of acts and scenes it seems that this play may have been given from Hardy's version as presented in London and Dorchester. The introduction to the playbill, however, is ambiguous. "This is a play of another Day—a Drama out of the past, presented in the manner in which Hardy wrote it—a play not of modern people, but of simple Wessex Country folk living as they lived in the Nineteenth Century."

Tess of the Vaudevilles and *Tess of Darbyville,* which were played in 1897 and 1898, are reflections of Mrs. Fiske's tremendous success at that time. The *New York Sun,* March 25, 1897, says:

Marie Dressler, Frederick Backus, Frederick Clifton, and A. R. Phillips unite at the Pleasure Palace in a comical assault on a current drama, which they style a musical and farcical spasm and to which they give the title "Tess of the Vaudevilles." Messrs. Backus and Clifton are responsible respectively for the words and music of the songs, and with Miss Dressler act in the sketch, while the fourth assistant wrote the sketch. For several minutes after it has

[1] *Boston Evening Transcript*, February 9, 1904.
[2] *Ibid.*, September 9, 1905.

begun there is no suggestion of the Hardy novel or the play that has been made from it, and Miss Dressler is seen as a housemaid caring for a room shared by an author and a composer. She is seen to hold and put down a duster, but after this convincing exposition of the fact that she is a servant, she gets at her more important duty in the establishment, which is to act in the author's play and to sing the composer's music. She makes a comical affair of singing a new composition with which she pretends to be unfamiliar, bending over her accompanist and counting time loudly. When she comes to interpret the untried drama she is Tess and her companions are Angel Food and Alec Stoutenbottle. Leading up to the murder scene, Angel Food shouts to Tess, "We must split, I am going to Brazil, Indiana," and departs in a frenzy. As Alec sends out from the wings a mocking laugh of many horse power, Tess sharpens a bread knife with a corrugated edge of her shoe and disappears in the direction of the laughter. A big racket indicates that she is using the knife, and she staggers in, brandishing the weapon. She has not had time to go half way across the stage when Alec steps up to enquire if he is dead. Being assured that he has been killed, he walks back, and Tess reaches a bureau and drops the knife behind it. At sight of blood on her hand she capers in agony for a moment, and then, opening a drawer frantically, hides the telltale stain with a boxing glove. On the entrance of an officer she collapses on the floor in surrender, whereat the officer removes his uniform, and the three burlesquers wind up with a selection from the composer's opera. A swell apartment on Cherry Hill is the scene of action, and lawless as the hodge-podge is, it makes Miss Dressler's fun-making more effective than did the inning of songs and recitations that she has been having.

The take-off on Mrs. Fiske's most tragic scenes with the knife, the glove, and the officer are, of course, obvious and indicate a widespread familiarity with Stoddard's play.

In Philadelphia, another farce, *Tess of Darbyville,* was very popular. The *Philadelphia Record,* January 25, 1898, carried this story: "*Tess of Darbyville* began the second week of its highly successful run at the Eleventh Street Opera House last night. As Baby Tess, bulky Mr. Woods provoked roars of laughter, and the antics of Hughey Drugherty, Alf. Gibson, and J. M. Kane delighted the large audience. Rarely has a more laughable sketch than *Tess of Darbyille* been acted at this theatre."

PLAYS GIVEN BY "HARDY PLAYERS"

The Trumpet-Major—interlude at lecture	Feb. 8, 1908
Ye Merrie Maie Fayre[1]—for Church schools	May 6, 7, 1908
The Trumpet-Major—Corn Exchange	Nov. 18, 19 (2),[2] 1908
" " Harrison	Dec. 31, 1908
Far from the Madding Crowd—Corn Exchange	Nov. 17, 18 (2), 1909
" " " " " Cripplegate, London	Nov. 24, 1909
" " " " " Harrison	Dec. 20, 1909
" " " " " Pavilion, Weymouth	Feb. 7, 1910
The Trumpet-Major—Pavilion, Weymouth	Feb. 8, 1910
The Mellstock Quire—Corn Exchange	Nov. 16, 17 (2), 1910
" " Cripplegate, London	Dec. 1, 1910
" " Pavilion, Weymouth	Feb. 9, 1911
The Three Wayfarers } —Corn Exchange *The Distracted Preacher* }	Nov. 15, 16 (2), 1911
" " Cripplegate, London	Nov. 27, 1911
" " Pavilion, Weymouth	Dec. 15, 1911
The Trumpet-Major (revised)—Corn Exchange	Nov. 27, 28 (2), 1912
" " " Cripplegate, London	Dec. 5, 1912
The Woodlanders—Corn Exchange	Nov. 19, 20 (2), 1913
" " Cripplegate, London	Dec. 8, 1913
" " Pavilion, Weymouth	Jan. 22, 1914

[1] Not "Hardy Players."
[2] (2) refers to matinee and evening performances.

Wessex Scenes from "The Dynasts"—Pavilion, Weymouth June 2, 1916
" " " " " Corn Exchange Dec. 6, 7 (2), 1916

The Mellstock Quire (revised)—Corn Exchange   Jan. 31 (2), 1918

The Return of the Native—Corn Exchange   Nov. 17, 18, 19, 20 (2), 1920

" " " " "   Guildhall School of   Jan. 27, 1921
Music, London

A Desperate Remedy—Corn Exchange   Nov. 15, 16, 17 (2), 1922
" " "   National Sporting Club,   Nov. 21, 1922
King's Hall,
Covent Garden, London

The Queen of Cornwall ⎱—Corn Exchange Nov. 28, 29, 30 (2), 1923
The Mumming Play ⎰
O Jan! O Jan! O Jan!

The Mumming Play ⎱ Broadcast BBC   Dec. 1, 1923
O Jan! O Jan! O Jan! ⎰

Old Time Rustic Wedding Scene ⎱ —King George's Hall,
O Jan! O Jan! O Jan! ⎰ Tottenham Court Road,
The Queen of Cornwall   London   Feb. 21 (2), 1924

Tess—Corn Exchange   Nov. 26, 27, 28, 29 (2), 1924
"   Pavilion, Weymouth   Dec. 11 (2), 1924

The Three Wayfarers—Broadcast from Bournemouth   Dec., 1926

Various scenes given at different places such as Melcome Bingham (on the bowling green which is bordered by a hedge dating from Henry VIII's time)   Twelve other performances

NOTE: This record taken from that kept by Mr. T. H. Tilley shows that the "Hardy Players" gave sixty full-length performances. This does not include the interlude at Mr. Broadley's lecture, *Ye Merrie Maie Fayre,* the broadcasts from BBC or Bournemouth studios, or the twelve performances given mostly about the country in places like Sturminster Newton and Melcome Bingham. With these included, the total number of presentations is seventy-six.

TESS OF THE D'URBERVILLES
Dramatization in Four Acts
by
LORIMER STODDARD

Original New York Cast

ANGEL CLARE	Edward M. Bell
ALEC D'URBERVILLE	Charles Coghlan
JOHN DURBEYFIELD	John Jack
ABRAHAM DURBEYFIELD	Alice Pierce
FARMER CRICK	W. L. Branscombe
JONATHAN	Wilfred North
JAMES	W. E. Butterfield
TIM	Alfred Hickman
SHERIFF	W. L. Branscombe
JOAN DURBEYFIELD	Mary E. Baker
TESS	Mrs. Fiske
LIZA LOO	Edith Wright
MARIAN	Annie Irish
IZZ	Nellie Lingard
RETTY	Bijou Fernandez

MANAGER—Harrison Grey Fiske

TESS OF THE D'URBERVILLES
DRAMATIZATION IN FOUR ACTS
by
LORIMER STODDARD

Cast at Tremont Theatre, Boston

ANGEL CLARE	Forrest Robinson
ALEC D'URBERVILLE	Frederick de Belleville
JOHN DURBEYFIELD	John Jack
ABRAHAM DURBEYFIELD	Anna Vislaire
FARMER CRICK	James Morley
JONATHAN	Wilfred North
JAMES	Frank McCormack
TIM	George Trader
SHERIFF	F. McCormack
JOAN DURBEYFIELD	Mary E. Baker
TESS	Mrs. Fiske
LIZA LOO	Edith Wright
MARIAN	Mary Shaw
IZZ	Dorothy Chester
RETTY	Sydney Cowell

MANAGER—Harrison Grey Fiske

TESS

Dramatization by H. A. Kennedy

Cast at Coronet Theatre
Nottinghill Gate
February 19, 1900

ANGEL CLARE	William Kittredge
ALEC TRANTRIDGE	Whitworth Jones
REVEREND CUTHBERT CLARE	Bangley Imeson
JOHN DURBEYFIELD	James Craig
DAIRYMAN CRICK	Leonard Hubert
A SHEPHERD	Leonard Buttress
ABRAHAM	Master Garnet Vayne
MRS. DURBEYFIELD	Lillian Hingston
MARIAN	Annie Webster
RETTY	Rosalind Ivan
IZZ	Gertrude Lovel
LIZA-LU	Miss Vayne
TESS	Mrs. Lewis Waller

TESS

Dramatization by H. A. Kennedy

Cast at Comedy Theatre
April 14, 1900

Angel Clare	Oswald Yorke
Alec Trantridge	Fred Terry
Reverend Cuthbert Clare	James Craig
John Durbeyfield	Cecil Brooking
Dairyman Crick	Leonard Hubert
A Shepherd	Leonard Buttress
Abraham	Master Garnet Vayne
Mrs. Durbeyfield	Lillian Hingston
Marian	Annie Webster
Retty	Rosalind Ivan
Izz	Elizabeth Kirby
Liza-Lu	Isla Vayne
Tess	Mrs. Lewis Waller

TESS: A Drama in Four Acts by Luigi Illica
Translation by C. Aveling
Music by Frederic d'Erlanger

Cast at Naples
Teatro San Carlo

Tess	Rina Giachetti
Jack	Michel Wigley
Joan	Sig.na Bernasconi
Aby	Emma Trentini
Angel Clare	Amedo Bassi
Alec D'Urberville	Mario Sammarco
Toronton	Angelo Bada
Dick	Angelo Bada
Nancy	Sig.na Manarini
Dark-Car	Sig.na Zaccaria

Conductor—Ettore Panizza

TESS: A DRAMA IN FOUR ACTS BY LUIGI ILLICA
Translation by C. Aveling
Music by Frederic d'Erlanger

Cast at Milan
Teatro Dal Verne

TESS	Tina Desana
JACK	Pompilio Malatesta
JOAN	Elvira Lucca
ABY	Albertina Cassani
ANGEL CLARE	Piero Schiavazzi
ALEC D'URBERVILLE	Ernesto Badini
TORONTON	Cesare Spadoni
DICK	Ugo Panerai
NANCY	Alfonsina Rolando
DARK-CAR	Elvira Lucca

CONDUCTOR—Tullio Serafin

TESS: A Drama in Four Acts by Luigi Illica
Translation by C. Aveling
Music by Frederic d'Erlanger

Cast at London
Royal Opera

Tess	Mlle. Destinn
Jack	M. Gilbert
Joan	Mme. Lejeune
Aby	Mlle. de Lys
Angel Clare	Signor Zenatello
Alec D'Urberville	Signor Sammarco
Toronton	Signor Zucchi
Dick	M. d'Oisly
Nancy	Mlle. Egener
Dark-Car	Mlle. Bourgeois

Conductor—Signor Panizza

TESS
OF THE D'URBERVILLES
A Tragedy
In Four Acts and an After-Scene
By
THOMAS HARDY

Given by the Hardy Players at the
Corn Exchange, Dorchester, 1924

ANGEL CLARE	Dr. E. W. Smerdon
ALEC D'URBERVILLE	Mr. N. J. Atkins
JOHN DURBEYFIELD	Mr. T. Pouncey
FELIX CLARE	Mr. R. Fare
JONATHAN KAIL	Mr. A. C. Cox
LABOURER	Mr. R. C. Barrow
TESS	Miss Gertrude Bugler
JOAN DURBEYFIELD	Mrs. Major
LIZA-LU	Miss A. Bugler
SARAH, A CLUB GIRL	Miss G. Lock
LABOURER'S WIFE	Miss G. Lock
MARIAN	Miss M. Dawes
IZZ	Miss E. Fare
LANDLADY OF LODGING-HOUSE	Mrs. Wacher
HER SERVANT	Miss A. Bugler

TESS OF THE D'URBERVILLES

A Tragedy
In Four Acts and an After-Scene
By
THOMAS HARDY

Barnes Production
London
September 7, 1925

ANGEL CLARE	Mr. Ion Swinley
ALEC D'URBERVILLE	Mr. Austin Trevor
JOHN DURBEYFIELD	Mr. Stanley Lathbury
MR. TRINGHAM	Mr. C. Leveson Lane
FELIX CLARE	Mr. Arthur J. Mayne
JONATHAN KAIL	Mr. H. Saxon-Snell
LABOURER	Mr. John Le Hay
BOY	Mr. Baron Salomons
TESS	Miss Gwen Ffrangçon-Davies
JOAN DURBEYFIELD	Miss Margaret Carter
LIZA-LU	Miss Gabrielle Casartelli
SARAH	Miss Natalie Moya
LABOURER'S WIFE	Miss Drusilla Wills
LANDLADY OF LODGING-HOUSE	Miss Elizabeth Webster
IZZ	Miss Phyllis de Lange
MARIAN	Miss Betty Belloc
HER MAIDSERVANT	Miss Tita Casartelli

TESS
OF THE D'URBERVILLES
A Tragedy
In Four Acts and an After-Scene

By

THOMAS HARDY

Duke of York's Theatre
London
July 23, 1929

ANGEL CLARE	Lawrence Anderson
MR. TRINGHAM	Drelincourt Odlum
JOHN DURBEYFIELD	A. S. Homewood
A BOY	Leonard Hayes
JOAN DURBEYFIELD	Barbara Gott
SARAH	Irene Barnett
TESS	Gertrude Bugler
ALEC D'URBERVILLE	Martin Lewis
LIZA-LU	Joyce Moore
FELIX CLARE	Arthur Mayne
JONATHAN KAIL	Harold Young
IZZ	Irene Barnett
MARIAN	Sonia Bellamy
LABOURER'S WIFE	Drusilla Wills
LABOURER	H. Saxon-Snell
LANDLADY OF LODGING-HOUSE	Marjorie Caldicott
HER MAIDSERVANT	Tita Casartelli

TESS OF THE D'URBERVILLES

A New Adaptation of THOMAS HARDY's Novel

By
RONALD GOW

New Theatre
London
November 26-30, 1946

MRS. CRUMB	Jane Henderson
JONATHAN KAIL, A COUNTRYMAN	Gerald Welch
ANGEL CLARE	William Devlin
TESS	Wendy Hiller
MRS. DURBEYFIELD, HER MOTHER	Everly Gregg
LIZA-LU, HER SISTER	Hilda Schroder
ALEC D'URBERVILLE	John Bailey
MRS. BROOKS	Nora Nicholson
A PORTER	Kenneth Connor
A SHEPHERD	Gerald Welch

Produced by HUGH HUNT
Settings and costumes by GUY SHEPPARD

www.ingramcontent.com/pod-product-compliance
Lightning Source LLC
Chambersburg PA
CBHW020352080526
44584CB00014B/999